# Bartending

maranGraphics™
&
THOMSON
COURSE TECHNOLOGY
Professional ■ Technical ■ Reference

## MARAN ILLUSTRATED™ Bartending

© 2005 by maranGraphics Inc. All rights reserved. No part of this book may be reproduced or transmitted in any form or by any means, electronic, mechanical or otherwise, including by photocopying, recording, or by any storage or retrieval system without prior written permission from maranGraphics, except for the inclusion of brief quotations in a review.

Distributed in the U.S. and Canada by Thomson Course Technology PTR. For enquiries about Maran Illustrated™ books outside the U.S. and Canada, please contact maranGraphics at international@maran.com

For U.S. orders and customer service, please contact Thomson Course Technology at 1-800-354-9706. For Canadian orders, please contact Thomson Course Technology at 1-800-268-2222 or 416-752-9448.

ISBN: 1-59200-944-1

Library of Congress Catalog Card Number: 2005926157

Printed in the United States of America

05 06 07 08 09 BU 10 9 8 7 6 5 4 3 2 1

## Trademarks

maranGraphics, Maran Illustrated, the Maran Illustrated logos and any trade dress related to or associated with the contents or cover of this book are trademarks of maranGraphics Inc. and may not be used without written permission.

The Thomson Course Technology PTR logo is a trademark of Course Technology and may not be used without written permission.

All other trademarks are the property of their respective owners.

## Important

maranGraphics and Thomson Course Technology PTR cannot provide software support. Please contact the appropriate software manufacturer's technical support line or Web site for assistance.

maranGraphics and Thomson Course Technology PTR have attempted throughout this book to distinguish proprietary trademarks by following the capitalization style used by the source. However, we cannot attest to the accuracy of the style, and the use of a word or term in this book is not intended to affect the validity of any trademark.

## Copies

Educational facilities, companies, and organizations located in the U.S. and Canada that are interested in multiple copies of this book should contact Thomson Course Technology PTR for quantity discount information. Training manuals, CD-ROMs, and portions of this book are also available individually or can be tailored for specific needs.

**DISCLAIMER:** PURCHASERS, READERS OR USERS OF THIS BOOK AGREE TO BE BOUND BY THE FOLLOWING TERMS.

INFORMATION CONTAINED IN THIS BOOK HAS BEEN OBTAINED BY MARANGRAPHICS AND FROM SOURCES BELIEVED TO BE RELIABLE. HOWEVER, NEITHER MARANGRAPHICS INC. NOR THOMSON COURSE TECHNOLOGY PTR NOR ANY OF THEIR RESPECTIVE AFFILIATES, DISTRIBUTORS, EMPLOYEES, AGENTS, CONTENT CONTRIBUTORS OR LICENSORS, IF ANY, MAKE ANY REPRESENTATION, WARRANTY, GUARANTEE OR ENDORSEMENT AS TO THE INFORMATION CONTAINED IN THIS BOOK OR AS TO THIRD-PARTY SUPPLIERS REFERENCED IN THIS BOOK, INCLUDING WITHOUT LIMITATION REGARDING THEIR ACCURACY, CORRECTNESS, TIMELINESS, RELIABILITY, USEFULNESS OR COMPLETENESS, OR THE RESULTS THAT MAY BE OBTAINED FROM THE USE OF THIS BOOK, AND DISCLAIM ALL EXPRESS, IMPLIED OR STATUTORY WARRANTIES, INCLUDING IMPLIED WARRANTIES OF MERCHANTABILITY, FITNESS OR SUITABILITY FOR A PARTICULAR PURPOSE, TITLE AND NON-INFRINGEMENT. THE SUBJECT MATTER OF THIS BOOK IS CONSTANTLY EVOLVING AND THE INFORMATION PROVIDED IN THIS BOOK IS NOT EXHAUSTIVE. IT SHOULD NOT BE USED AS A SUBSTITUTE FOR CONSULTING WITH A QUALIFIED PROFESSIONAL WHERE PROFESSIONAL ASSISTANCE IS REQUIRED OR APPROPRIATE, INCLUDING WHERE THERE MAY BE ANY RISK TO HEALTH OR PROPERTY, AND THE PURCHASER, READER OR USER UNDERSTANDS AND ACKNOWLEDGES THAT THE AFOREMENTIONED PARTIES ARE NOT HEREBY PROVIDING ANY PROFESSIONAL ADVICE, CONSULTATION OR OTHER SERVICES.

IN NO EVENT WILL ANY OF MARANGRAPHICS INC., THOMSON COURSE TECHNOLOGY PTR, OR ANY OF THEIR RESPECTIVE AFFILIATES, DISTRIBUTORS, EMPLOYEES, AGENTS, CONTENT CONTRIBUTORS OR LICENSORS BE LIABLE OR RESPONSIBLE FOR ANY DAMAGES INCLUDING ANY DIRECT, INDIRECT, SPECIAL, CONSEQUENTIAL, INCIDENTAL, PUNITIVE OR EXEMPLARY LOSSES, DAMAGE OR EXPENSES (INCLUDING BUSINESS INTERRUPTION, LOSS OF PROFITS, LOST BUSINESS, OR LOST SAVINGS) IRRESPECTIVE OF THE NATURE OF THE CAUSE OF ACTION, DEMAND OR ACTION, INCLUDING BREACH OF CONTRACT, NEGLIGENCE, TORT OR ANY OTHER LEGAL THEORY.

**maranGraphics™**

maranGraphics Inc.
5755 Coopers Avenue
Mississauga, Ontario
L4Z 1R9
www.maran.com

COURSE TECHNOLOGY
Professional ■ Technical ■ Reference

Thomson Course Technology PTR, a division of Thomson Course Technology
25 Thomson Place ■ Boston, MA 02210 ■ http://www.courseptr.com

maranGraphics is a family-run business

At **maranGraphics**, we believe in producing great books—one book at a time.

Each maranGraphics book uses the award-winning communication process that we have been developing over the last 30 years. Using this process, we organize photographs and text in a way that makes it easy for you to learn new concepts and tasks.

We spend hours deciding the best way to perform each task, so you don't have to! Our clear, easy-to-follow photographs and instructions walk you through each task from beginning to end.

We want to thank you for purchasing what we feel are the best books money can buy. We hope you enjoy using this book as much as we enjoyed creating it!

Sincerely,

**The Maran Family**

We would love to hear from you! Send your comments and feedback about our books to family@maran.com

To sign up for sneak peeks and news about our upcoming books, send an e-mail to newbooks@maran.com

Please visit us on the Web at:

**www.maran.com**

## CREDITS

**Author:**
maranGraphics
Development Group

**Content Architect:**
Jill Maran Dutfield

**Content Architect for Spirits & Liqueurs, Beer & Wine Sections:**
Wanda Lawrie

**Technical Consultant:**
Gavin MacMillan

**Project Manager & Editor:**
Judy Maran

**Copy Developer:**
Andrew Wheeler

**Photographer & Layout Designer:**
Sarah Kim

**Layout Artist:**
Richard Hung

**Post Production:**
Robert Maran

**Publisher and General Manager, Thomson Course Technology PTR:**
Stacy L. Hiquet

**Associate Director of Marketing, Thomson Course Technology PTR:**
Sarah O'Donnell

**National Sales Manager, Thomson Course Technology PTR:**
Amy Merrill

**Manager of Editorial Services, Thomson Course Technology PTR:**
Heather Talbot

Special thanks to Gavin MacMillan for creating all of the cocktails photographed in this book.

## ACKNOWLEDGMENTS

Thanks to the dedicated staff of maranGraphics, including Richard Hung, Kelleigh Johnson, Sarah Kim, Jill Maran Dutfield, Judy Maran, Robert Maran, Ruth Maran and Andrew Wheeler.

Finally, to Richard Maran who originated the easy-to-use graphic format of this guide. Thank you for your inspiration and guidance.

## ABOUT THE TECHNICAL CONSULTANT...

### Gavin MacMillan

After graduating in 1997, Gavin MacMillan traveled the world for 3 years putting "a different spin" on his Honors Business degree. While plying his trade in 13 countries on 4 continents, Gavin perfected his style as a classic mixologist and performance bartender. His experience in a broad range of hospitality concepts in roles from master bartender to corporate trainer, won Gavin his 2001 ranking as the UK's top bartender while working at TGI Friday's flagship location in London, England.

Currently ranked #1 in Canada, Gavin has been featured in music videos, newspapers, the Travel Channel, A&E and in many world championship competition videos. Gavin continues to work, train, and compete with the world's finest entertainment flair bartenders. Gavin writes a monthly column entitled "Raising the Bar" for *Food Service News*, a national resource for bar owners and managers.

Gavin owns BartenderOne (www.bartenderone.com), a premier hospitality training facility, and The Movers'n'Shakers (www.themoversnshakers.com), Canada's largest team of entertainment flair bartenders which caters to corporate and private events of all types.

### A few words from Gavin:

Cocktail culture is on the rise again... everything old is new. I'd like to extend a big thank you to maranGraphics for their meticulous attention to detail. You hold in your hands one of the most well assembled drink guides to date.

Once you're comfortable with the drink making techniques covered in this book, you'll discover the real pleasure of learning to adapt ingredients to create a custom cocktail that you can truly call your own. I encourage you to experiment and taste each ingredient first to learn how it will interact with the rest of the cocktail. If you find yourself staring blankly at your liquor cabinet wondering what you can make, check out the online cabinet at www.bartenderone.com for ideas. It's an invaluable tool and it's simple to use. Lastly... as if it needs to be said, please enjoy your cocktail creations responsibly. Have fun!

## SPECIAL THANKS TO...

A special thank you to Libbey for suppling the majority of the glassware featured in this book.

Based in Toledo, Ohio, Libbey operates glass tableware manufacturing plants in Louisiana and Ohio, and in the Netherlands and Portugal. Libbey Foodservice companies include Libbey Glassware, Royal Leerdam, Crisal, Syracuse China, World Tableware, and Traex. They are the leading providers of glass and other tableware products to the foodservice industry through their broad glassware, dinnerware, flatware, and plastic products offerings and extensive sales and distribution network—among the largest in the foodservice industry. Libbey is also one of the most recognized brand names in consumer housewares in the United States and the leading brand name in glass tableware.

## THANK YOU TO THE FOLLOWING COMPANIES FOR ALLOWING US TO SHOW PHOTOGRAPHS OF THEIR PRODUCTS IN OUR BOOK...

### Broadbent Wines

Wine Enthusiast Magazine calls Broadbent Selections one of the five best wine importers. Broadbent features the highest quality and most unique of wines, such as New Zealand's Spy Valley and Lebanon's Ch. Musar. Broadbent brands differentiate the ordinary bar from a sophisticated establishment and Andrea Immer always says, when buying wine, to look for the importer, highly recommending Broadbent.

### Diageo

## Campari Group

The Campari Group is a major player in the global beverage sector, trading in over 190 nations around the world with a leading position in the Italian and Brazilian markets and a strong presence in the US, Germany and Switzerland. The Group has an extensive portfolio that spans three business segments: spirits, wines and soft drinks. The Group's portfolio includes a combination of strong international brands, such as Campari, SKYY Vodka, Cynar and Cinzano and leading local brands, such as CampariSoda, Campari Mixx, Crodino, Aperol, Aperol Soda, Sella & Mosca, Zedda Piras, Biancosarti, Lemonsoda, Oransoda and Pelmosoda in Italy, Ouzo 12 in Greece and in Germany, Dreher, Old Eight, Drury's and Liebfraumilch in Brazil, Gregson's in Uruguay, Riccadonna in Australia and New Zealand and Mondoro in Russia. The Group has over 1,500 employees and shares of the parent company Davide Campari-Milano S.p.A are listed on the Italian stock exchange.

## Fonseca Guimaraens

Fonseca Guimaraens was founded in 1822 and remains one of the leading Port wine houses. It maintains its ardent quest for quality, complexity and structure, maintaining its position as one of the leading wine producers in the world. Today Fonseca Guimaraens is still a family wine shipper, with a house style that produces beautiful luscious dark berry fruit that has the intensity, structure and balance to last for decades.

## Foster's Wine Estates

Foster's Wine Estates is the world's leading premium wine business, producing and marketing an international portfolio of top quality wines—with Beringer, Lindemans, Penfolds, Rosemount Estate and Wolf Blass being the best known. Other key market-leading or boutique estates owned by the company include Chateau St Jean, Meridian Vineyards, Castello di Gabbiano, Chateau Souverain, Etude Wines, Greg Norman Estates, Stags' Leap Winery, and Matua Valley. More information can be found at www.Fosterswineestates.com.

## González Byass

Since it was founded in 1835, González Byass has based its policy on one principle, the passion of its founder, Manuel María González, for excellence in wine. The company, 100% family owned by the González family, produces high quality wines and spirits from different regions of Spain, such as world's best known Fino Tío Pepe, brandies Lepanto and Soberano, Rioja wines Beronia, and Tierra de Castilla wines Altozano.

# Table of Contents

CHAPTER 1 Bartending Basics



CHAPTER 2 Bartending Techniques



CHAPTER 3 Spirits & Liqueurs

## CHAPTER 4 Martinis



## CHAPTER 5 Classic Cocktails

# Table of Contents

## CHAPTER 10 Warmers



## CHAPTER 11 Alcohol-Free Cocktails



## CHAPTER 12 Wine & Beer Essentials



## CHAPTER 13 Measurements & Reference

# Introduction to Bartending

Bartending is more than opening bottles and pouring alcohol. The skilled bartender must know the tools, garnishes and techniques of the trade. This section of the book will help you stock your bar with the right tools, glasses and an appropriate selection of alcohol. You will also learn the techniques for creating great garnishes.

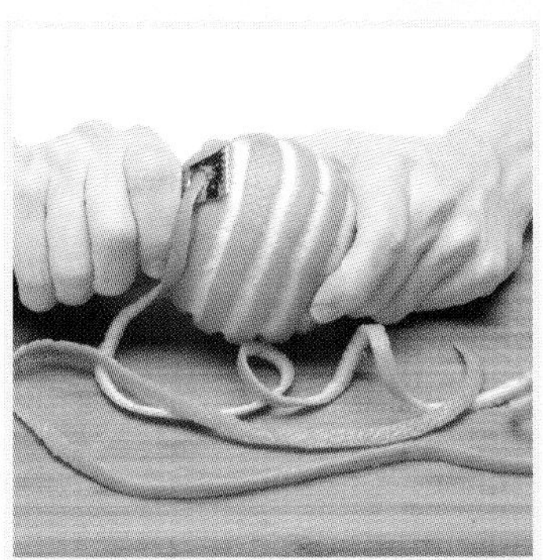

# Basic Bar Tools

To do any job well, you need the right tools. Mixing drinks is no different. Anyone can pop open a can of beer, but bar tools such as shakers, strainers and barspoons are essential for putting together a proper cocktail. Many of these basic bartending tools can be purchased as part of a starter's kit and most are readily available in houseware stores.

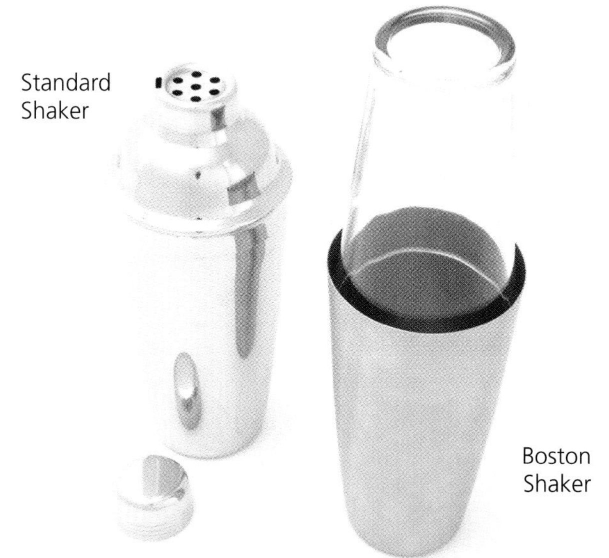


## Shakers

Cocktail shakers generally come in one of two forms—the standard shaker and the Boston shaker.

Standard shakers are comprised of three stainless-steel pieces: a can between 8 and 24 ounces, a lid that contains a strainer and a tight-fitting cap.

Boston shakers are composed of two pieces: a tapered stainless steel can between 26 and 30 ounces and a smaller tapered glass that is generally 16 ounces in size. Boston shakers are preferred by professional bartenders because they are generally bigger and allow more drinks to be mixed at once.

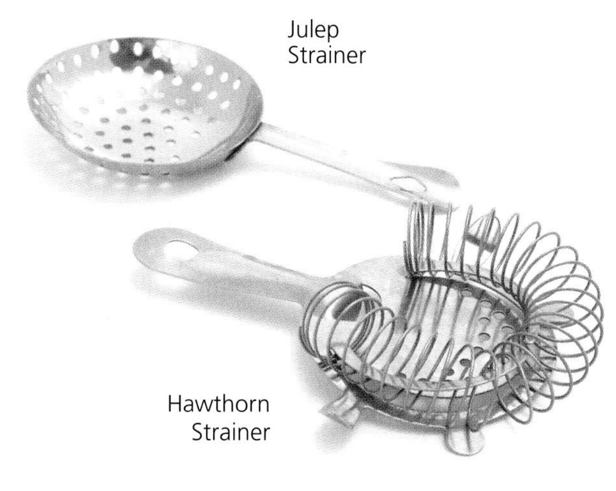


## Strainers

There are two main types of strainers used by bartenders who use Boston shakers, the julep strainer and the Hawthorn strainer.

The julep strainer looks like an over-sized metal spoon studded with holes. It fits well inside a mixing glass to strain ice and citrus seeds out of a stirred drink.

The Hawthorn strainer is a slotted metal disc with a metal coil on its underside and is attached to a handle. The Hawthorn strainer fits on top of a Boston shaker's metal can with the spring inside the can to filter ice and citrus seeds out of a cocktail that has been shaken.

## Blender

Blenders are used to blend fresh or frozen fruits and to create drinks that contain ice. Ice cubes should be broken up in a bag with a rolling pin before being added to a blender to avoid unnecessary strain on the blender's motor. Some blenders also have a setting that allows you to grind ice cubes into crushed ice.

## Measured Shot Glasses & Jiggers

Measured shot glasses and jiggers are used to measure cocktail ingredients. These essential tools come in a wide variety of styles and typically range in size from 1 to 6 oz. Measured shot glasses are typically marked with graduated measurements. Jiggers feature two different-sized cups stacked end-to-end like an hourglass—one cup is normally double the size of the other cup.

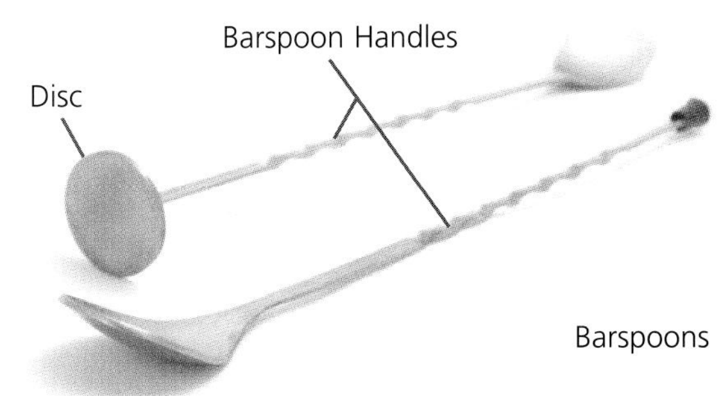


## Barspoons

Barspoons are spoons used to stir cocktails that are not shaken. Barspoon handles are frequently twisted and are long enough to reach the bottom of a pitcher or large cocktail shaker. Some barspoons also have a flat disc on the end that can be used to muddle cocktail ingredients. For information on how to muddle, see page 44. In cocktails where the ingredients are layered, the liquors are often poured over the back of a barspoon. For information on how to layer drinks, see page 45.

## Wine Opener

Wine openers are used for removing the corks from wine bottles. Wine openers come in a wide variety of styles, most featuring a screw that winds down into and pulls out a bottle's cork. Professional bartenders often use a "waiter's corkscrew" to open bottles. A waiter's corkscrew is a folding multipurpose tool that features a foil cutter, a bottle-cap remover and a simple corkscrew mechanism.

## Knives

Knives are essential for preparing garnishes. An eight-inch chef's knife is handy for slicing larger fruits such as pineapples and grapefruits.

## Channel Knife

A channel knife is a small tool featuring a square or rounded head with a hole and small blade for cutting long slices of peel from citrus fruits.

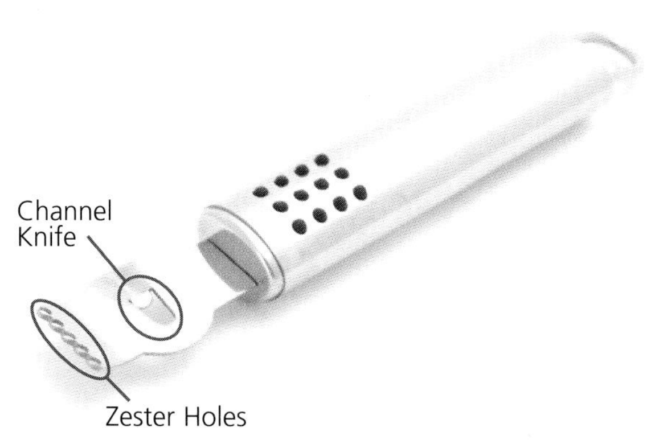


## Citrus Zester

A citrus zester is a hand-held tool with five or six small, sharp, stainless steel holes used to remove threadlike strips of peel from the rind of a citrus fruit. Combination tools featuring both a channel knife and zester are common.

## Muddler

A muddler is a wooden bat that is used to crush ingredients such as herbs, fruit and sugar in the bottom of a glass or cocktail shaker. Most muddlers are six or more inches long and flattened on one end.

Here are some other tools that are valuable for the home bar.

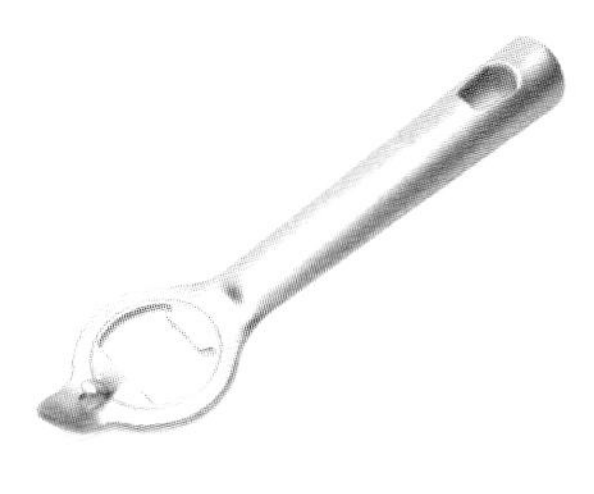

### Bottle Opener

A bottle opener is a handy device to quickly remove the caps on beer bottles.

### Nutmeg Grater

A nutmeg grater is useful for grating nutmeg, cinnamon and other spices over drinks.

### Cocktail Pitcher

A tall cocktail pitcher with a rim designed to hold back ice is useful for mixing punches and drinks for large crowds.

### Pourer

A pourer is a spout that is plugged into a bottle to regulate the flow of liquor. Bartenders use pourers to measure out ingredients by the number of seconds they pour.

### Cutting Board

A cutting board is necessary for preparing fruit to be used for juicing as well as garnishes.

### Reamer

A citrus reamer is a pointed tool that is designed to extract juice when pressed into citrus fruits that have been cut in half.

### Ice Bucket, Tongs and Scoop

An ice bucket is essential for storing fresh ice when serving cocktails. Ice tongs and scoops are used to add ice to glasses when preparing drinks.

### Mixing Glass

A mixing glass can be used instead of a shaker for making drinks that need to be stirred rather than shaken.

### Straws, Stir Sticks and Cocktail Sticks

Straws and stir sticks are used to sip and stir drinks. Cocktail sticks can be used to skewer a garnish in a drink.

### Tea Strainer

A fine-mesh tea strainer is useful for removing small seeds and ice chips from cocktails. For information on how to fine strain, see the top of page 77.

# Glassware

Unless you are hosting a Super Bowl party for the beer-and-bratwurst crowd, your alcoholic beverages deserve something a little better than plastic cups. From tall champagne flutes to tiny shot glasses, glassware has been custom-developed to compliment the wide range of drinks available from the bar. If you are just setting up your bar, it's good to know that it is not critical to have every single glass—many of these specialized glasses will do double-duty. Your guests will not walk out in disgust, for example, if you serve them a margarita in a cocktail glass.

## Highball and Collins Glasses

Highball glasses are tall, narrow, stemless glasses that are commonly used to serve drinks that hold a combination of liquor and soda.

A Collins glass is slightly taller and narrower than a highball glass.

Common drinks served in this glass: Alabama Slammer, Long Island Iced Tea

## Rocks/Old-Fashioned Glasses

Rocks glasses, also known as old-fashioned glasses, are used for drinks which are served with ice or "on the rocks."

Common drinks served in this glass: Brown Cow, Rusty Nail, Screwdriver

## Shot Glasses

A shot glass is used as a measuring cup when mixing drinks. A shot glass can also be used for serving a single serving of alcohol that is consumed in one gulp.

Common drinks served in this glass: B-52, Broken Down Golf Cart, Lemon Drop

TIP

*Anatomy of a Glass*

Most glasses consist of some combination of bowl, stem and base which vary in size and height depending on the beverages they are designed to hold. Some glasses, such as beer mugs, also feature a handle. The top edge of a glass' bowl is called the rim.

## Wine Glasses

Wine glasses are used to serve wine. White wine glasses are typically smaller than red wine glasses which feature wider bowls that allow more oxygen to interact with the wine and enhance its aroma and flavors.

Common drinks served in this glass:
Red and white wine

## Champagne Flutes

Champagne flutes are designed to show off the delicate bubbles of a sparkling wine and to prevent the bubbles from escaping.

Common drinks served in this glass:
Champagne, Mimosa, Kir Royale

# GLASSWARE

Most pieces of glassware have been developed to somehow enhance the type of drink for which they were designed. The wide rim of a margarita glass is ideal for rimming, the practice of coating the rim of the glass with sugar, salt or some other powdered coating that will compliment the flavor of the drink. Sometimes the shape of the glass just enhances the look of a drink. The classic martini would just not look the same if it were served in a hefty beer mug.

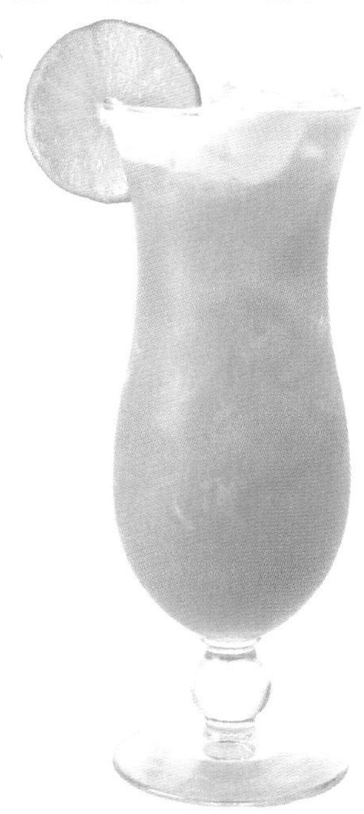

### Cocktail/Martini Glasses

A cocktail glass, also called a martini glass, is used for cocktails that are served without ice, or "straight up."

Common drinks served in this glass:
Classic Manhattan, Cosmopolitan, Sour Apple Martini

### Hurricane Glasses

Hurricane glasses are shaped like hurricane lamps with tall, tulip-shaped bowls mounted on a wide base.

Common drinks served in this glass:
Mudslide, Mai Tai, Killer Kool-aid

### Margarita Glasses

Margarita glasses feature a wide, two-tiered bowl atop a slender stem and wide base. If you don't have a margarita glass available, you can use a cocktail glass instead.

Common drinks served in this glass:
Strawberry Margarita,
Raspberry Daiquiri

**TIP** *Essential Glassware*

Having one set of each of the following types of glasses will allow you the versatility to serve most kinds of drinks.

- Beer Mugs
- Champagne Flutes
- Cocktail/Martini Glasses
- Highball/Collins Glasses
- Rocks Glasses
- Shot Glasses
- Wine Glasses
- Coffee Glasses

## Brandy Snifter

A brandy snifter is designed to be cupped in the hand rather than being held by the stem or base. Cupping the bowl warms the drink in the glass.

Common drinks served in this glass:
Brandy or Cognac, Blueberry Tea

## Coffee Glasses

Coffee glasses are used to serve hot drinks. If you don't have a coffee glass available, you can use a highball glass instead.

Common drinks served in this glass:
Spanish Coffee, B-52 Coffee, Irish Coffee

## Beer Mugs

Beer mugs are wide, heavy glasses with a large handle attached on the side. The thicker glass of a beer mug and the fact that it is held by a handle helps keep the beer inside it cold. If you don't have a beer mug available, you can use a highball glass instead.

Common drinks served in this glass:
Beer

# Garnish your Drinks

What would a martini be without its signature olive or lemon twist? A great garnish is the crowning glory of a well-made cocktail. Any self-respecting bartender, professional or amateur, will put as much effort into creating fine garnishes as he or she does into creating extraordinary drinks. A garnish should compliment the cocktail in every way—the flavor of the garnish should enhance the taste of the drink and the garnish's appearance should compliment the look of the drink. Using fresh, top-quality ingredients is mandatory.

## Fruits

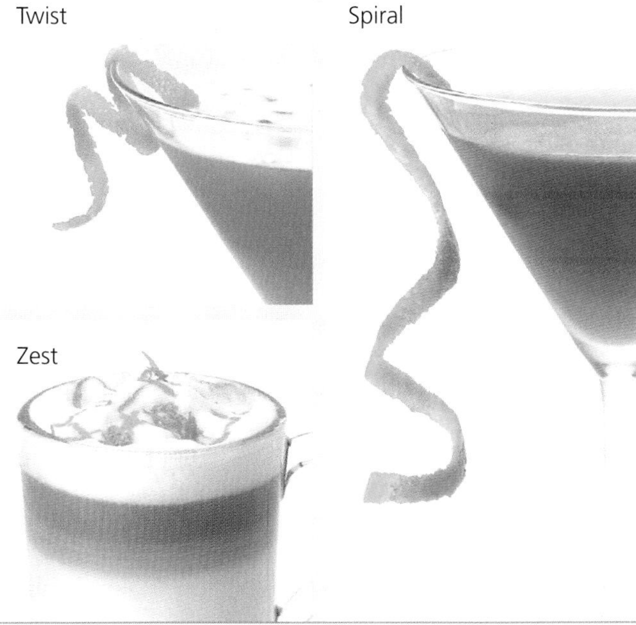


### Citrus Wheels, Slices and Wedges

Lemons, limes and oranges can all be cut up into wheels, slices and wedges. A wheel is a round cross section of fruit and a slice is a wheel cut in half. Wheels and slices are generally mounted on the rim of a glass or floated in a drink. A wedge, also called a squeeze, is a thick slice of fruit designed to add flavor to a cocktail. Wedges are usually mounted on the rim of a glass and can be squeezed into a drink before consuming.

### Citrus Twists, Spirals and Zest

The peels of citrus fruit offer a number of attractive garnish options. Twists, spirals and zest of lemons, limes and oranges look great and contain essential oils that give cocktails delicious, concentrated citrus flavors. Twists and spirals are created by cutting long strips of peel. Citrus zest is created by removing fine threads of peel from a fruit. Zest is typically added to the surface of a cocktail.

## Fruits (continued)

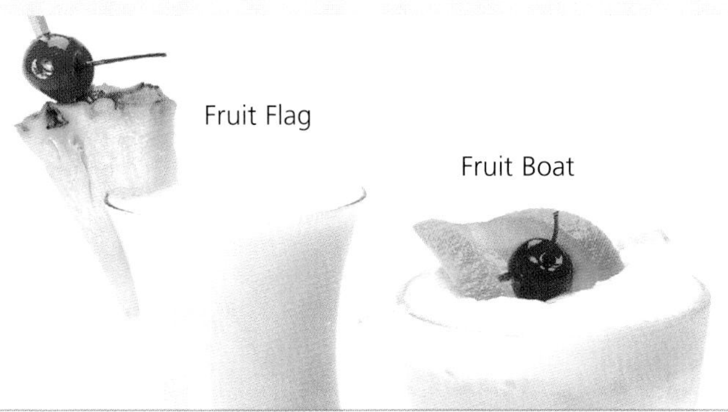


### Fruit Flags and Boats

Fruit flags and boats are flamboyant fruit garnishes. A flag, also called a sail, is a maraschino cherry skewered on top of another piece of fruit, such as a pineapple wedge. Flags are placed on the rim of a glass. A boat is a wheel of a citrus fruit that has been folded in half with a maraschino cherry skewered in the center. A boat is placed across the opening of a glass.

### Maraschino Cherries

You cannot successfully tend bar without a plentiful supply of maraschino cherries. These classic garnishes are extremely versatile—they can be skewered on a cocktail stick, dropped into a drink or used as part of a garnish, such as a fruit flag. When used as a garnish, maraschino cherries that have their stems attached are best.

### Berries

Fresh field berries, like blueberries, raspberries and strawberries, make colorful and delicious garnishes for many cocktails. Blueberries and raspberries are typically skewered and placed in a cocktail glass. Strawberries can be used whole or cut in half and are usually placed on the rim of a glass.

### Other Fresh Fruits

Almost any fresh fruit can be used as a garnish. Fruits provide lots of color and taste great. Popular choices of fruit that can be added to the rim of a glass include pineapple, kiwi, peach and banana. Exotic-looking cross sections of star fruit and elegant skewers of grapes also look stunning in cocktails.

# GARNISH YOUR DRINKS

Vegetables like celery, cucumbers and different types of herbs make great drink garnishes. As is the case with any garnish, it is crucial to use only the freshest and highest-quality vegetables and herbs. When you decide to get creative with your vegetable garnishes, all you have to remember is to match the garnish to the cocktail. For example, if you are mixing a spicy cocktail, try a fiery garnish such as a jalapeno pepper or habanero-stuffed olive.

## Vegetables

### Fresh Vegetables

Fresh vegetables are great options for garnishing salty, bitter or spicy cocktails. Celery stalks, cucumber slices and cherry tomatoes are all examples of vegetables that can be used creatively as garnishes. For example, a leafy celery stalk is the classic garnish for the Bloody Caesar.

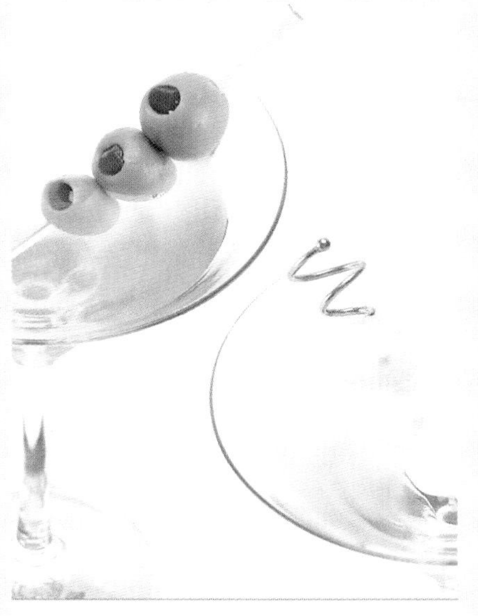

### Cocktail Olives and Onions

Olives and onions are popular garnishes. Both olives and onions are most often skewered and served in a cocktail. When a recipe calls for an olive, it usually refers to green olives with pimento stuffing, such as in the Classic Martini. When garnishing with olives or onions, be sure to use odd numbers which are more visually pleasing.

### Herbs and Spices

Herbs and spices can be used in numerous ways to garnish your cocktails. These garnishes not only look striking, but often provide a potent punch of flavor. For example, mint is a very popular garnish used in cocktails like the Orange Razz Smoothie. Cinnamon sticks are also popular garnishes because they make good stir sticks and add a distinctive flavor to drinks.

## Toppings and Specialty Garnishes

Toppings are the finishing touch, the ingredients that complete a cocktail. Whipped cream and cocoa powder make great toppings for drinks such as the Almond Hot Chocolate. Grated nutmeg adds just a hint of spice in drinks like the Brandy Alexander Martini. Coffee beans can even be used to garnish cocktails like the Espresso Martini.

## Rimming Glasses

Some drink recipes call for the rim of a glass to be coated with a powdered garnish. This technique is called rimming. Rimming a glass enhances the flavor of a cocktail with every sip.

### Salt and Celery Salt

Both salt and celery salt are popular rim garnishes for cocktails. Salt is famously used as the rimmer for the Lime Margarita. Celery salt, which is a flavorful blend of salt and ground celery seed, packs more of a punch and can be found on the rim of the Bloody Caesar.

### White Sugar

White sugar is used to rim the glasses of sweet cocktails such as the Lemon Drop Martini and warmers like the B-52 coffee. While both granulated sugar and superfine sugar are suitable for rimming glasses, superfine sugar is preferred for rimming. Brown sugar can also be used on a rim for its uniquely rich flavor.

### Others Rimmers

Just about any powdered, crumbled or granulated ingredient can be used as a rimmer. Cocoa powder is a great rimming option for chocolaty drinks like the Classic Chocolate Martini. Even graham cracker crumbs are used to rim the Key Lime Pie Martini for authentic flavor.

# Stock Your Bar

If you plan to boast about your newfound bartending skills to friends and family, you had better stock your home supply appropriately. There is nothing more embarrassing than being asked for an elegant cocktail and sheepishly having to offer a ho-hum rum and cola because you do not have the right ingredients. If you are starting from scratch, it may seem like a lot of alcohol to buy at once, but you will be able to create a huge array of cocktails by having some basics on hand.

## Spirits

We suggest that you purchase one 750 ml bottle of each of the following spirits.

Bourbon Brandy Gin Light Rum Rye Whiskey Scotch Tequila Vodka

## Beer, Wine and Fortified Wines

We suggest that you purchase 12 bottles of beer, three bottles of both red and white wine, one bottle of sparkling wine and one 750 ml bottle of both Dry Vermouth and Sweet Vermouth.

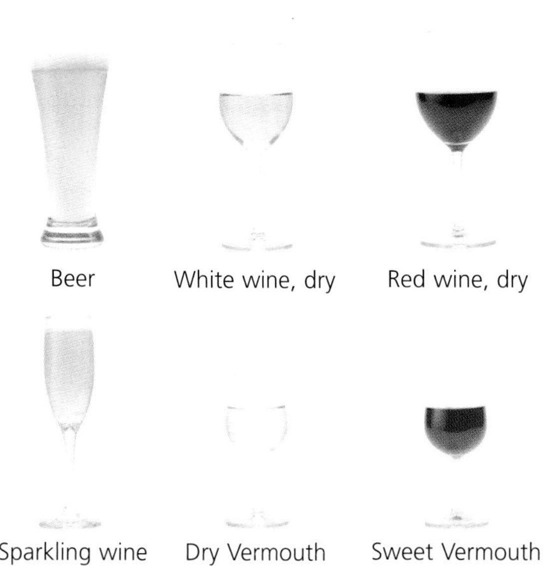

Beer White wine, dry Red wine, dry

Sparkling wine Dry Vermouth Sweet Vermouth

### *Buying a Limited Selection*

If you are hosting a party on a tight budget, it is perfectly acceptable to offer a limited selection of beverages rather than stocking up the whole bar. Come up with two or three special cocktails. All you will have to buy are the ingredients and garnishes necessary to make those cocktails, as well as beer and wine.

## Liqueurs, Cordials and Apéritifs

We suggest that you purchase one 750 ml bottle of an apéritif and three to four 750 ml bottles of any of the following liqueurs or cordials.

Amaretto

Baileys

Campari (or apéritif of choice)

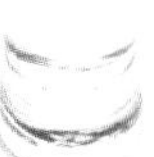

Triple Sec

White Crème de Cacao

Crème de Menthe or Peppermint Schnapps

Kahlua

Peach Schnapps

Sambuca

Southern Comfort

## Non-Alcoholic Beverages

There will always be guests who cannot or do not wish to drink alcohol. Here's a list of drinks you'll need to have on hand to keep them from feeling left out.

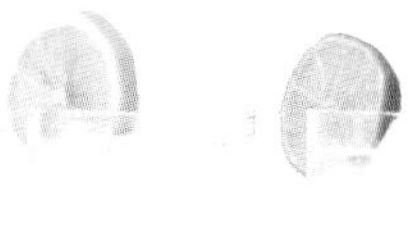

Water, still and sparkling

Soda

Alcohol-Free Punch

Fruit Juice

Tea & Coffee

# Stock your Bar

After you have purchased a basic selection of spirits, liqueurs, beer and wine, you will still need to buy the necessary extras before you can open the bar to your guests. Quality mixers and condiments are absolutely essential for concocting the best-tasting cocktails. Fine-looking garnishes, rimmers and toppings will make your drinks stand out, so be sure to buy the best you can find. Finally, don't forget the ice. Fresh ice is virtually indispensable if you will be serving anything besides beer and wine.

## Mixers

Club Soda

Cola & Diet Cola

Cranberry Juice

Fresh Lemon Juice

Fresh Lime Juice

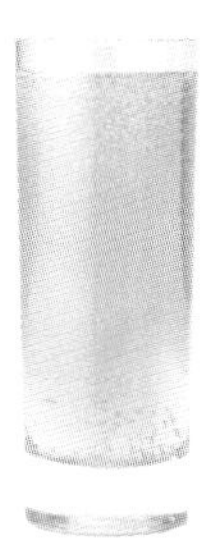

Ginger Ale

Half & Half Cream and 2% Milk

Lemon-Lime Soda

Orange Juice

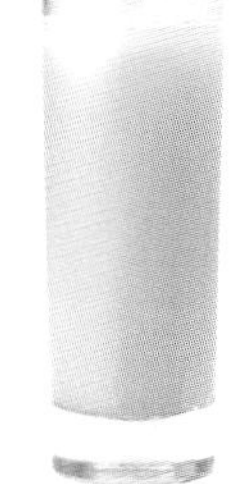

Pineapple Juice

Tomato Juice

Tonic Water

## Condiments

Bitters

Grenadine

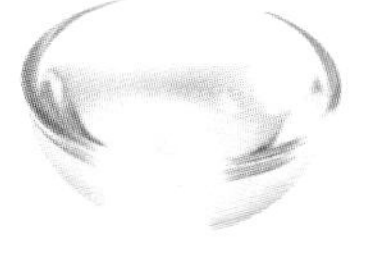

Rose's Lime Cordial

Simple Syrup

Tabasco Sauce

Worchestershire Sauce

## Garnishes

Limes

Lemons

Oranges

Mint

Cocktail Onions

Cocktail Olives

Maraschino Cherries

## Rimmers & Toppings

Cinnamon

Cocoa Powder

Nutmeg

Pepper

Salt

Superfine Sugar

## Ice

Cubed Ice

Crushed Ice

# CREATE CITRUS WEDGES, WHEELS & SLICES

Serving your drinks unadorned is no way to impress your guests. Most cocktails need to be dressed up and few garnishes are more popular than citrus wedges, wheels and slices. Creating perfect citrus wedges, wheels and slices is a basic skill that is easy to learn and will serve you well as you tend bar. Remember that you must use fresh fruit and store it properly—nothing looks worse than a cocktail with a dried out garnish. Also, be sure to wash the fruits you will be using to make garnishes.

## Create Citrus Wedges

Step 2

Step 3

Step 4

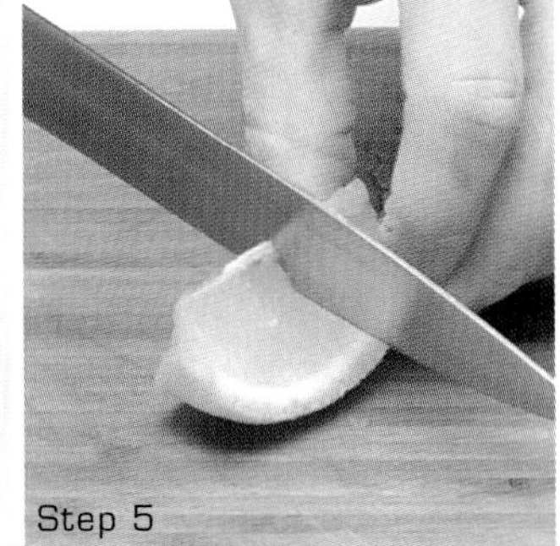

Step 5

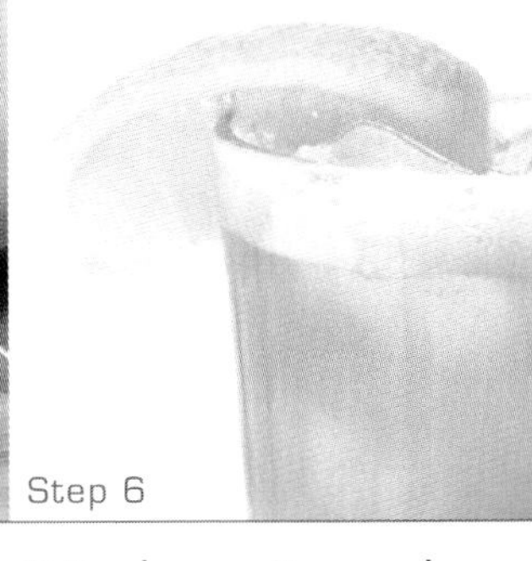

Step 6

- Lemon and lime wedges are commonly placed on the rims of glasses to decorate drinks and can be squeezed over drinks to add flavor.

1 To make citrus wedges, start by cutting off and discarding the ends of the fruit.

2 Cut the fruit in half lengthwise.

3 Place each half of the fruit on the cutting board, cut-side down, and cut the fruit lengthwise in half again.

4 Cut each half of the fruit lengthwise again, creating two wedges. Each lemon or lime should produce eight wedges.

5 To place a citrus wedge on the rim of a glass, make a cut approximately 1/4 inch deep into the wedge.

6 Place the citrus wedge on the rim of a glass.

**TIP** *When should I prepare my citrus garnishes?*

Ice melts and drinks dilute quickly, so prepare your garnishes well ahead of time. Citrus garnishes prepared in advance will keep for several hours stored in a bowl underneath a damp paper towel. Just remember: garnishes should be prepared first and added last.

**TIP** *Should I remove the seeds from my citrus garnishes?*

If you have the time, it's a great idea to remove the seeds from any wedges, wheels or slices you create. Taking the seeds out of your citrus garnishes will save you from serving a drink that has unsightly seeds floating around the bottom of the glass. Seed removal is mandatory if you are muddling your citrus wedges, wheels or slices—crushed seeds may give the drink an unpleasant bitter taste. For information on muddling, see page 44.

## Create Citrus Wheels & Slices

Step 2

Step 3

Step 4

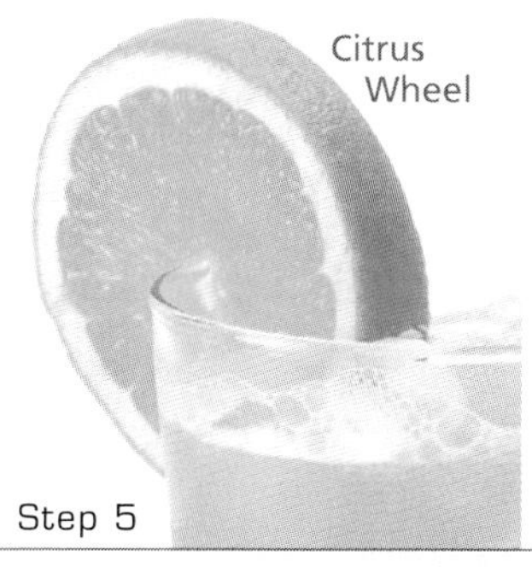

Step 5

- Wheels and slices of orange, lemon and lime are commonly used to decorate drinks. Citrus wheels and slices are not usually squeezed over drinks to add flavor.

1 Cut off and discard the ends of the fruit.

2 To make citrus wheels, position the fruit on its side. Starting at one end of the fruit, cut the fruit widthwise into 1/4 inch wheels.

3 To make citrus slices, cut the citrus wheels in half.

4 To place a citrus wheel or slice on the rim of a glass, make a cut 1/2 way through the wheel or approximately a 1/4 inch deep into the slice.

5 Place the citrus wheel or slice on the rim of a glass.

# CREATE CITRUS TWISTS & SPIRALS

Citrus twists and spirals are all about glamour. While a pineapple flag (page 36) is flamboyant and skewered cocktail onions are elegant, you cannot top the look of a slinky lemon twist or gorgeous orange spiral for sheer drama. Twists and spirals will also add a dose of flavor to your cocktails if you gently twist the garnishes, peel-side down, over the drink to release the peel's essential oils. Twists and spirals can be made in advance and frozen to save time. To create a twisted shape, you can wrap a twist or spiral around a straw before placing it in the freezer.

## Create Citrus Twists

- Citrus twists are 1 to 1 1/2 inch long pieces of citrus peel that are used in drinks as a garnish and to add flavor.

1 To make a citrus twist, start by cutting off and discarding the ends of the fruit with a knife.

2 Using a channel knife tool, cut off a slice of peel, starting at the top of the fruit and working your way downward to the bottom of the fruit.

- Perform step 2 until all of the peel is sliced off the fruit.

- To place a citrus twist in a cocktail, twist the garnish over the cocktail, rub the peel around the rim of the glass and then drop into the drink.

**TIP** *What does a twist and spiral look like?*

A twist is a 1 to 1 1/2 inch long piece of citrus peel.

A spiral is typically a 3 to 4 inch long piece of citrus peel.

## Create Citrus Spirals

- Citrus spirals are typically 3 to 4 inch long pieces of citrus peel that are used in drinks as a garnish and to add flavor.

*Note: For a more dramatic effect, you can make citrus spirals longer, such as 6 to 8 inches or longer.*

1. To make a citrus spiral, hold the fruit firmly in one hand. At one end of the fruit, place your thumb on the peel and dig a channel knife tool into the peel.
2. Gently bring the tool towards you, cutting a slice of peel.
3. Continue to cut the peel, working around the circumference of the fruit until you reach the other end of the fruit.
4. Cut the peel into 3 to 4 inch pieces.

- To place a citrus spiral in a cocktail, twist the garnish over the cocktail and rub the peel around the rim of the glass. Position a third of the spiral in the drink and drape the rest of the spiral over the edge of the glass.

*Note: You can also place the entire spiral in the drink.*

# CREATE PINEAPPLE WEDGES

Few things bring the sunny tropics to mind like fresh, juicy pineapples. It's no wonder that so many tropical cocktails feature pineapple wedges as a garnish. Bright yellow and bursting with sweet flavor, a pineapple wedge garnish is simple to create and makes a nice snack once you have finished your drink. You also need a pineapple wedge to create a pineapple flag, which is a showy garnish with a maraschino cherry skewered on top of a pineapple wedge. To make pineapple flags, see page 36.

## Creating Pineapple Wedges

Step 1

Step 2

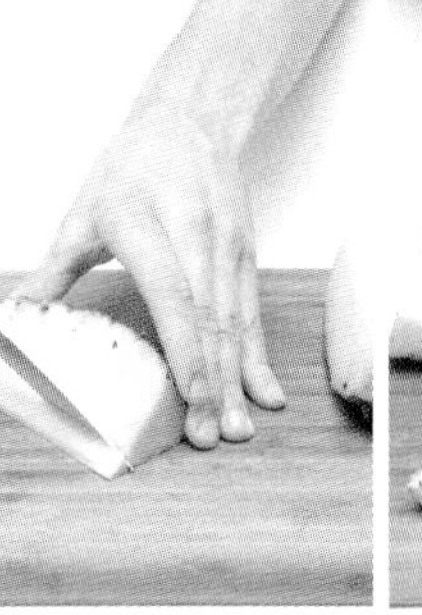

Step 5

Step 6

Step 3

Step 4

Step 7

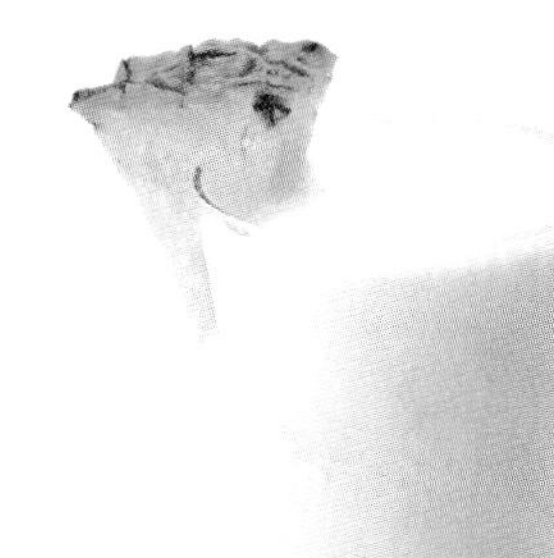

Step 8

- Pineapple wedges are commonly placed on the rims of glasses to decorate drinks.

1 To make pineapple wedges, start by cutting off and discarding the ends of the fruit.

2 Cut the fruit in half lengthwise.

3 Place each half of the fruit on the cutting board, cut-side down, and cut the fruit lengthwise in half again.

4 Cut each section of fruit lengthwise in half again.

5 Slice off the core of the pineapple from each section of pineapple.

6 Cut each section of pineapple into 1/4 to 1/2 inch thick wedges.

7 To place a pineapple wedge on the rim of a glass, make a cut approximately 1/2 inch deep into the wedge.

8 Place the pineapple wedge on the rim of a glass.

# Zest & Juice
## Citrus Fruits

Citrus fruits contain two sources of flavor: juice and zest. While citrus juices can be purchased, nothing tastes better than fresh-squeezed juice. Citrus zest, which contains flavorful oils and looks great as a garnish, is removed from the peel of the fruit with a zester. A citrus zester is a hand-held tool with five or six small, sharp stainless steel holes used to remove threadlike strips of peel from the rind of a citrus fruit. Generally, a medium orange yields 4 teaspoons of zest, a medium lemon delivers 2 to 3 teaspoons of zest and a medium lime yields 1 teaspoon of zest.

### Zesting Citrus Fruits

Steps 1 & 2

Step 3

- You can use a citrus zester to create citrus zest, which is fine threads of fruit peel.

1 To make citrus zest, position the fruit on its side on a cutting board.

2 Stabilizing the fruit with one hand, position the edge of the citrus zester at the top of the fruit with your other hand.

3 Using firm and even pressure, move the citrus zester downward to the bottom of the fruit.

4 Repeat steps 2 to 3 until you have produced the desired amount of zest.

### Juicing Citrus Fruits

*How much juice do lemons and limes produce?*

| 1 Medium Lemon |
|---|
| 1 lemon = 2 oz |
| 3/4 lemon = 1 1/2 oz |
| 1/2 lemon = 1 oz |
| 1/4 lemon = 1/2 oz |

| 1 Medium Lime |
|---|
| 1 lime = 1 oz |
| 3/4 lime = 3/4 oz |
| 1/2 lime = 1/2 oz |
| 1/4 lime = 1/4 oz |

- Many recipes call for fresh lemon and lime juice. Here are some tips to make juicing quick and easy.
- Fruits stored at room temperature are easier to squeeze and produce more juice than fruit that is refrigerated.
- Before juicing a fruit, firmly roll the fruit on a hard surface with the palm of your hand a few times.
- You can store fresh juice in the refrigerator for one week. If you have a large amount of juice, pour the juice into an ice cube tray and freeze for later use.

# Create Flags & Boats

Fruit flags and boats are the flashiest of the standard cocktail garnishes. Flags are garnishes that skewer a maraschino cherry on top of another garnish, such as an orange slice or pineapple wedge. Think of the cherry as a flag being planted on top of the other garnish. Boats are made from citrus fruit wheels that have been folded in half with a maraschino cherry pinned into the fold.

## How to Make an Orange Flag

Step 1

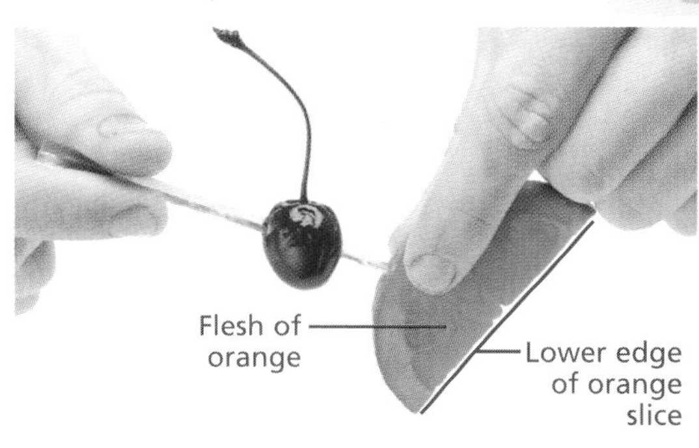


Steps 2 & 3

- An orange flag is a maraschino cherry skewered on top of an orange slice.

1 Push a cocktail stick through a maraschino cherry.

2 Hold an orange slice between your thumb and index finger.

*Note: To make an orange slice, see page 31.*

3 Gently push the cocktail stick through the peel of the orange slice and down through the flesh. The cocktail stick should not go beyond the lower edge of the orange slice.

## How to Make a Pineapple Flag

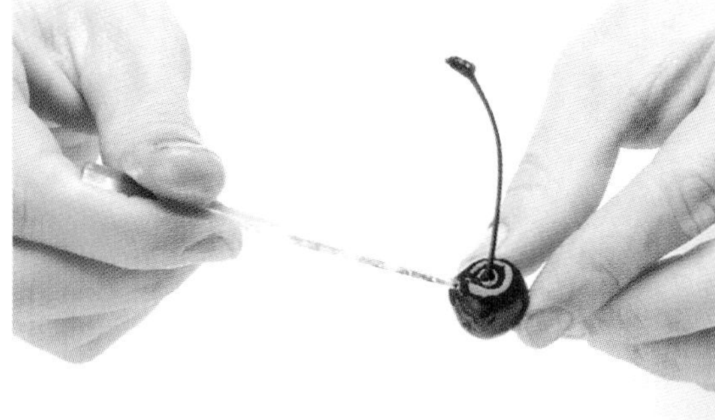

Step 1

Steps 2 & 3

- A pineapple flag is a maraschino cherry skewered on top of a pineapple wedge.

1 Push a cocktail stick through a maraschino cherry.

2 Hold a pineapple wedge between your thumb and index finger.

*Note: To make a pineapple wedge, see page 34.*

3 Gently push the cocktail stick through the skin of a pineapple wedge and down through the flesh. The cocktail stick should not go beyond the lower edge of the pineapple wedge.

**TIP** *How do I place a flag and boat on the rim of a glass?*

Before placing an orange flag or a pineapple flag on the rim of a glass, you must make a cut approximately 1/4 inch deep into the orange slice of an orange flag and a 1/2 inch cut into the pineapple wedge of the pineapple flag. Then place the flag on the rim. Boats are much easier to place. You simply place the boat across the opening of a glass.

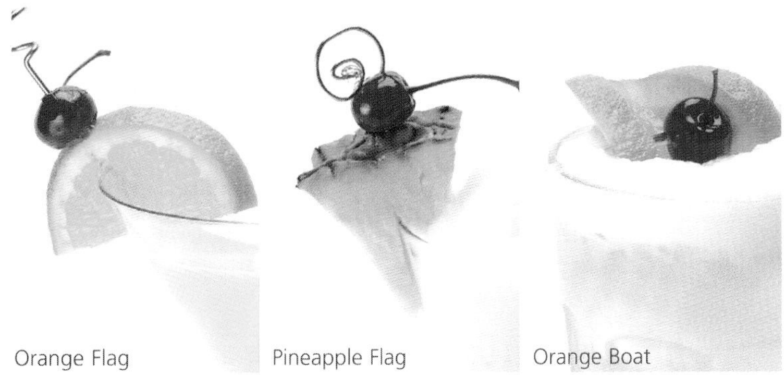

Orange Flag Pineapple Flag Orange Boat

## How to Make a Boat

Step 1

Step 2

Step 3

White pith

- A boat is a citrus fruit wheel that has been folded in half with a maraschino cherry skewered in the center.

1 Push a cocktail stick just below the white pith of an orange wheel.

*Note: To make an orange wheel,* *see page 31.*

2 Push the cocktail stick through a maraschino cherry.

3 Bend the orange wheel into a "U" shape. Push the cocktail stick just below the white pith on the other side of the orange wheel.

# SHAKE THE PERFECT COCKTAIL

Aside from the ability to open a bottle, shaking a cocktail is the most basic skill in bartending. Cocktails are typically shaken to thoroughly mix the drink's ingredients. There are two main types of shakers. Preferred by the pros, Boston shakers are comprised of a tapered, stainless steel can and a smaller tapered glass. Standard shakers are comprised of a large can, a lid that contains a strainer and a tight-fitting cap. Whichever shaker you use, shaking should be done with one hand on either end and vigorous enough that the ingredients travel the entire length of the shaker.

## Boston Shaker

Steps 1 & 2

1 To shake a cocktail in a Boston shaker, fill the glass halfway with ice cubes.

*Note: If the recipe you are following does not call for ice cubes in the shaker, see the top of page 39.*

2 Pour the ingredients into the glass and place the stainless steel can securely over the glass.

3 Holding the bottom of the glass in one hand and the top of the can in your other hand, turn the shaker upside down. The can should now be on the bottom.

4 Shake the Boston shaker with an up and down movement for 5 to 10 seconds.

5 Remove the glass from the can.

6 Place a Hawthorn strainer at the top of the can.

*Note: For information on Hawthorn strainers, see page 14.*

7 With one hand holding the can and the strainer, firmly place your index finger against the raised tab or at the back of the Hawthorn strainer.

8 Holding a glass in your other hand, strain the drink into the glass.

TIP *How do I shake a cocktail that does not have ice in the shaker?*

The method for shaking a cocktail with or without ice is the same. The only difference is how you transfer the drink from the shaker to the glass. If you shake a cocktail that does not have ice in the shaker, simply pour the drink into the glass without using a strainer. However, you may want to use a strainer if you are using fresh lime, lemon or other citrus fruits in your cocktails. Straining will filter out any seeds that may have fallen into the shaker.

## Standard Shaker

1 To shake a cocktail in a standard shaker, fill the can halfway with ice cubes.

*Note: If the recipe you are following does not call for ice cubes in the shaker, see the top of page 39.*

2 Pour the ingredients into the can. Then place the cap with its lid securely on the can.

3 Hold the bottom of the can in one hand and the top of the can with your other hand, securing the lid. Shake the standard shaker with an up and down movement for 5 to 10 seconds.

4 Remove the lid from the cap.

5 Holding the can where the cap and can meet, strain the drink into a glass.

# Coat the Rim of a Glass

Often seen on margaritas and Bloody Marys, rim coatings are a unique way to add extra interest and flavor to your cocktails. After moistening the outside of the rim with a lemon wedge or other citrus fruit, almost any powdered or crystallized ingredient, such as sea salt, sugar, cocoa powder and celery salt, can be used to "rim" a glass. Coatings should be on the outside of the rim only—the idea is to have the coating hit the tongue before the drink does.

## Coat the Rim of a Glass

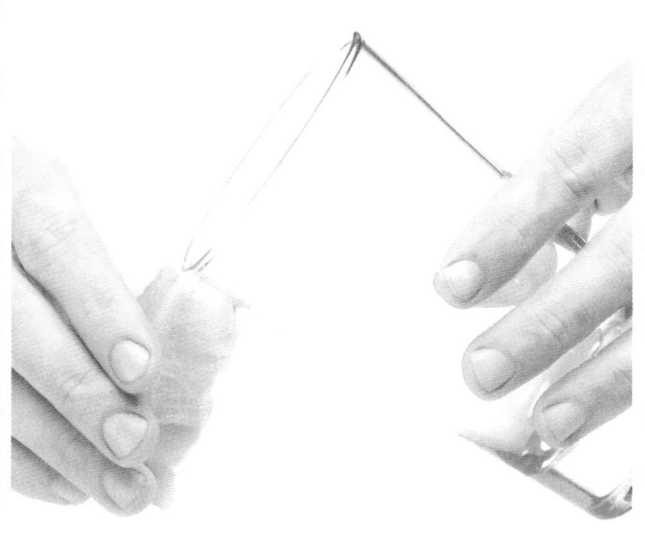

1 Pour the sugar, salt or other ingredient you want to use to coat the rim of a glass onto a small plate.

2 Rub a lemon wedge around the outside edge of the glass rim.

*Note: Do not rub the lemon wedge around the inside edge of the glass rim. This may cause the rimming ingredient to stick to the inside of the glass rim and eventually fall into the drink, altering its taste.*

3 Holding the glass at a 90-degree angle, slowly rotate the outside edge of the glass in the rimming ingredient until it is fully coated.

- If the rimming ingredient appears on the inside edge of the glass rim, gently wipe the inside rim with a moistened napkin or paper towel.

# CHILL & PREHEAT GLASSWARE

Chilling and preheating your glassware is crucial to keeping your beverages at the ideal temperature. Also, when preparing cocktails while entertaining, chilling or preheating glasses in front of your guests shows that you are taking extra care in creating their cocktails. If a cocktail does not include ice in the glass, then the glass should be chilled. Chilling a glass simply requires some ice and water. To heat a glass, boiling water does an excellent job. A specialty coffee or hot chocolate served in a preheated glass will warm your guests to the last sip.

## Chill a Glass

1 Fill the glass you want to chill with ice cubes and pour cold water up to the rim of the glass.

2 Prepare your cocktail in a shaker. For information on shaking cocktails, see page 38.

3 Pick the glass up by the stem and pour the ice cubes and water out of the glass. Shake the glass a few times to get rid of any remaining drops of water.

4 Pour or strain your cocktail into the chilled glass.

## Preheat a Glass

1 Fill the glass you want to preheat up to the rim with boiling water.

2 Let the boiling water sit in the glass for 10 seconds.

3 Pick the glass up by the stem or handle and pour the boiling water out of the glass. Shake the glass a few times to get rid of any remaining drops of water.

4 Prepare your hot beverage in the preheated glass. For recipes of hot beverages, see pages 178 to 197.

# MAKE SIMPLE SYRUP

Remember when you learned in chemistry class that sugar dissolves more readily in hot water than cold? That lesson applies to bartending. When mixing icy cocktails, you'll shake your arms off before regular sugar dissolves. Fortunately, we have simple syrup, a water and sugar mixture that has been heated so that the sugar is dissolved and will easily blend with your beverages. Simple syrup is easy to make and will keep for several weeks in the refrigerator.

## Make Simple Syrup

2 cups sugar
1 cup water

Step 1 Step 2

Step 5

- This recipe makes 18 oz, or 2 1/8 cups, of simple syrup.

1 Add the water and sugar to a saucepan and stir.

2 Using medium-high heat, bring the mixture to a gentle boil and continue to stir.

3 Reduce to low heat and continue to stir the mixture for 3 to 4 minutes until the sugar has completely dissolved.

4 Remove the saucepan from the heat and let the simple syrup cool to room temperature.

*Note: Simple syrup should have a consistency between maple syrup and warm molasses.*

5 Using a funnel, pour the mixture into a glass container with a tight fitting lid and refrigerate.

*Note: You should not store simple syrup in a plastic container as the plastic may affect the taste of the simple syrup.*

# MAKE FRUIT PUREE

Fruit puree adds fresh fruit flavor to any cocktail. It can, however, be difficult to find. Fortunately, making your own is simple and inexpensive. Aside from strawberries and peaches, you can make puree from any fresh, juicy fruit—try raspberries, pears, apricots, blueberries or mangos. One of the best things about making fruit puree is that you can adjust the sweetness to suit your tastes. If your puree is too thick, blend in a splash of fresh lemon or lime juice. Homemade puree can be refrigerated for a week or frozen in an ice-cube tray to create small portions.

## Strawberry Puree

1 pint ripe strawberries
1/4 cup sugar

Steps 1, 2 & 3

Step 4

- Strawberry puree is a mixture of strawberries and sugar that has been blended to a smooth, thick liquid consistency. Purees give cocktails fresh fruit flavor and a thicker texture.
- This recipe makes approximately 1 3/4 cups or 14 oz of puree.

1. Wash and remove the stems from the strawberries. Cut the strawberries in half.
2. Place the strawberries and sugar into a blender.
3. Blend until smooth.
4. Pour the puree into a container with a tight-fitting lid and refrigerate.

## Peach Puree

2 large, ripe peaches
3 tablespoons sugar

Steps 1, 2 & 3

Step 4

- Peach puree is a mixture of peaches and sugar that has been blended to a smooth, thick liquid consistency. Purees give cocktails fresh fruit flavor and a thicker texture.
- This recipe makes approximately 1 1/4 cups or 10 oz of puree.

1. Wash and cut the peaches into 1/2 inch cubes.
2. Place the peach cubes and sugar into a blender.
3. Blend until smooth.
4. Pour the puree into a container with a tight-fitting lid and refrigerate.

# HOW TO MUDDLE

Muddling is a great way to release both stress and flavor. Using a small, wooden bat called a muddler, muddling involves mashing up cocktail ingredients to release their flavors. Fruits, herbs and sugars are all prime candidates for muddling. Typically, the ingredients are placed in the bottom of a sturdy glass and mashed firmly. In drinks like the Bourbon Smash (page 137), muddling releases fruit juices and herbal flavors. In the Caipirinha (page 117), muddling extracts essential oils from the citrus peels.

## How to Muddle

- Muddling refers to crushing ingredients such as herbs, fruit and sugar to release their flavors into the cocktail.

1 Place the ingredients you want to muddle at the bottom of a sturdy glass.

*Note: In this example, we are muddling a lime.*

- If you are muddling fruit, make sure the fruit is cut up into pieces no larger than 1/2 inch chunks.

2 Holding the glass with one hand, hold the base of the muddler with your other hand. Place the wide end of the muddler on the ingredients at the bottom of the glass.

3 Press down and twist the muddler in one direction to crush the ingredients. Continue to press down and twist the muddler until the ingredients are completely crushed.

# HOW TO LAYER DRINKS

Layering is a bartending technique that is guaranteed to impress. Typically prepared in shot glasses, layered drinks feature liqueurs and liquors that stay separated in distinct layers in a glass. It's possible to achieve this striking effect because liquids of different densities will stay separate if you pour slowly and layer from most-dense to least-dense, bottom to top. A steady hand and lots of practice are the keys to mastering this technique. A barspoon is the best tool for layering—if you don't have one, you can pour over the back of a teaspoon instead.

## How to Layer Drinks

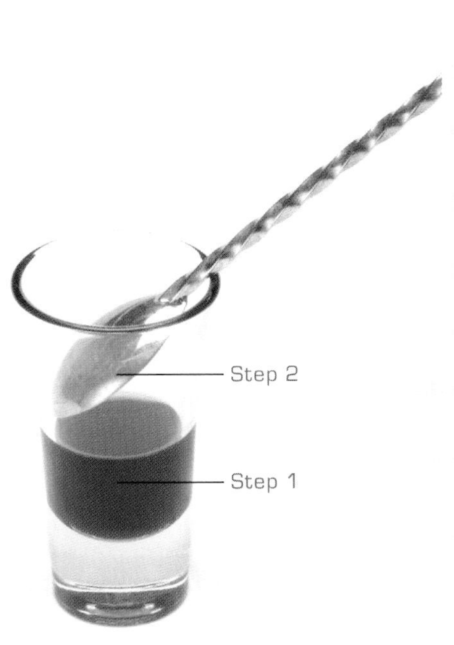


Step 3

Step 5

- A layered drink features different liqueurs and liquors that are poured on top of the other. The different liqueurs and liquors appear "layered" and are not mixed together.

1. Pour the first ingredient in the glass.
2. Place the back of a barspoon just above the first ingredient in the glass.
3. Pour the next ingredient very slowly over the back of the barspoon.

- The liquid flows over the back of the barspoon. The barspoon spreads the liquid over the layer below without mixing the ingredients.

4. Once you have finished pouring the layer, slowly remove the barspoon and clean with a cloth.
5. Repeat steps 3 to 4 for each ingredient you want to layer.

# Spirits & Liqueurs

Without alcohol, bartending would be pretty dull. Becoming familiar with the extensive variety of spirits and liqueurs available is absolutely crucial if you wish to become a first-rate bartender. This section of the book explores the six main spirits and many liqueurs that are used to create the range of cocktails served today.

# 3 Spirits & Liqueurs

Gin

Vodka

Rum

Tequila

Whiskey

Brandy

Liqueurs

# GIN

Gin is a popular distilled spirit with a very distinctive flavor. Gin is different from other clear spirits because it is flavored with juniper berries and other botanical ingredients. When a recipe lists "gin" as an ingredient, it is referring to a type of gin called London dry gin. Originally produced in Holland for medicinal purposes, gin is now also produced in England and the United States. Gin should be stored in a cool, dark place out of direct sunlight.

## Gin Overview

- Gin is a distilled, colorless spirit that has an alcohol content of approximately 40% by volume or 80 proof. Gin is made from grain such as barley, corn or rye.
- Gin is infused with the flavor of several natural ingredients which gives this spirit its distinct aroma and taste.
- The most common style of gin is London dry gin. There are several brands of London dry gin available.
- Gin is a key ingredient in cocktails such as the Classic Gin Martini (page 66) and Tom Collins (page 100).

## Quality Gin

- Quality gins are readily available and are a good choice when making cocktails.
- Gordon's gin is consumed at a rate of 10 bottles/min around the world. Only 12 people know the top-secret recipe used to make Gordon's.
- Beefeater is the only London dry-labeled gin to still be produced in London. The recipe has been virtually unchanged since 1820.
- Seagram's Extra Dry is produced in the United States and is aged in whiskey barrels, which gives this gin a slightly yellow hue.

TIP *Are there other flavors of gin available?*

While plain London dry gins are popular, flavored gins are also available. Noted gin producer Beefeater produces several flavored gins. Beefeater Lime and Beefeater Orange are flavored London dry gins that are ideal for using as mixers. Wet by Beefeater is a lighter, fruiter tasting gin that is infused with pear flavor. Hendrick's Gin is a Scottish gin that adds rose petals and cucumber to the flavor mix to create a very unique taste.

TIP *What does "distilled" mean?*

Distilled spirits are made by *distillation*, a process where a fermented liquid, which contains small amounts of alcohol, is heated so the alcohol evaporates. The vapor is then condensed into a liquid that contains a much higher amount of alcohol. Gin, as well as vodka, rum, whiskey, tequila and brandy are all made in this manner. The alcohol content of a distilled spirit is higher than that of beer or wine.

## Premium Gin

- Premium gins are higher-quality and more expensive gins. Premium gins offer a smooth, clean taste and are a good choice when making cocktails for special occasions.
- Britain's Tanqueray is made from high-quality grains and herbs and is distilled four times to ensure a smooth taste.
- Bombay Sapphire is packaged in a distinct blue bottle. This premium gin is produced in Britain and is made from the traditional juniper berries along with nine other plant extracts.

## Super Premium Gin

- No. Ten by Tanqueray is a super premium gin. This gin is produced in small batches and is made from whole fresh herbs and fruit.
- No. Ten has a higher alcohol content than other gins and is distilled at 47.3% alcohol by volume or 94.6 proof.
- No. Ten offers gin drinkers a silky-smooth texture and fresh fruit aromas and flavors. This super premium gin is often served chilled, with or without ice and without a mixer.

# VODKA

Vodka is a versatile spirit that is distilled and filtered to such a point that it has virtually no flavor or aroma. This versatility has made vodka one of the most popular liquors in the world. Vodka originated in Russia and Poland, but today it is produced around the world. Quality vodkas, such as Absolut, are ideal for making cocktails. Premium and super premium vodkas, such as Skyy and Grey Goose, are good choices for mixing up in cocktails for special occasions as well as drinking on their own, with or without ice.

## Vodka Overview

- Vodka is a colorless and odorless spirit that has an alcohol content of approximately 40% by volume or 80 proof. Vodka is used in numerous recipes including the Screwdriver (page 98) and Cosmopolitan (page 72).
- Vodka is most often made from grain, such as wheat, barley or rye.
- Vodka is made by a process called *distillation*, which concentrates the alcohol content of the spirit. Vodka is then filtered to remove impurities. The more vodka is distilled and filtered, the higher quality the vodka is.

## Quality Vodka

- Quality vodkas are readily available and are a good choice when making cocktails.
- Smirnoff is produced in the United States and is the largest selling vodka in the world.
- Finlandia is distilled in Finland and is a leading brand of quality vodka.
- Absolut is a popular brand of vodka and is produced in Sweden.

TIP *How should I store vodka?*

Vodka is customarily served ice cold and, since it will not freeze because of its high alcohol content, the best place to store vodka is in the freezer. You can store an open bottle of vodka in the freezer for up to three years.

TIP *What are flavored vodkas?*

Flavored vodkas are vodkas that have had various flavors added to them. These vodkas have become extremely popular and most vodka producers have responded to this trend with their own lines of flavored vodka. Absolut offers a line of lemon, vanilla, peach, orange, raspberry, black currant and even pepper vodkas. Stolichnaya offers lemon, cranberry, peach, strawberry, vanilla, orange and raspberry variations. Even super premium Grey Goose offers vodkas infused with orange, lemon and vanilla flavors.

## Premium Vodka

- Premium vodkas are higher-quality and more expensive vodkas. Premium vodkas offer a smooth, clean taste and are a good choice when making cocktails for special occasions or for serving on ice.
- Skyy is produced in the United States. This brand of premium vodka is distilled four times and filtered three times.
- Stolichnaya, often simply called Stoli, is a Russian vodka. Stoli is distilled twice and filtered four times through charcoal and quartz sand to remove impurities.

## Super Premium Vodka

- Super premium vodkas are the highest-quality and most expensive vodkas. These vodkas offer the smoothest taste and are often served chilled, with or without ice and without a mixer.
- Poland's Belvedere is made in small batches and is distilled four times to ensure superior quality.
- France's Grey Goose uses the finest French wheat to produce its vodka. It also uses a five-step distillation process.

# RUM

Rum is a spirit that is distilled from sugar cane and comes in several distinct forms. Originally produced in the Caribbean, rum is still mainly made in this region. There are several types of rum, including light, dark and gold rums, as well as spiced rum and overproof rum. Popular brands of rum include Bacardi, Captain Morgan and Appleton Estate. Rum should be stored in a cool, dark place out of direct sunlight.

## Rum Overview

- Rum is used in hundreds of cocktail recipes and has an alcohol content of approximately 40% by volume or 80 proof.
- Rum is a distilled spirit made from sugar cane. Most of the world's rum is produced in the Caribbean.
- Rum is available in several varieties including light and dark. Light rum is aged in stainless steel tanks. Dark rum gets its color from the addition of caramel and being aged in charred oak barrels.

## Light Rum

- Light rum, also called white rum, is colorless. This type of rum is dry, light-bodied and has a delicate, sweet flavor.
- Light rum is commonly used to make tropical cocktails such as Daiquiris (pages 138 to 141) and Coladas (pages 142 to 143).
- Bacardi Superior, Captain Morgan White Rum and Appleton White Jamaica Rum are popular examples of light rum.

TIP *What is gold rum?*

Gold rum, also called amber rum, is a medium-bodied rum that is golden in color. Gold rum is made by blending dark and light rum. Appleton Estate V/X Jamaica Rum and Bacardi Gold are examples of popular gold rums. Gold rum is also used in the making of spiced rums like Captain Morgan Original Spiced Rum.

TIP *What is overproof rum?*

Overproof rum is a type of rum that has a much higher alcohol content than the 40% alcohol by volume of normal rum. Bacardi 151°, with an alcohol content of 75.5% by volume, is an example of overproof rum. Due to its high alcohol content, overproof rum is frequently used in flaming drinks.

## Dark Rum

- Dark rum is dark brown or black in color. This full-bodied rum is characterized by a rich, complex flavor that often includes hints of molasses or caramel.
- Dark rum is an ingredient in several cocktails including the Bees Knees and Bella Donna (page 91).
- Bacardi Black and Captain Morgan Black Label are popular examples of dark rum.

## Flavored Rum

- Flavored rum generally has a lower alcohol content than other types of rum and can be used in place of light rum in cocktail recipes.
- Captain Morgan offers Parrot Bay which is available in mango, pineapple and coconut flavors.
- Bacardi's line of flavored rum includes Bacardi Limón, Bacardi O, Bacardi Cóco, Bacardi Vaníla and Bacardi Razz.
- Malibu is a popular rum-based liqueur that comes in coconut, mango, pineapple and passion fruit flavors.

# Tequila

Imported from Mexico, tequila is a unique type of liquor. Instead of being made from grapes, grains, potatoes or some other edible plant, tequila is made from the blue agave plant, a member of the lily family. Once mainly thought of as a shooter and the prime ingredient for margaritas, tequila has become popular as the base spirit for a great number of cocktails. There is a wide range of tequilas to suit a variety of tastes and uses.

## Tequila Overview

- Tequila is a distilled spirit from Mexico and is named for the town of Tequila, where most of the spirit is produced.
- All tequila must contain at least 51% agave. Tequila labeled 100% agave is the highest quality.
- Tequila is most often distilled twice before bottling and has an alcohol content of 40% by volume or 80 proof.
- Tequila is an ingredient in Margaritas (page 144) and the Long Island Iced Tea (page 106).

## Blanco

- Blanco, which means white, is a colorless tequila. This type of tequila may also be labeled Plata, meaning silver.
- Blanco can be bottled immediately after distillation or kept for up to two months in stainless steel tanks. Blanco has a strong flavor and aroma.
- Jose Cuervo Clásico, Sauza Tequila Blanco and Cabo Wabo Tequila Blanco are popular examples of Blanco tequila.

TIP *What is gold tequila?*

Gold tequila, also known as Joven Abocado or Oro, is Blanco tequila that has had colorings and flavorings, such as caramel, added to it. These additives mellow the flavor of the tequila. Gold is the ideal choice for making cocktails. Sauza Extra Gold and Jose Cuervo Especial are popular examples of gold tequila.

TIP *What is mezcal?*

Mezcal, sometimes spelled mescal, is a distilled spirit that is related to tequila. While tequila can only be made from the blue agave plant, mezcal can be made from several varieties of the agave plant. Most mezcal is produced around the city of Oaxaca. Monte Alban is one popular brand of mezcal.

## Reposado

- Reposado, meaning rested, is tequila that has been aged from two months to a year in oak tanks or barrels before being bottled.
- Reposado tequila has a smooth, complex flavor and ranges in color from pale straw to gold.
- This tequila is a good choice when making special cocktails.
- Jose Cuervo Tradicional, Cabo Wabo Tequila Reposado and Patrón Reposado are popular examples of this tequila.

## Añejo

- Añejo, which means aged, is tequila that has been aged in oak barrels for at least a year before being bottled for sale.
- The aging process gives Añejo tequila a smooth taste and a subtle, woodsy flavor. This tequila ranges in color from gold to amber and is meant to be enjoyed on its own without ice.
- Jose Cuervo Reserva de la Familia, Patrón Añejo and Herradura Añejo are popular examples of this tequila.

# WHISKEY

Distilled from various grains, whiskey is a spirit that is produced in various forms around the world. Production of whiskey began in Ireland and Scotland sometime around the 17th century. Two distinct varieties of whiskey, Irish whiskey and Scotch whisky, continue to be produced there today. In North America, a number of different varieties have been developed including bourbon, Canadian whisky and Tennessee whiskey.

## Whiskey Overview

- Whiskey is a distilled spirit made from grain and aged in wooden barrels. The aging process mellows the flavor of the whiskey.
- Whiskey has an alcohol content of approximately 40% by volume or 80 proof. Whiskey may be enjoyed on its own with or without ice or used in cocktails.
- Whiskey is produced in several countries and is available in many styles. Depending on where the spirit is produced, it may be spelled "whiskey" or "whisky."

## Scotch Whisky

- Scotch whisky, also called Scotch, is produced in Scotland and is aged for at least three years in oak barrels and is known for its smoky flavor.
- Single Malt Scotch is the highest quality whisky available and is produced at a single distillery. Glenfiddich and Glenlivet are popular brands.
- Blended Scotch is made from barley and other grains and is the most commonly consumed type of Scotch. Popular brands include J&B and Johnnie Walker.

**TIP** *What is Tennessee whiskey?*

Tennessee whiskey is an American whiskey that is very similar to bourbon. Tennessee whiskey is made mainly from corn and is aged for at least two years in new, charred oak barrels. Tennessee whiskey differs from bourbon in that it is filtered though maple charcoal before aging. This filtering process gives Tennessee whiskey a subtle, sweet flavor. Jack Daniel's is the best-known Tennessee whiskey.

**TIP** *What is Irish whiskey?*

Irish whiskey is a mellow, sweeter type of whiskey which is produced in Ireland. Unlike Scotch whisky, Irish whiskey does not generally have a smoky flavor. Instead, it derives much of its flavor from aging in barrels that have previously held sherry, rum or bourbon. Like Scotch, Irish whiskey is available in single-malt and blended varieties. Well-known producers of Irish whiskey include Jameson, Bushmills and Midleton.

## Bourbon

- Bourbon, also known as Kentucky whiskey, is an American whiskey produced in the state of Kentucky. Bourbon is generally considered a high-quality whiskey.
- Bourbon is made from corn along with smaller amounts of wheat, rye and barley.
- Bourbon must be aged for at least two years in oak barrels.
- Popular brands of bourbon include Jim Beam, Wild Turkey and Knob Creek.

## Canadian Whisky

- Most of the whisky produced in Canada is blended and is made from a combination of rye, corn and barley.
- Canadian whisky is aged for at least three years in wooden barrels and tends to be lighter tasting than other types of whiskey.
- Crown Royal and Canadian Club are popular brands of Canadian whisky.

# Brandy

Distilled from wine or fermented fruit juice, brandy is a unique liquor that was created quite unintentionally. In the 16th century, Dutch traders began removing water from wine so that it would take up less cargo space. Water would be added back to the wine when it reached its destination. It was soon discovered, however, that this concentrated wine took on intriguing characteristics and was delicious undiluted. At that moment brandy was born.

## Brandy Overview

- Brandy is a distilled spirit made from wine or fermented fruit juice.
- Brandy has an alcohol content of approximately 40% by volume or 80 proof.
- Younger, less expensive brandy is a good choice when making cocktails such as the Brandy Alexander (page 96). Older, more expensive brandy is meant to be enjoyed on its own without ice.

## Cognac

- Cognac is brandy produced in the Cognac region of France. Cognac is made from wine and is the best known brandy.
- Cognac is distilled twice before being aged in oak barrels for many years. The aging process allows cognac to develop its distinct aroma and smooth taste, as well as darken in color.
- Almost all cognacs are a blend of brandies from different years.
- Popular brands of cognac include Rémy Martin, Hennessy and Courvoisier.

**TIP** *What do the letters on a bottle of cognac or armagnac mean?*

The letters on a bottle of cognac or armagnac indicate the spirit's age. V.S. ("Very Special") means the youngest brandy in the blend has been aged at least 3 years, V.S.O.P. ("Very Superior Old Pale") means the youngest brandy in the blend has been aged at least 5 years and X.O. ("Extra Old") means the youngest brandy in the blend has been aged at least 6 years.

**TIP** *How do I serve cognac or armagnac?*

Older cognac and armagnac is ideally served at room temperature in a brandy snifter. To serve, preheat your brandy snifter. For information on preheating glassware, see page 41. Then pour 2 oz of brandy into the snifter. Holding the bowl of the snifter in the palm of your hand, with the stem between your index finger and middle finger, gently swirl the brandy to release its aroma.

## Armagnac

- Armagnac is brandy produced from grapes grown in the Armagnac region of France.
- This brandy is produced using a single distillation process and is then aged in oak barrels. A long aging process mellows the flavor of armagnac and gives the brandy its amber to mahogany color.
- Like cognac, most armagnacs are a blend of brandies from different years.
- Janneau, Samalens and de Montal are well known brands of armagnac.

## Fruit Brandy

- Fruit brandy is made from fermented fruit juice. Fruit brandy is available in many flavors including apple, plum, peach, apricot and cherry.
- Fruit brandy can be enjoyed in cocktails or served over ice.
- Popular examples of fruit brandy include calvados, which is apple brandy from France and kirsch, which is cherry brandy.

# Liqueurs

Liqueurs are sweet, alcoholic beverages that are generally made up of a spirit that has been flavored with fruits, nuts, herbs, spices and other ingredients. Today, consumers can choose from a mind-boggling selection of delicious liqueurs from around the world.

Originally served as after-dinner drinks, liqueurs now play a crucial role as ingredients in the broad range of cocktails made today. Instead of serving just straight spirits, liqueurs allow you to serve up interesting cocktails that contain an array of unique flavors.

## Advocaat

Advocaat is a creamy, yellow liqueur made from egg yolks, sugar, spices and brandy. Of Dutch origin, advocaat's flavor is somewhat similar to that of eggnog which makes advocaat the perfect ingredient for Christmas-themed warmers.

## Alizé

Alizé is made in France and is a brandy-based liqueur blended with passion fruit juice. Alizé is available in several varieties, with Red Passion being the most popular.

## Amaretto

Amaretto is an almond-flavored liqueur made from apricot pits. Disaronno is the most popular brand of amaretto and is made in Italy with 17 herbs and fruits.

## Apricot Brandy

Apricot brandy is a brandy created from apricots and select cognacs. Apricot brandy has a slight almond flavor.

## Asian Pear Liqueur

Asian pear liqueur is a green liqueur that is made from pears. While the predominant flavor is that of pears, there are also hints of vanilla and apple in this liqueur.

## B & B

B&B is a combination of Benedictine liqueur and fine brandy. Benedictine is a liqueur comprised of 27 herbs and spices, such as saffron, ginger and cloves.

## Baileys Irish Cream

Baileys Irish Cream is a liqueur made up of dairy cream and Irish whiskey. The whiskey acts as a preservative, so Baileys does not need to be refrigerated.

## Banana Liqueur

Banana liqueur is a bright yellow liqueur that tastes like bananas. Also called crème de banane, banana liqueur has vanilla and almond undertones.

## Butterscotch Schnapps

Butterscotch schnapps is a brandy-based, butterscotch-flavored liqueur. The butterscotch flavor comes from a mixture of butter and brown sugar.

## Campari

Campari is a bright-red, bittersweet apéritif and is typically served chilled. This dry-tasting Italian liqueur is made from a secret recipe of herbs, plants and fruits.

## Cassis

Cassis is a liqueur made from black currants. Originally produced only in France, Cassis is now produced in the United States as well.

## Chambord

Chambord is a premium raspberry liqueur. Produced in France, this dark purple liqueur tastes of black raspberries with a hint of honey, herbs and other berry fruits.

## Chartreuse

Chartreuse is a herbal liqueur containing over 130 herbs and spices. Of French origin, Chartreuse is available in both yellow and green varieties.

## Cherry Brandy

Cherry brandy is brandy made from cherries and select cognacs. Cherry brandy has undertones of cinnamon, almonds, cloves and spices.

## Cointreau

Cointreau is an orange-flavored liqueur. Clear in color, Cointreau is a brandy-based liqueur infused with orange peel.

## Crème de Cacao

Crème de cacao is a chocolate-flavored liqueur with hints of vanilla. Available in white and dark varieties, both types of crème de cacao taste very similar.

## Crème de Menthe

Crème de menthe is a mint-flavored liqueur. Available in green and white varieties, both types of crème de menthe taste very similar.

## Curacao

Curacao is an orange-flavored liqueur. Available in both orange and blue varieties, both types of curacao taste very similar.

## Drambuie

Drambuie is a scotch-based liqueur. Produced in Scotland, Drambuie is flavored with a secret recipe of honey, herbs and various spices.

## Frangelico

Frangelico is a hazelnut-flavored liqueur. Produced in Italy, Frangelico is based upon a 300-year-old recipe and features vanilla and cinnamon undertones.

# Liqueurs

The exact ingredients and methods for making well-known liqueurs, such as orange-flavored Grand Marnier and coffee-flavored Kahlua, are closely guarded secrets. In general, however, the various fruits, herbs and spices used to flavor liqueurs are mixed directly into the base spirit. Natural extracts and essential oils are also used to flavor some liqueurs. Less-expensive liqueurs often use artificial flavors and will produce lesser-quality cocktails.

## Galliano

Galliano is a gold-colored liqueur. Produced in Italy, Galliano contains over 40 herbs with predominant flavors of vanilla and anise.

## Goldschlager

Goldschlager is a cinnamon schnapps liqueur. Produced in Switzerland, Goldschlager contains real flakes of gold. The gold flakes are not harmful if ingested.

## Grand Marnier

Grand Marnier is a premium orange-flavored liqueur. Produced in France, Grand Marnier is a cognac-based liqueur that lends sophistication to any cocktail.

## Hpnotiq

Hpnotiq is a cognac-based, tropical-fruit-flavored liqueur. Produced in France, Hpnotiq is famous for its deep blue color.

## Jägermeister

Jägermeister is a liqueur made up of 56 herbal ingredients. Produced in Germany, Jägermeister is traditionally known for its digestive benefits.

## Kahlua

Kahlua is a rum-based, coffee-flavored liqueur with undertones of vanilla. Produced in Mexico, Kahlua is the most popular coffee liqueur in the world.

## Limoncello

Limoncello is a tangy, lemon-flavored liqueur. Produced in Italy, Limoncello is flavored with the zest of Sorrento lemons and should be served chilled.

## Lychee liqueur

Lychee liqueur is a lychee-flavored liqueur. Clear in color, lychee liqueur is quickly becoming a popular ingredient in many martini recipes.

## Malibu

Malibu is a rum-based liqueur. Malibu is offered in four different varieties: coconut, pineapple, passion fruit and mango.

## Midori

Midori is a green, honeydew-melon liqueur. Produced by a Japanese company, Midori is the Japanese word for "green."

## Ouzo

Ouzo is an anise-flavored liqueur. Produced in Greece, ouzo is clear when served on its own. When served with water, Ouzo turns a cloudy white.

## Peach Schnapps

Peach schnapps is a dry, peach-flavored liqueur. Peach schnapps is a common ingredient in shooters and is often mixed with orange and cranberry juice in cocktails.

## Peppermint Schnapps

Peppermint schnapps is a peppermint-flavored liqueur. Peppermint schnapps should not be confused with crème de menthe, which is much sweeter.

## Pernod

Pernod is an anise-flavored liqueur made in France. Created in 1805, Pernod is traditionally served with cold water, but can also be mixed into cocktails.

## Sambuca

Sambuca is a licorice-flavored liqueur made from elderberry flowers. Available in both white and black varieties, both types of sambuca taste very similar.

## Sloe Gin

Sloe gin is made from the sloe berry, a small plum-like fruit with a berry taste and aroma. Despite its name, sloe gin has very little in common with the spirit gin.

## Sour liqueurs

Sour liqueurs are sour-tasting, fruit-based liqueurs. Available in different varieties, the most popular sour liqueurs are apple, peach, raspberry and blueberry.

## Southern Comfort

Southern Comfort is a peach-flavored, bourbon-based liqueur. An American creation, Southern Comfort is made from a secret recipe of over 100 ingredients.

## Tia Maria

Tia Maria is a coffee-flavored, rum-based liqueur. Of Jamaican origin, Tia Maria was first made in the 1600s and has a hint of vanilla flavor.

## Triple Sec

Triple sec is an orange-flavored liqueur. Triple sec is the generic name for this liqueur. Grand Marnier and Cointreau are both brand-name triple secs.

# RECIPES

Great recipes are the key to a bartender's success. From icy blended drinks and classic cocktails to stunning shooters and piping-hot warmers, serving fantastic drinks is the quickest way to impress. This section of the book will show you how to make the best-tasting and most-popular drinks. You will also learn how to make alcohol-free mocktails for nondrinkers.

# CLASSIC Martinis

While the martini is almost universally recognized as the definitive cocktail, what exactly constitutes a martini is often the subject of much debate. Every bartender has his or her own perfect ratio of gin or vodka to vermouth. The beauty of the martini, however, is its simplicity and versatility. The possibilities are endless. You can use vodka for a clean taste or gin for its aromatic bite. Changing the amount of vermouth or even the garnish can also create numerous variations with different subtleties.

## Classic Gin Martini

2 1/2 oz gin
1/2 oz dry vermouth
3 cocktail olives or
1 lemon twist

1 Fill a shaker halfway with ice cubes.

2 Add the gin and vermouth to the shaker.

3 Gently stir the ingredients in a circular motion for 8 to 10 seconds being careful not to break the ice cubes.

4 Strain the contents of the shaker into a chilled cocktail glass and garnish with cocktail olives or a lemon twist.

## Classic Vodka Martini

2 1/2 oz vodka
1/2 oz dry vermouth
1 lemon twist or
3 cocktail olives

1 Fill a shaker halfway with ice cubes.

2 Add the vodka and vermouth to the shaker.

3 Gently stir the ingredients in a circular motion for 8 to 10 seconds being careful not to break the ice cubes.

4 Strain the contents of the shaker into a chilled cocktail glass and garnish with a lemon twist or cocktail olives.

**TIP** *How can I make a really dry martini?*

To make a dry martini, decrease the amount of dry vermouth to a 1/4 oz. If you would like a bone dry martini, simply splash a dash of dry vermouth over ice in a shaker, stir and then pour out the dry vermouth before adding the gin or vodka. To make the driest martini known to man, coat the inside of a cocktail glass with a 1/4 oz of scotch. Then pour any remaining scotch out of the glass before pouring in 2 1/2 oz of ice-cold gin or vodka.

**TIP** *How do I make James Bond's favorite martini?*

In the first James Bond novel, Agent 007 defines his favorite martini as a mix of gin, vodka and dry vermouth with a lemon twist. Of course, it was shaken not stirred. This martini variation has become known as a Vesper. To make a Vesper, shake together ice cubes, 1 1/2 oz of gin, 1/2 oz of vodka and 1/4 oz of dry vermouth. Strain into a cocktail glass and garnish with a lemon twist.

## Gibson

2 1/2 oz gin or vodka
1/2 oz dry vermouth
3 cocktail onions

1. Fill a shaker halfway with ice cubes.
2. Add the gin or vodka and vermouth to the shaker.
3. Gently stir the ingredients in a circular motion for 8 to 10 seconds being careful not to break the ice cubes.
4. Strain the contents of the shaker into a chilled cocktail glass and garnish with cocktail onions.

## Dirty Martini

2 1/2 oz gin or vodka
1/2 oz dry vermouth
1/2 oz olive brine
3 cocktail olives

1. Fill a shaker halfway with ice cubes.
2. Add the gin or vodka, vermouth and olive brine to the shaker.

   *Note: Olive brine is the salt and water solution found inside a jar of cocktail olives.*
3. Gently stir the ingredients in a circular motion for 8 to 10 seconds being careful not to break the ice cubes.
4. Strain the contents of the shaker into a chilled cocktail glass and garnish with cocktail olives.

# Classic Cocktail

## Martinis

While there have never been so many new and interesting cocktail options, it was not always that way. There was a time when liquor was mainly consumed without any mixers. Today's cocktails have their roots in early experimentation that combined those spirits with various liqueurs and non-alcoholic mixers. Many drinks have since come and gone, but the cocktails below have stood the test of time to become classics and there's good reason—they taste great.

### Scarlet O'Hara

- 2 oz Southern Comfort
- 3 oz red cranberry juice
- 1/4 lime
- 3 cranberries

1 Fill a shaker halfway with ice cubes.

2 Add the Southern Comfort and cranberry juice to the shaker and squeeze the juice from the lime into the shaker.

3 Shake the mixture vigorously for 5 to 10 seconds.

4 Strain the drink into a chilled cocktail glass and garnish with cranberries.

### Sidecar

- superfine sugar
- 1 1/2 oz cognac
- 1 oz triple sec
- 1/4 lemon
- 1 oz sparkling water (optional)

1 Coat the rim of a chilled cocktail glass with superfine sugar.

*Note: To coat the rim of a glass, see page 40.*

2 Fill a shaker halfway with ice cubes.

3 Add the cognac, triple sec and juice from the lemon into the shaker.

4 Shake the mixture vigorously for 5 to 10 seconds.

5 Strain the drink into the chilled cocktail glass and add the sparkling water.

**TIP** *What is a Cable Car?*

The Cable Car is a variation on the Sidecar first created in, you guessed it, San Francisco. To mix a Cable Car, combine 1 1/2 oz of spiced rum, 1 oz of triple sec, juice from a 1/4 lemon, a 1/4 oz of simple syrup and 1/2 an egg white in an ice-filled shaker. Shake and then strain the drink into a cocktail glass, garnishing with a lemon twist.

**TIP** *Why isn't the Blue Blazer actually blue?*

The Blue Blazer's name comes from the way it was originally served by its creator, bartending legend Jerry Thomas. After adding the Scotch to the other ingredients, Thomas would set it ablaze and the ingredients would burn with a blue flame. The drink was then mixed by pouring the flaming mixture back and forth between two mixing glasses until the flames went out. Don't try this at home, kids.

## Blue Blazer

- 2 oz scotch
- 2 tsp honey
- 1/4 lemon
- 1 oz boiling water
- 1 lemon spiral

1. Add the honey, juice from the lemon and boiling water to a mixing glass.
2. Gently stir the mixture until the honey has dissolved.
3. Add the scotch to the ingredients in the mixing glass and gently stir for 5 seconds.
4. Pour the drink into a cocktail glass and garnish with a lemon spiral.

## Between the Sheets

- 1 oz rum
- 1 oz cognac
- 1/2 oz triple sec
- 1 oz water
- 1/4 lemon
- 1/4 oz simple syrup
- 1 orange spiral

1. Fill a shaker halfway with ice cubes.
2. Add the rum, cognac, triple sec, water, juice from the lemon and simple syrup to the shaker.

   *Note: To make simple syrup, see page 42.*
3. Shake the mixture vigorously for 5 to 10 seconds.
4. Strain the drink into a chilled cocktail glass and garnish with an orange spiral.

# MANHATTANS

The Manhattan is a classic. Originally concocted in New York (where else?) back in the 1870s, this cocktail remains popular today providing a rich somewhat smoky flavor with a pleasant bite. Just like any classic, many variations have spun off from the original Manhattan recipe. The Rob Roy puts the spotlight on scotch as its base ingredient. The New York, New York is a sweet variation, while the Martinez ditches the bourbon for gin and throws in a splash of triple sec.

## Classic Manhattan

2 1/2 oz bourbon
1/2 oz sweet vermouth
1 maraschino cherry

1. Fill a shaker halfway with ice cubes.
2. Add the bourbon and vermouth to the shaker.
3. Gently stir the ingredients in a circular motion for 8 to 10 seconds being careful not to break the ice cubes.
4. Strain the contents of the shaker into a chilled cocktail glass and garnish with a maraschino cherry.

## Rob Roy

2 1/2 oz scotch
1/2 oz sweet vermouth
1 maraschino cherry

1. Fill a shaker halfway with ice cubes.
2. Add the scotch and vermouth to the shaker.
3. Gently stir the ingredients in a circular motion for 8 to 10 seconds being careful not to break the ice cubes.
4. Strain the contents of the shaker into a chilled cocktail glass and garnish with a maraschino cherry.

**TIP** *How can I make my Manhattans more dry?*

To make a dry Manhattan, substitute dry vermouth for the sweet vermouth and garnish with a lemon twist. If you prefer a cocktail that is not too sweet and yet not too dry, you can prepare a "perfect" Manhattan which features a 1/4 oz each of sweet and dry vermouth and is garnished with both a lemon twist and a maraschino cherry.

**TIP** *Why is the Manhattan sometimes served in a rocks glass?*

While legend has it that the Manhattan was created for Lady Churchill, the American-born mother of Winston, it soon became known as more of a "gentleman's drink." To give the Manhattan more of a macho look, it is sometimes served in a rocks glass.

## New York, New York

2 1/2 oz bourbon
1/2 oz grenadine
1/2 lemon
1 orange spiral

1 Fill a shaker halfway with ice cubes.

2 Add the bourbon and grenadine to the shaker.

3 Squeeze the juice from the lemon into the shaker and shake the mixture vigorously for 5 to 10 seconds.

4 Strain the contents of the shaker into a chilled cocktail glass and garnish with an orange spiral.

## Martinez

1 1/2 oz gin
1/2 oz sweet vermouth
1/2 oz triple sec
1 orange spiral

1 Fill a shaker halfway with ice cubes.

2 Add the gin, vermouth and triple sec to the shaker.

3 Gently stir the ingredients in a circular motion for 8 to 10 seconds being careful not to break the ice cubes.

4 Strain the contents of the shaker into a chilled cocktail glass and garnish with an orange spiral.

# Cosmopolitans

The world is divided into two types of people: those who love Cosmopolitans and those who have yet to taste one. While that may be a bit of an overstatement, there's no denying that the Cosmopolitan is hugely popular. In fact, no other beverage has done more to bring about the modern cocktail renaissance than this tangy cranberry-lime-based sensation. If you have yet to join the revolution, prepare your taste buds and whip up a Cosmopolitan or one of these tasty variations.

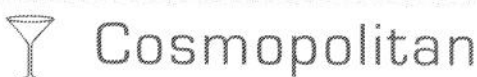

## Cosmopolitan

1 1/4 oz vodka
3/4 oz triple sec
3 oz red cranberry juice
1/2 lime
1 orange spiral

1 Fill a shaker halfway with ice cubes.

2 Add the vodka, triple sec and cranberry juice to the shaker.

3 Squeeze the juice from the lime into the shaker and shake the mixture vigorously for 5 to 10 seconds.

4 Strain the mixture into a chilled cocktail glass and garnish with an orange spiral.

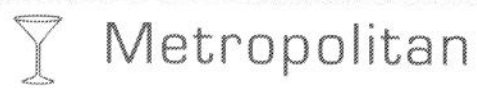

## Metropolitan

1 1/4 oz currant vodka
3/4 oz triple sec
3 oz red cranberry juice
1/2 lime
1 orange spiral

1 Fill a shaker halfway with ice cubes.

2 Add the currant vodka, triple sec and cranberry juice to the shaker.

3 Squeeze the juice from the lime into the shaker and shake the mixture vigorously for 5 to 10 seconds.

4 Strain the mixture into a chilled cocktail glass and garnish with an orange spiral.

**TIP** *What other Cosmopolitan variations can I make?*

**Crantini**
Turn up the tang by substituting lime cordial for the triple sec.

**White Cosmopolitan**
Change the color and make the drink a little less tart by using white cranberry juice instead of red cranberry juice.

**Apri-cosmo**
Add a delightful taste of apricot by swapping the triple sec out for apricot brandy.

**Grand Cosmopolitan**
Go upscale by using premium vodka and substituting Grand Marnier for triple sec.

## Blue Cosmopolitan

- 1 1/4 oz vodka
- 3/4 oz blue curacao
- 3 oz white cranberry juice
- 1/2 lime
- 1 orange spiral

1. Fill a shaker halfway with ice cubes.
2. Add the vodka, blue curacao and cranberry juice to the shaker.
3. Squeeze the juice from the lime into the shaker and shake the mixture vigorously for 5 to 10 seconds.
4. Strain the mixture into a chilled cocktail glass and garnish with an orange spiral.

## Razzmopolitan

- 1 1/4 oz raspberry vodka
- 3/4 oz triple sec
- 3 oz red cranberry juice
- 1/2 lime
- 3 raspberries

1. Fill a shaker halfway with ice cubes.
2. Add the raspberry vodka, triple sec and cranberry juice to the shaker.
3. Squeeze the juice from the lime into the shaker and shake the mixture vigorously for 5 to 10 seconds.
4. Strain the mixture into a chilled cocktail glass and garnish with raspberries.

# SOUR
## Martinis

Pucker up! These recipes pack a serious sour punch that will create more puckered lips than you would find in a dark theater full of teenagers. From the popular Sour Apple Martini to the delicious peach, raspberry and blueberry variations, your guests will love these tart and colorful cocktails. You can even add an extra surge of fruit flavor to these concoctions by replacing the vodka in the recipes with one of the many flavored vodkas now available.

### Sour Apple Martini

- 1 1/4 oz vodka
- 3/4 oz sour apple liqueur
- 3 oz apple juice
- 1/2 lime
- 1 lime wheel

1. Fill a shaker halfway with ice cubes.
2. Add the vodka, sour apple liqueur and apple juice to the shaker.
3. Squeeze the juice from the lime into the shaker.
4. Shake the mixture vigorously for 5 to 10 seconds.
5. Strain the contents of the shaker into a chilled cocktail glass and garnish with a lime wheel.

### Sour Peach Martini

- 1 1/4 oz vodka
- 3/4 oz sour peach liqueur
- 3 oz peach or pineapple juice
- 1/2 lime
- 1 peach slice

1. Fill a shaker halfway with ice cubes.
2. Add the vodka, sour peach liqueur and peach or pineapple juice to the shaker.
3. Squeeze the juice from the lime into the shaker.
4. Shake the mixture vigorously for 5 to 10 seconds.
5. Strain the contents of the shaker into a chilled cocktail glass and garnish with a peach slice.

**TIP** *What other garnishes can I use for the Sour Apple and Sour Peach Martinis?*

Try using an apple or peach wheel to garnish your Sour Apple and Sour Peach Martinis. Just cut a thin disc from near the center of an apple or next to the pit of a peach. Then, rather than placing the wheel on the rim of the glass, float it on the surface of the cocktail. Your unique garnish will also make a tasty liqueur-soaked treat when your guests have finished their drinks.

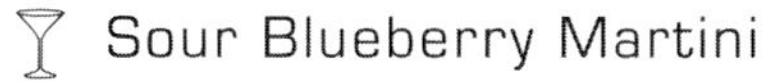

## Sour Raspberry Martini

- 1 1/4 oz vodka
- 3/4 oz sour raspberry liqueur
- 3 oz red cranberry juice
- 1/2 lime
- 3 raspberries

1 Fill a shaker halfway with ice cubes.

2 Add the vodka, sour raspberry liqueur and cranberry juice to the shaker.

3 Squeeze the juice from the lime into the shaker.

4 Shake the mixture vigorously for 5 to 10 seconds.

5 Strain the contents of the shaker into a chilled cocktail glass and garnish with raspberries.

## Sour Blueberry Martini

- 1 1/4 oz vodka
- 3/4 oz sour blueberry liqueur
- 3 oz white cranberry juice
- 1/2 lime
- 5 blueberries

1 Fill a shaker halfway with ice cubes.

2 Add the vodka, sour blueberry liqueur and cranberry juice to the shaker.

3 Squeeze the juice from the lime into the shaker.

4 Shake the mixture vigorously for 5 to 10 seconds.

5 Strain the contents of the shaker into a chilled cocktail glass and garnish with blueberries.

# Springtime in Paris

If you yearn to visit Paris in the spring, where even the air seems to be infused with love, passion and romance, these martinis are the next best thing. Romantics will swoon over the sweet names, like Cupid's Arrow and P.S. I Love You, while the rest of us will adore the flavors, from rich and complex to fruity and light. Consider serving these delicious martinis at a Valentine's Day get together or a romantic dinner for two.

## P.S. I Love You

- 1 oz amber rum
- 1/2 oz Baileys
- 1/2 oz Kahlua
- 1/2 oz amaretto
- 2 oz half & half cream
- 1 maraschino cherry
- cinnamon

1. Fill a shaker halfway with ice cubes.
2. Add the rum, Baileys, Kahlua, amaretto and cream to the shaker.
3. Shake the mixture vigorously for 5 to 10 seconds.
4. Strain the drink into a chilled cocktail glass and garnish with a maraschino cherry and a sprinkle of cinnamon.

## Passion Fruit Martini

- 1 1/2 oz vodka
- 1 oz passion fruit liqueur
- 3 oz apple juice
- 1/2 egg white
- 1/2 passion fruit
- 1 orange spiral

1. Fill a shaker halfway with ice cubes.
2. Add the vodka, passion fruit liqueur, apple juice and egg white to the shaker.
3. Scoop the flesh from the half passion fruit into the shaker.
4. Shake the mixture vigorously for 5 to 10 seconds.
5. Fine strain the drink into a chilled cocktail glass and garnish with an orange spiral.

*Note: For information on fine straining, see the top of page 77.*

**TIP** *How do I fine strain a cocktail?*

You may need to fine strain a cocktail when mixing drinks that contain fruit pulp or small seeds. Fine straining is an extra filtration step performed when you pour a drink out of a shaker. Hold either a Boston shaker can topped with a Hawthorn strainer or a standard shaker with its strainer cap attached in one hand and a tea strainer in the other hand. Pour the cocktail through the tea strainer into a glass. For information on using Boston and standard shakers, see page 38.

## Cupid's Arrow

1 1/2 oz citrus vodka
1 oz sloe gin
1/2 lime
3 raspberries

1. Fill a shaker halfway with ice cubes.
2. Add the citrus vodka and sloe gin to the shaker.
3. Squeeze the juice from the lime into the shaker.
4. Shake the mixture vigorously for 5 to 10 seconds.
5. Strain the drink into a chilled cocktail glass and garnish with raspberries.

## Rose Petal

1 1/2 oz vodka
1/2 oz white crème de cacao
1/2 oz lychee liqueur
dash grenadine
1 rose petal

1. Fill a shaker halfway with ice cubes.
2. Add the vodka, crème de cacao, lychee liqueur and grenadine to the shaker.
3. Shake the mixture vigorously for 5 to 10 seconds.
4. Strain the drink into a chilled cocktail glass and garnish with a rose petal.

# CHOCOLATE Martinis

Chocolate is universally adored and martinis are popular all over the world so a combination of the two was inevitable. The Classic Chocolate Martini is a delicious cocktail infused with rich crème de cacao liqueur. It is also the base for a number of other tasty chocolate martini variations including the Vanilla Chocolate Martini, White Chocolate Martini and Chocolate Mint Martini. Martini purists tend to look down upon all of these chocolate-flavored concoctions but that's ok—it just means more for the rest of us.

## Classic Chocolate Martini

- cocoa powder
- 1 3/4 oz vodka
- 3/4 oz white crème de cacao
- 1 maraschino cherry

1. Coat the rim of a chilled cocktail glass with cocoa powder and set aside.

   *Note: To coat the rim of a glass, see page 40.*

2. Fill a shaker halfway with ice cubes.
3. Add the vodka and crème de cacao to the shaker.
4. Shake the mixture vigorously for 5 to 10 seconds.
5. Strain the contents of the shaker into the chilled cocktail glass and garnish with a maraschino cherry.

## Vanilla Chocolate Martini

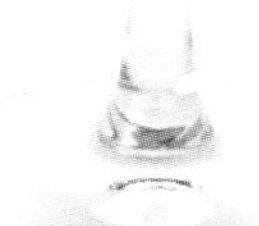

- 1 3/4 oz vanilla vodka
- 3/4 oz white crème de cacao
- 1 maraschino cherry

1. Fill a shaker halfway with ice cubes.
2. Add the vanilla vodka and crème de cacao to the shaker.
3. Shake the mixture vigorously for 5 to 10 seconds.
4. Strain the contents of the shaker into a chilled cocktail glass and garnish with a maraschino cherry.

**TIP** *How can I make a Raspberry Chocolate Martini?*

A delicious Raspberry Chocolate Martini is easy to create. Just replace the vodka in the Classic Chocolate Martini recipe with raspberry vodka and garnish with 3 fresh raspberries. You will be pleasantly surprised by how beautifully the fruit flavor complements the chocolate flavored crème de cacao.

**TIP** *Why do chocolate martinis seem so small?*

Unlike other types of martinis, chocolate martinis are all alcohol with no extra juices mixed in. This makes most chocolate martinis around 2 1/2 oz in size. In a serious breach of martini etiquette, some bartenders will serve chocolate martinis with ice in an effort to make them appear larger when all it really does is produce a thin, watered down chocolate martini.

## White Chocolate Martini

- 1 1/2 oz vanilla vodka
- 1/2 oz white crème de cacao
- 1/2 oz Baileys
- 1 maraschino cherry

1 Fill a shaker halfway with ice cubes.

2 Add the vanilla vodka, crème de cacao and Baileys to the shaker.

3 Shake the mixture vigorously for 5 to 10 seconds.

4 Strain the contents of the shaker into a chilled cocktail glass and garnish with a maraschino cherry.

## Chocolate Mint Martini

- 1 1/2 oz vanilla vodka
- 1/2 oz white crème de cacao
- 1/2 oz white crème de menthe
- 1 maraschino cherry
- 1 sprig of mint

1 Fill a shaker halfway with ice cubes.

2 Add the vanilla vodka, crème de cacao and crème de menthe to the shaker.

3 Shake the mixture vigorously for 5 to 10 seconds.

4 Strain the contents of the shaker into a chilled cocktail glass and garnish with a maraschino cherry and a sprig of mint.

# LYCHEE Martinis

Lychee martinis are great for serving to your guests when you want to surprise them with cocktails that are exotic and sweet. If you have never tasted this unique Asian fruit, you will be pleasantly surprised by the lychee's fragrance and flavor which is similar to that of a Muscat grape. Any one of these variations—from the sugary Classic Lychee Martini to the cranberry-and-lime infused Cosmopo-lychee—are sure to be crowd pleasers.

## Classic Lychee Martini

- 1 3/4 oz vodka
- 3/4 oz lychee liqueur
- 1 oz lychee syrup
- 1 lychee, peeled and pitted

1 Fill a shaker halfway with ice cubes.

2 Add the vodka, lychee liqueur and lychee syrup to the shaker.

*Note: For information on lychee syrup, see the top of page 81.*

3 Shake the mixture vigorously for 5 to 10 seconds.

4 Strain the contents of the shaker into a chilled cocktail glass and garnish with a lychee.

## Lychee Pinetini

- 1 3/4 oz vodka
- 3/4 oz lychee liqueur
- 2 oz pineapple juice
- 1/2 lime
- 1 maraschino cherry

1 Fill a shaker halfway with ice cubes.

2 Add the vodka, lychee liqueur and pineapple juice to the shaker.

3 Squeeze the juice from the lime into the shaker.

4 Shake the mixture vigorously for 5 to 10 seconds.

5 Strain the contents of the shaker into a chilled cocktail glass and garnish with a maraschino cherry.

**TIP** *What is lychee syrup?*

Lychee syrup is a sweet liquid flavored with lychee fruits. It is available in the soda or juice aisle of some grocery stores, as well as in specialty food shops and online stores. If you have trouble finding lychee syrup, you can use the juice from a can of lychee fruit.

**TIP** *How can I make the Classic Lychee Martini less sweet?*

The Classic Lychee Martini is so decadently sweet that many people find it hard to indulge in more than one. To balance out the sweetness, you can add a 1/4 oz splash of fresh-squeezed lime juice to the recipe.

## Cosmopo-lychee

- 1 3/4 oz vodka
- 3/4 oz lychee liqueur
- 3 oz red cranberry juice
- 1/2 lime
- 1 lychee, peeled and pitted

1. Fill a shaker halfway with ice cubes.
2. Add the vodka, lychee liqueur and cranberry juice to the shaker.
3. Squeeze the juice from the lime into the shaker.
4. Shake the mixture vigorously for 5 to 10 seconds.
5. Strain the contents of the shaker into a chilled cocktail glass and garnish with a lychee.

## Meloncholy-chee

- 1 1/2 oz vodka
- 1/2 oz lychee liqueur
- 1/2 oz Midori melon liqueur
- 2 oz pineapple juice
- 1 maraschino cherry

1. Fill a shaker halfway with ice cubes.
2. Add the vodka, lychee liqueur, melon liqueur and pineapple juice to the shaker.
3. Shake the mixture vigorously for 5 to 10 seconds.
4. Strain the contents of the shaker into a chilled cocktail glass and garnish with a maraschino cherry.

# ASIAN-INSPIRED Martinis

These four martinis are characterized by unique flavors from the Orient, from light-tasting melon liqueur to complex Japanese sake, sweet lychee syrup to refreshing Asian pear liqueur. For those who feel intimidated by the task of pairing drinks with Asian foods, these cocktails are the answer. If you have never tasted some of these ingredients, don't be scared off by their exotic sounding names. You just might find a new favorite, your own personal Zen in a glass.

## Japanese Slipper Martini

- superfine sugar
- 1 3/4 oz tequila
- 3/4 oz Midori melon liqueur
- 1/2 oz simple syrup
- 1/2 lemon

1 Coat the rim of a chilled cocktail glass with superfine sugar.

*Note: To coat the rim of a glass, see page 40.*

2 Fill a shaker halfway with ice cubes.

3 Add the tequila, melon liqueur and simple syrup to the shaker and squeeze the juice from the lemon into the shaker.

*Note: To make simple syrup, see page 42.*

4 Shake the mixture vigorously for 5 to 10 seconds and strain the drink into the chilled cocktail glass.

## Sake-tini

- 1 1/2 oz sake
- 1/2 oz gin
- 1/2 oz triple sec
- 1 orange spiral

1 Fill a shaker halfway with ice cubes.

2 Add the sake, gin and triple sec to the shaker.

3 Gently stir the ingredients in a circular motion for 8 to 10 seconds being careful not to break the ice cubes.

4 Strain the drink into a chilled cocktail glass and garnish with an orange spiral.

**TIP** *Shouldn't sake be served warm?*

While you may have heard of sake being served warm, this is not necessarily the best way to drink it. Most connoisseurs agree that sake is best served chilled. So there's no need to feel that you are breaching some sort of sake etiquette when you stir your sake cocktails with ice.

**TIP** *Is sake a liquor or wine?*

Sake is a uniquely-flavored Japanese drink made from fermented rice. It is neither a liquor, because it is not distilled, nor a true wine, because it is not derived from grapes. In terms of alcohol content, sake places somewhere between wine and liquor as it contains around 15% alcohol by volume.

## Lotus Martini

- 2 oz gin
- 1/2 oz blue curacao
- 2 oz lychee syrup
- 1/2 oz grenadine
- 1 sprig of mint

1 Fill a shaker halfway with ice cubes.

2 Add the gin, blue curacao, lychee syrup and grenadine to the shaker.

*Note: You can use the liquid from canned lychees as lychee syrup.*

3 Shake the mixture vigorously for 5 to 10 seconds.

4 Strain the drink into a chilled cocktail glass and garnish with a sprig of mint.

## Asian Pear Martini

- 1 1/2 oz sake
- 1 oz Asian pear liqueur
- 1 oz apple juice
- 1/2 lemon
- 1 pear slice

1 Fill a shaker halfway with ice cubes.

2 Add the sake, pear liqueur and apple juice to the shaker.

*Note: If you do not have Asian pear liqueur, you can substitute with pear liqueur.*

3 Squeeze the juice from the lemon into the shaker.

4 Gently stir the ingredients in a circular motion for 8 to 10 seconds being careful not to break the ice cubes.

5 Strain the drink into a chilled cocktail glass and garnish with a pear slice.

# FRUITY
## Martinis I

Thanks to the huge array of fruit-flavored liqueurs and liquors available today, you can get very creative when mixing delicious fruity martinis. And we're not just talking about simple fruit juice creations here. Think of cocktails with in-your-face fruit flavors and names like the Lemon Drop and the Candy Apple Martini. Your guests will love these scrumptious treats in a cocktail glass.

### Banana Popsicle Martini

- 1 oz banana liqueur
- 1 oz blue curacao
- 3 oz white cranberry juice
- 1 banana slice

1. Fill a shaker halfway with ice cubes.
2. Add the banana liqueur, blue curacao and cranberry juice to the shaker.
3. Shake the mixture vigorously for 5 to 10 seconds.
4. Strain the drink into a chilled cocktail glass and garnish with a banana slice.

### Lemon Drop Martini

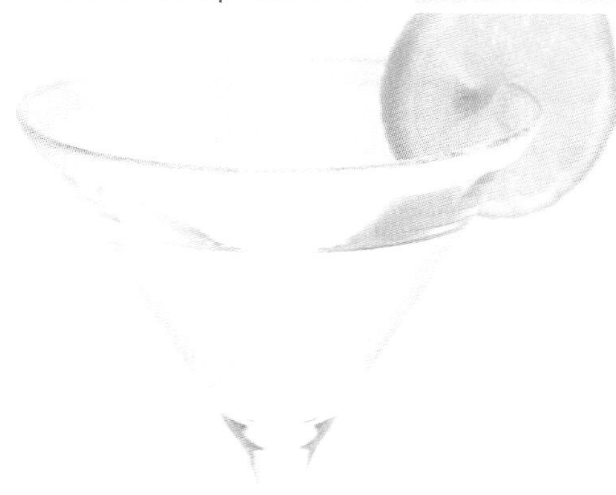

- superfine sugar
- 2 oz citrus vodka
- 1/2 oz triple sec
- 1/2 lemon
- 1 lemon wheel

1. Coat the rim of a chilled cocktail glass with superfine sugar.

   *Note: To coat the rim of a glass, see page 40.*

2. Fill a shaker halfway with ice cubes.
3. Add the citrus vodka and triple sec to the shaker and squeeze the juice from the lemon into the shaker.
4. Shake the mixture vigorously for 5 to 10 seconds.
5. Strain the drink into the cocktail glass and garnish with a lemon wheel.

TIP

*How can I "electrify" the Banana Popsicle Martini?*

By adding more alcohol to the Banana Popsicle Martini, you can create an Electric Banana Popsicle Martini. Simply add 1 1/2 oz of vodka to the Banana Popsicle Martini recipe and reduce the amount of banana liqueur and blue curacao to a 1/2 oz each.

*How can I make a Candy Apple Tart Martini?*

To make a deliciously tart version of the Candy Apple Martini, all you have to do is replace the apple juice in the recipe with 3 oz of red cranberry juice.

## Melon Ball Martini

- 1 3/4 oz citrus vodka
- 3/4 oz Midori melon liqueur
- 3 oz orange juice
- 1 orange flag

1. Fill a shaker halfway with ice cubes.
2. Add the citrus vodka, melon liqueur and orange juice to the shaker.
3. Shake the mixture vigorously for 5 to 10 seconds.
4. Strain the drink into a chilled cocktail glass and garnish with an orange flag.

*Note: To create an orange flag, see page 36.*

## Candy Apple Martini

- 1 1/2 oz green apple vodka
- 1/2 oz sour apple liqueur
- 1/2 oz butterscotch schnapps
- 3 oz apple juice
- 1 apple slice

1. Fill a shaker halfway with ice cubes.
2. Add the vodka, sour apple liqueur, butterscotch schnapps and apple juice to the shaker.
3. Shake the mixture vigorously for 5 to 10 seconds.
4. Strain the drink into a chilled cocktail glass and garnish with an apple slice.

# FRUITY
## Martinis II

If you like fruit flavors, you are going to love these delectable martinis. They all have big fruit taste. The kaleidoscope of flavors that you will discover in the Jolly Rancher Martini is unparalleled. The Raspberry Tartini is sure to subdue the cravings of even the most serious raspberry fan. The grapey Saturn's Moons Martini features Chardonnay, while the Tropical Cream Martini combines tropical fruit flavors with rich cream.

### Jolly Rancher Martini

- 1 oz raspberry vodka
- 1/2 oz sour apple liqueur
- 1/2 oz sour raspberry liqueur
- 1/2 oz banana liqueur
- 3 oz red cranberry juice
- 1 lemon wheel

1. Fill a shaker halfway with ice cubes.
2. Add the vodka, sour apple liqueur, sour raspberry liqueur, banana liqueur and cranberry juice to the shaker.
3. Shake the mixture vigorously for 5 to 10 seconds.
4. Strain the drink into a chilled cocktail glass and garnish with a lemon wheel.

### Raspberry Tartini

- 1 1/2 oz raspberry vodka
- 1/2 oz Chambord
- 1/2 oz sour raspberry liqueur
- 3 oz red cranberry juice
- 1/2 lime
- 3 raspberries

1. Fill a shaker halfway with ice cubes.
2. Add the vodka, Chambord, sour raspberry liqueur and cranberry juice to the shaker.
3. Squeeze the juice from the lime into the shaker.
4. Shake the mixture vigorously for 5 to 10 seconds.
5. Strain the drink into a chilled cocktail glass and garnish with raspberries.

**TIP** *What can I do to lower the calories in fruity martinis?*

Many fruity cocktails call for cranberry juice which contains more sugar than most other mixers. That's not good for those who are trying to cut back on calories. Light cranberry juice, however, is a great option for the calorie-conscious.

**TIP** *Can I use white cranberry juice instead of red cranberry juice?*

You can substitute white cranberry juice for red in any recipe. You will notice two major differences. First, the color of your cocktail will change because white cranberry juice is virtually clear. Second, your cocktail will taste a little less tart because white cranberry juice has a milder flavor than red cranberry juice.

## Saturn's Moons

- 2 oz citrus vodka
- 2 oz Chardonnay
- 1 1/2 oz white grape juice
- 1 tsp honey
- 3 grapes

1. Fill a shaker halfway with ice cubes.
2. Add the vodka, Chardonnay, grape juice and honey to the shaker.
3. Shake the mixture vigorously for 5 to 10 seconds.
4. Strain the drink into a chilled cocktail glass and garnish with grapes.

## Tropical Cream Martini

- 1/2 oz vodka
- 1/2 oz Midori melon liqueur
- 1/2 oz peach schnapps
- 1/2 oz coconut rum
- 1/2 oz Frangelico
- 2 oz orange juice
- 1 oz half & half cream
- 1 kiwi fruit wheel

1. Fill a shaker halfway with ice cubes.
2. Add the vodka, melon liqueur, peach schnapps, coconut rum, Frangelico, orange juice and cream to the shaker.
3. Shake the mixture vigorously for 5 to 10 seconds.
4. Strain the drink into a chilled cocktail glass and garnish with a kiwi fruit wheel.

# CAKE & PIE
## Martinis

Have your cake and drink it too! Believe it or not, you can recreate some of your favorite desserts at the bar. The flavors from decadent treats like key lime pie and black forest cake can be found amongst the liqueurs and mixers behind your bar. The talented mixologist (that's you, by the way) can use just the right proportions of these tastes to deliver a luscious liquid treat.

### Black Forest Cake Martini

- 1 1/2 oz vodka
- 1/2 oz white crème de cacao
- 1/2 oz Chambord
- 1 1/2 oz half & half cream
- nutmeg

1. Fill a shaker halfway with ice cubes.
2. Add the vodka, crème de cacao, Chambord and cream to the shaker.
3. Shake the mixture vigorously for 5 to 10 seconds.
4. Strain the drink into a chilled cocktail glass and sprinkle with nutmeg.

### Key Lime Pie Martini

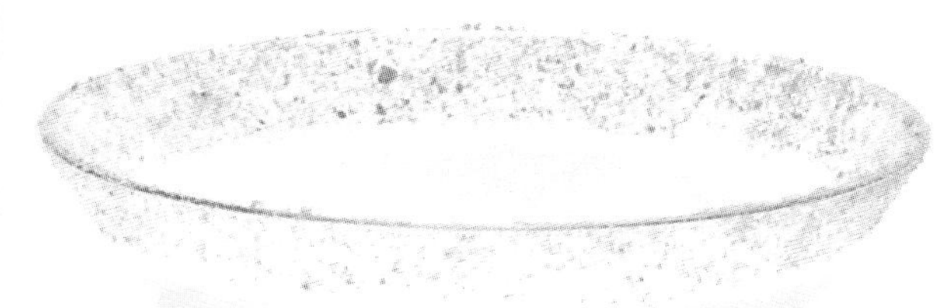

- crushed graham crackers
- 2 oz vanilla vodka
- 1/2 oz triple sec
- 2 1/2 oz pineapple juice
- 1/2 oz lime cordial
- 1/2 lime

1. Coat the rim of a chilled cocktail glass with crushed graham crackers.

   *Note: To coat the rim of a glass, see page 40.*
2. Fill a shaker halfway with ice cubes.
3. Add the vodka, triple sec, pineapple juice and lime cordial to the shaker.
4. Squeeze the juice from the lime into the shaker.
5. Shake the mixture vigorously for 5 to 10 seconds and strain the drink into the cocktail glass.

**TIP** *Can I make my Apple Pie Martini "a la mode?"*

Some people simply cannot have their apple pie without a little ice cream on the side. For those folks, you can create an Apple Pie a la mode Martini. Simply add 1 oz of half & half cream to the Apple Pie Martini recipe and remove the red cranberry juice. Top off the finished drink with cinnamon.

**TIP** *How can I add a little something extra to my cocktails?*

As you can see in several of these recipes, you sometimes add that elusive flavor to your cocktail by coating the rim of the glass with an imaginative ingredient. Sometimes a coating of ground cinnamon, nutmeg, cocoa powder, crushed graham crackers or crushed Oreo cookies can make the difference between a good cocktail and a great one.

## Apple Pie Martini

- 1 3/4 oz vodka
- 3/4 oz Goldschlager
- 1 1/2 oz apple juice
- 1 1/2 oz red cranberry juice
- 1 apple slice

1 Fill a shaker halfway with ice cubes.

2 Add the vodka, Goldschlager, apple juice and cranberry juice to the shaker.

3 Shake the mixture vigorously for 5 to 10 seconds.

4 Strain the drink into a chilled cocktail glass and garnish with an apple slice.

## Banana Cream Pie

- crushed graham crackers
- 1 oz banana liqueur
- 1 oz amaretto
- 1/2 oz Baileys
- 1 oz half & half cream
- 1 banana slice

1 Coat the rim of a chilled cocktail glass with crushed graham crackers.

*Note: To coat the rim of a glass, see page 40.*

2 Fill a shaker halfway with ice cubes.

3 Add the banana liqueur, amaretto, Baileys and cream to the shaker.

4 Shake the mixture vigorously for 5 to 10 seconds.

5 Strain the drink into a chilled cocktail glass and garnish with a banana slice.

# RUM Martinis

Who doesn't love rum? A generally rich and casual spirit, rum is the flavor and essence of the Caribbean where it was originally produced. Rum is the delicious base for many tall drinks, but you may not have considered it as the main spirit in a martini. Paired with the right flavors, however, rum can be used to concoct some very delicious martinis. These four martinis will take you through the range of rums from light to dark—a thoroughly enjoyable journey indeed.

## redruM Martini

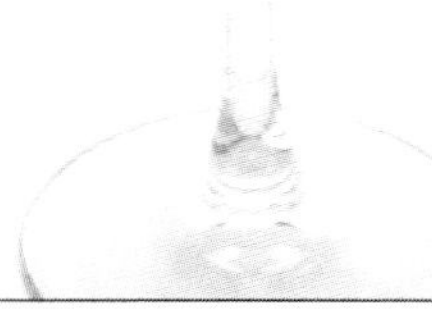

- 1 oz amber rum
- 1 oz vanilla vodka
- 1/2 oz sloe gin
- 1/2 lemon
- 1 maraschino cherry

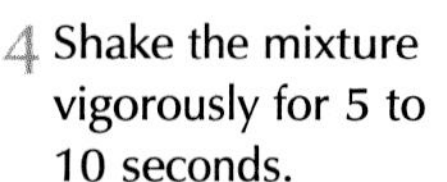

1. Fill a shaker halfway with ice cubes.
2. Add the rum, vodka and sloe gin to a shaker.
3. Squeeze the juice from the lemon into the shaker.
4. Shake the mixture vigorously for 5 to 10 seconds.
5. Strain the drink into a chilled cocktail glass and garnish with a maraschino cherry.

## Azure Martini

- 2 oz spiced rum
- 1/2 oz Goldschlager
- 2 oz apple juice
- 1/2 lime
- 1 cinnamon stick

1. Fill a shaker halfway with ice cubes.
2. Add the rum, Goldschlager and apple juice to a shaker.
3. Squeeze the juice from the lime into the shaker.
4. Shake the mixture vigorously for 5 to 10 seconds.
5. Strain the drink into a chilled cocktail glass and garnish with a cinnamon stick.

TIP *Light rum, amber rum, dark rum—aren't all rums the same?*

Rum is a spirit that is made from sugar cane and comes in many very different forms. Light rums have very little flavor, like vodka and other clear spirits. Golden or amber rums have smooth, mellow flavors. Dark rums have rich, full-bodied flavors. Rums infused with spice or fruit flavors are also available.

TIP *Can I substitute a flavored rum for light rum?*

Using a flavored rum instead of light or amber rum in a cocktail will completely change the flavor of the drink. When substituting, use a flavored rum that will complement the other flavors in the cocktail. For example, if you want to replace the amber rum in the redruM Martini, try a raspberry-infused rum that will complement the berry-flavored sloe gin.

## Bees Knees

- 1 1/2 oz light rum
- 1 oz dark rum
- 1 tsp honey
- 1 1/2 oz orange juice
- 1/2 oz half & half cream
- 1 orange spiral

1. Add the light rum, dark rum and honey to a shaker.
2. Stir the mixture until the honey is dissolved.
3. Fill the shaker halfway with ice cubes.
4. Add the orange juice and cream to the shaker.
5. Shake the mixture vigorously for 5 to 10 seconds.
6. Strain the drink into a chilled cocktail glass and garnish with an orange spiral.

## Bella Donna

- 1 1/2 oz dark rum
- 1 oz amaretto
- 1 oz water
- 1/2 oz simple syrup
- 1/2 lemon
- 1 cinnamon stick

1. Fill a shaker halfway with ice cubes.
2. Add the dark rum, amaretto, water and simple syrup to the shaker.

   *Note: To make simple syrup, see page 42.*
3. Squeeze the juice from the lemon into the shaker.
4. Shake the mixture vigorously for 5 to 10 seconds.
5. Strain the drink into a chilled cocktail glass and garnish with a cinnamon stick.

# French Riviera Martinis

Palm trees, stunning ocean views and the occasional world-renowned film festival—that's how many sum up the French Riviera. To sum it up in a cocktail glass, you can try one of these four delicious martinis that capture the sophisticated essence of the Riviera. Infused with bright flavors and gorgeous colors, these martinis will instantly transport your taste buds to the *Cote d'Azure*. If you're not careful, you may find yourself rolling a red carpet up to the bar.

## French Martini

- 1 3/4 oz raspberry vodka
- 3/4 oz Chambord
- 3 oz pineapple juice
- 3 raspberries

1. Fill a shaker halfway with ice cubes.
2. Add the vodka, Chambord and pineapple juice to the shaker.
3. Shake the mixture vigorously for 5 to 10 seconds.
4. Strain the drink into a chilled cocktail glass and garnish with raspberries.

## Baby Blue Martini

- 1 3/4 oz gin
- 3/4 oz blue curacao
- 1 1/2 oz pineapple juice
- 1 1/2 oz pink grapefruit juice
- 1 orange twist

1. Fill a shaker halfway with ice cubes.
2. Add the gin, blue curacao, pineapple juice and grapefruit juice to the shaker.
3. Shake the mixture vigorously for 5 to 10 seconds.
4. Strain the drink into a chilled cocktail glass and garnish with an orange twist.

TIP *What is a Baby Doll Martini?*

A Baby Doll Martini is just a lighter-colored more feminine-looking version of the Baby Blue Martini. To make a Baby Doll Martini, substitute 3/4 oz of triple sec for the blue curacao. Both martinis taste the same since the only difference between triple sec and blue curacao is the color.

TIP *What variations of the Bellini-tini can I mix up?*

The Bellini-tini is extremely versatile. You can substitute your favorite fruit liqueurs or cordials for the peach schnapps. Consider using banana liqueur, Chambord, apricot brandy, Midori melon liqueur or whatever strikes your fancy.

## Bellini-tini

- 1 3/4 oz vodka
- 3/4 oz peach schnapps
- 3 oz white cranberry juice
- 1 peach slice or maraschino cherry

1. Fill a shaker halfway with ice cubes.
2. Add the vodka, peach schnapps and cranberry juice to the shaker.
3. Shake the mixture vigorously for 5 to 10 seconds.
4. Strain the drink into a chilled cocktail glass and garnish with a peach slice or a maraschino cherry.

## Bikini Martini

- 1 1/2 oz gin
- 1/2 oz blue curacao
- 1/2 oz peach schnapps
- 1/2 lemon
- 1 orange spiral

1. Fill a shaker halfway with ice cubes.
2. Add the gin, blue curacao and peach schnapps to the shaker.
3. Squeeze the juice from the lemon into the shaker.
4. Shake the mixture vigorously for 5 to 10 seconds.
5. Strain the drink into a chilled cocktail glass and garnish with an orange spiral.

# COFFEE Martinis

If you have never had coffee in anything but a paper cup, prepare yourself for a new caffeinated experience. Cold shots of espresso and Kahlua make excellent cocktail ingredients. These distinctly flavored martinis give new meaning to the phrase "strong coffee" and, just like your early morning cup of java, you may find that they give you an energy boost. After sipping coffee from a cocktail glass, you may never go back to the old paper-cup variety.

## Espresso Martini

1 1/2 oz vodka
1 oz Kahlua
1 oz espresso, cold
1/2 oz simple syrup
3 espresso beans

1 Fill a shaker halfway with ice cubes.

2 Add the vodka, Kahlua, espresso and simple syrup to the shaker.

*Note: To make simple syrup,* *see page 42.*

3 Shake the mixture vigorously for 5 to 10 seconds.

4 Strain the drink into a chilled cocktail glass and garnish with espresso beans.

## Raspberry Mochatini

1 1/2 oz raspberry vodka
1/2 oz dark crème de cacao
1/2 oz Chambord
1 oz espresso, cold
3 raspberries

1 Fill a shaker halfway with ice cubes.

2 Add the vodka, crème de cacao, Chambord and espresso to the shaker.

3 Shake the mixture vigorously for 5 to 10 seconds.

4 Strain the drink into a chilled cocktail glass and garnish with raspberries.

**TIP** *Are there any shortcuts to making coffee martinis?*

Instead of making espresso each time you want to make a coffee martini, you can easily make espresso syrup which will keep in the fridge for a couple of weeks. To make espresso syrup, boil a 1/2 cup of water and stir in 1 cup of sugar. Once the sugar has dissolved, add 4 oz of espresso. Give it a couple of stirs and then pour the syrup into a sealable container.

**TIP** *Can I substitute regular coffee for espresso?*

If you don't have an espresso maker, you can substitute strong coffee for espresso. To brew a batch of extra-strength java, use only 1/2 of the amount of water that you would normally use to make coffee.

## Russians on Alert

1 1/2 oz vodka
1 oz Kahlua
1 oz espresso, cold
1 maraschino cherry

1 Fill a shaker halfway with ice cubes.

2 Add the vodka, Kahlua and espresso to the shaker.

3 Shake the mixture vigorously for 5 to 10 seconds.

4 Strain the drink into a chilled cocktail glass and garnish with a maraschino cherry.

## Toasted Almond Martini

1 1/2 oz amaretto
1 oz Kahlua
1 1/2 oz half & half cream
1 maraschino cherry

1 Fill a shaker halfway with ice cubes.

2 Add the amaretto, Kahlua and cream to the shaker.

3 Shake the mixture vigorously for 5 to 10 seconds.

4 Strain the drink into a chilled cocktail glass and garnish with a maraschino cherry.

# Alexanders

When planning a light dinner for friends, consider serving Alexanders to your guests afterward. Alexanders are rich, chocolaty variations on the Martini and make ideal after-dinner cocktails. Of these variations, the Brandy Alexander is the most popular. It is a sensuous cocktail, certain to delight chocolate lovers and overwhelm calorie counters. Gin enthusiasts will no doubt go for the Gin Alexander while the Barbary Coast and Bird of Paradise offer pairings of Scotch-gin and tequila-amaretto, respectively.

## Brandy Alexander

- 1 3/4 oz brandy
- 3/4 oz dark crème de cacao
- 1 1/2 oz half & half cream
- nutmeg

1. Fill a shaker halfway with ice cubes.
2. Add the brandy, crème de cacao and cream to the shaker.
3. Shake the mixture vigorously for 5 to 10 seconds.
4. Strain the drink into a chilled cocktail glass and sprinkle with nutmeg.

## Gin Alexander

- 1 3/4 oz gin
- 3/4 oz white crème de cacao
- 1 1/2 oz half & half cream
- nutmeg

1. Fill a shaker halfway with ice cubes.
2. Add the gin, crème de cacao and cream to the shaker.
3. Shake the mixture vigorously for 5 to 10 seconds.
4. Strain the drink into a chilled cocktail glass and sprinkle with nutmeg.

**TIP** *Is there any way to cut the richness of an Alexander?*

Cream can be a bit too much for some. Delicious, yes. Health conscious, not so much. Feel free to switch out the half & half cream for whole or even 2% milk. For those who are lactose intolerant, soy milk is an acceptable and interesting substitute.

**TIP** *What's the difference between white and dark crème de cacao?*

Although the difference is subtle, dark crème de cacao has a more robust flavor than white crème de cacao. Dark crème de cacao is created by roasting and percolating cacao beans, which results in a darker color and fuller flavor. The cacao beans used for white crème de cacao are not percolated, which gives the liqueur a smooth flavor and clear color.

## Barbary Coast

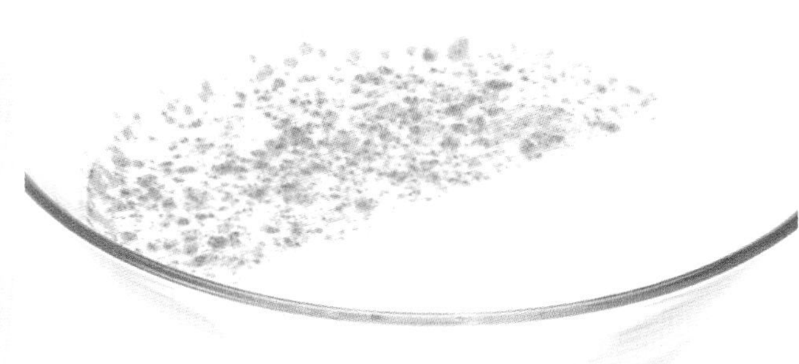

- 1 oz scotch
- 3/4 oz gin
- 3/4 oz white crème de cacao
- 1 1/2 oz half & half cream
- cinnamon

1. Fill a shaker halfway with ice cubes.
2. Add the scotch, gin, crème de cacao and cream to the shaker.
3. Shake the mixture vigorously for 5 to 10 seconds.
4. Strain the drink into a chilled cocktail glass and sprinkle with cinnamon.

## Bird of Paradise

- 1 oz tequila
- 1 oz white crème de cacao
- 1/2 oz amaretto
- 1 1/2 oz half & half cream
- nutmeg

1. Fill a shaker halfway with ice cubes.
2. Add the tequila, crème de cacao, amaretto and cream to the shaker.
3. Shake the mixture vigorously for 5 to 10 seconds.
4. Strain the drink into a chilled cocktail glass and sprinkle with nutmeg.

# SCREWDRIVERS

Considered by some to be a beginner's cocktail, the beauty of the Screwdriver lies in its simplicity. If you have orange juice and a bottle of vodka, you've got yourself a great tasting cocktail—no fuss, no muss. The Screwdriver's simplicity also gives it versatility. By adding a liqueur, you can create a number of unique variations. You can add Galliano to create a Harvey Wallbanger or melon liqueur to make a Melon Ball. You can also try throwing in some peach schnapps to create the delicious Fuzzy Navel.

## Screwdriver

1 oz vodka
4 oz orange juice

1 Fill a rocks glass with ice cubes.

2 Add the vodka to the glass.

3 Fill the glass with the orange juice and stir the drink.

## Harvey Wallbanger

1 oz vodka
1/2 oz Galliano
4 oz orange juice

1 Fill a highball glass with ice cubes.

2 Add the vodka and Galliano to the glass.

3 Fill the glass with the orange juice and stir the drink.

TIP *How do I make a Green Eyes cocktail?*

The Green Eyes is an emerald colored variation of the classic Screwdriver. To make a Green Eyes cocktail, just add 1/2 oz of blue curacao to the Screwdriver recipe. Garnish the green drink with two maraschino cherries.

TIP *What is a Blood Orange Screwdriver?*

A Blood Orange Screwdriver is a ruby colored variation of the Screwdriver. Mixing a Blood Orange Screwdriver is easy. Just make a normal Screwdriver and add 1/2 oz of Campari. Naturally, the ideal garnish is a wedge of blood orange.

## Melon Ball

1 oz vodka
1/2 oz Midori melon liqueur
4 oz orange juice
1 melon ball

1 Fill a highball glass with ice cubes.

2 Add the vodka and melon liqueur to the glass.

3 Fill the glass with the orange juice.

4 Garnish the drink with a melon ball and stir the drink.

## Fuzzy Navel

1 oz vodka
1/2 oz peach schnapps
4 oz orange juice

1 Fill a highball glass with ice cubes.

2 Add the vodka and peach schnapps to the glass.

3 Fill the glass with the orange juice and stir the drink.

# COLLINS Cocktails

If you like citrus flavors, you will love Tom Collins and his brothers. The tangy Tom Collins cocktail is a summer classic, a surefire hit for a hot afternoon with friends. While the recipe may look simple, the Tom Collins is anything but boring and Tom's brothers are equally as intriguing. A John Collins replaces the gin with rye whiskey whereas the Juan Collins includes tequila and a Comrade Collins features vodka.

## Tom Collins

1 1/2 oz gin
2 oz lime juice
1/4 oz simple syrup
1 oz club soda
1 lime wedge

1 Fill a highball glass with ice cubes.

2 Add the gin, lime juice and simple syrup to the glass.

*Note: To make simple syrup, see page 42.*

3 Top the drink with club soda, garnish with a lime wedge and stir the drink.

## John Collins

1 1/2 oz rye whiskey
2 oz lime juice
1/4 oz simple syrup
1 oz club soda
1 lime wedge

1 Fill a highball glass with ice cubes.

2 Add the rye whiskey, lime juice and simple syrup to the glass.

*Note: To make simple syrup, see page 42.*

3 Top the drink with club soda, garnish with a lime wedge and stir the drink.

**TIP** *Is there an easier way to mix Collins cocktails for a crowd?*

While using lime juice and simple syrup is the most authentic and freshest tasting way to add that sour zing to a Collins cocktail, you can use store bought Collins mix. Pre-made Collins mix is available in many grocery stores and can be a real time saver when you have to serve a lot of people at once.

**TIP** *What other Collins cocktails can I create?*

There are plenty of interesting variations on the Tom Collins that replace the gin with another base spirit. For example, you can make a Sandy Collins using scotch, a Jack Collins using applejack liqueur or a Pedro Collins using your favorite rum.

## Juan Collins

- 1 1/2 oz tequila
- 2 oz lime juice
- 1/4 oz simple syrup
- 1 oz club soda
- 1 lime wedge

1 Fill a highball glass with ice cubes.

2 Add the tequila, lime juice and simple syrup to the glass.

*Note: To make simple syrup, see page 42.*

3 Top the drink with club soda, garnish with a lime wedge and stir the drink.

## Comrade Collins

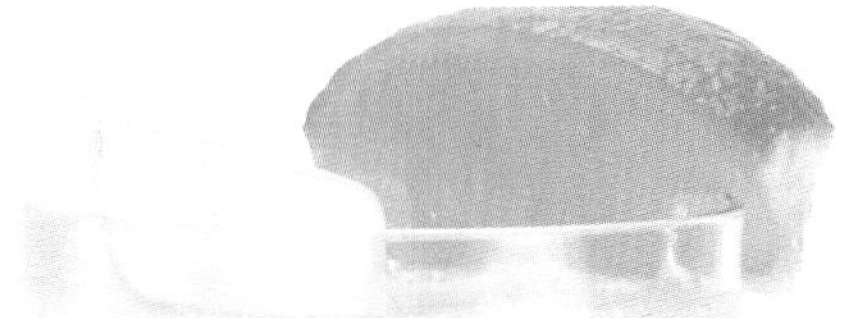

- 1 1/2 oz vodka
- 2 oz lime juice
- 1/4 oz simple syrup
- 1 oz club soda
- 1 lime wedge

1 Fill a highball glass with ice cubes.

2 Add the vodka, lime juice and simple syrup to the glass.

*Note: To make simple syrup, see page 42.*

3 Top the drink with club soda, garnish with a lime wedge and stir the drink.

# CAPE COD

## Cocktails I

The Cape Cod is a wonderfully simple cocktail: vodka, cranberry juice and a splash of club soda. Like its distant cousin, the Screwdriver, the Cape Cod is a drink capable of spawning many delicious and intriguing variations. The Watermelon with melon liqueur, the Woo Woo featuring peach schnapps and the classic Sex on the Beach with peach schnapps and orange juice are all fantastic cocktails that can trace their roots back to the Cape Cod.

### Cape Cod

- 1 oz vodka
- 4 oz red cranberry juice
- 1 oz club soda
- 1 lime wedge

1. Fill a rocks glass with ice cubes.
2. Add the vodka and cranberry juice to the glass.
3. Add the club soda, garnish with a lime wedge and stir the drink.

### Watermelon

- 1 oz vodka
- 1/2 oz Midori melon liqueur
- 4 oz red cranberry juice
- 1 melon ball

1. Fill a rocks glass with ice cubes.
2. Add the vodka, melon liqueur and cranberry juice to the glass.
3. Garnish with a melon ball and stir the drink.

**TIP** *What is the secret to eternal youth?*

The Forever Young is a simple variation on the Cape Cod cocktail. Simply substitute 1 oz of gin for the 1 oz of vodka. It makes for a deliciously dry and tart drink.

**TIP** *What is a Georgia Peach?*

The Georgia Peach is a variation of the Woo Woo cocktail. To mix a Georgia Peach, simply substitute 1 oz of light rum for the 1 oz of vodka that is called for in the Woo Woo recipe.

## Woo Woo

- 1 oz vodka
- 1/2 oz peach schnapps
- 4 oz red cranberry juice
- 1 lime wedge

1. Fill a rocks glass with ice cubes.
2. Add the vodka, peach schnapps and cranberry juice to the glass.
3. Garnish with a lime wedge and stir the drink.

## Sex on the Beach

- 1 oz vodka
- 1/2 oz peach schnapps
- 2 oz red cranberry juice
- 2 oz orange juice
- 1 lime wedge

1. Fill a rocks glass with ice cubes.
2. Add the vodka, peach schnapps, cranberry juice and orange juice to the glass.
3. Garnish with a lime wedge and stir the drink.

# Cape Cod
## Cocktails II

For a drink to fit into the Cape Cod family, it has to feature a fair amount of sourness. It is the cranberry juice that usually imparts this pucker power, but Cape Cod cocktails can also utilize grapefruit juice. The Greyhound is a variation of the Cape Cod that swaps out the cranberry juice in favor of grapefruit juice. The Seabreeze, Bay Breeze and Madras all temper their cranberry flavor with grapefruit, pineapple or orange juices, respectively.

### Greyhound

1 oz vodka
4 oz white grapefruit juice
1 lemon wedge

1 Fill a rocks glass with ice cubes.

2 Add the vodka and grapefruit juice to the glass.

3 Garnish with a lemon wedge and stir the drink.

### Seabreeze

1 oz vodka
2 oz white grapefruit juice
2 oz red cranberry juice
1 lemon wedge

1 Fill a rocks glass with ice cubes.

2 Add the vodka, grapefruit juice and cranberry juice to the glass.

3 Garnish with a lemon wedge and stir the drink.

TIP *What is a Salty Dog?*

A Salty Dog is a variation of the Greyhound cocktail that substitutes 1 oz of gin for the vodka. To live up to its name, the Salty Dog is served in a highball glass with a salted rim.

TIP *How can I make an Arizona Cooler?*

To mix up an Arizona Cooler, you simply combine 1 oz of gin with 2 oz each of grapefruit and cranberry juices in an ice-filled highball glass. Garnish the drink with a lemon wedge.

## Bay Breeze

- 1 oz vodka
- 2 oz pineapple juice
- 2 oz red cranberry juice
- 1 lime wedge

1 Fill a rocks glass with ice cubes.

2 Add the vodka, pineapple juice and cranberry juice to the glass.

3 Garnish with a lime wedge and stir the drink.

## Madras

- 1 oz vodka
- 2 oz orange juice
- 2 oz red cranberry juice
- 1 lime wedge

1 Fill a rocks glass with ice cubes.

2 Add the vodka, orange juice and cranberry juice to the glass.

3 Garnish with a lime wedge and stir the drink.

# Iced Teas

The Long Island Iced Tea is a wolf in sheep's clothing. Few cocktails are as easy drinking while being so potent. According to legend, the Long Island Iced Tea dates back to the days of Prohibition. Those with a hankering for a stiff drink would ask a sympathetic bartender for this cocktail which looked like a harmless iced tea but packed a serious punch. Despite alcohol's improved legal standing, the Long Island Iced Tea and its variations remain popular to this day.

## Long Island Iced Tea

1/2 oz vodka
1/2 oz light rum
1/2 oz gin
1/2 oz tequila
1/2 oz triple sec
1 oz lemon juice
1/2 oz simple syrup
1 oz cola
1 lemon wedge

1 Fill a highball glass with ice cubes.

2 Add the vodka, rum, gin, tequila, triple sec, lemon juice and simple syrup to a shaker.

*Note: To make simple syrup, see page 42.*

3 Shake the mixture vigorously for 5 to 10 seconds.

4 Pour the mixture into the glass.

5 Add the cola to the glass, garnish with a lemon wedge and stir the drink.

## Long Beach Iced Tea

1/2 oz vodka
1/2 oz light rum
1/2 oz gin
1/2 oz tequila
1/2 oz triple sec
1 oz lemon juice
1/2 oz simple syrup
1 oz red cranberry juice
1 lime wedge

1 Fill a highball glass with ice cubes.

2 Add the vodka, rum, gin, tequila, triple sec, lemon juice and simple syrup to a shaker.

*Note: To make simple syrup, see page 42.*

3 Shake the mixture vigorously for 5 to 10 seconds.

4 Pour the mixture into the glass.

5 Add the cranberry juice to the glass, garnish with a lime wedge and stir the drink.

**TIP** *What is a Gilligan's Island Iced Tea?*

The Gilligan's Island Iced Tea is a red-tinged tribute to the Skipper's favorite little buddy. Based on the Long Island Iced Tea recipe, 1 oz of red grape juice is used as a substitute for the cola. Garnish with a floppy white hat if you have one, otherwise a lime wedge will do.

**TIP** *How can I put a tropical twist on the Long Island Iced Tea?*

You can create a Hawaiian Iced Tea by substituting one simple ingredient. Instead of using the 1 oz of cola called for in the Long Island Iced Tea, add 1 oz of pineapple juice to the mix and garnish with a lime wedge.

## Miami Beach Iced Tea

- 1/2 oz vodka
- 1/2 oz light rum
- 1/2 oz gin
- 1/2 oz tequila
- 1/2 oz blue curacao
- 1 oz lemon juice
- 1/2 oz simple syrup
- 1 oz lemon-lime soda
- 1 lemon wedge

1. Fill a highball glass with ice cubes.
2. Add the vodka, rum, gin, tequila, blue curacao, lemon juice and simple syrup to a shaker.

   *Note: To make simple syrup, see page 42.*
3. Shake the mixture vigorously for 5 to 10 seconds.
4. Pour the mixture into the glass.
5. Add the lemon-lime soda to the glass, garnish with a lemon wedge and stir the drink.

## Beverly Hills Iced Tea

- 1/2 oz vodka
- 1/2 oz light rum
- 1/2 oz gin
- 1/2 oz tequila
- 1/2 oz triple sec
- 1 oz lemon juice
- 1/2 oz simple syrup
- 1 oz sparkling white wine
- 1 lemon wedge

1. Fill a highball glass with ice cubes.
2. Add the vodka, rum, gin, tequila, triple sec, lemon juice and simple syrup to a shaker.

   *Note: To make simple syrup, see page 42.*
3. Shake the mixture vigorously for 5 to 10 seconds.
4. Pour the mixture into the glass.
5. Add the sparkling white wine to the glass, garnish with a lemon wedge and stir the drink.

# SOURS

Brace yourself. These cocktails will hit you with a pucker punch. Making use of tangy lemon juice, these sour cocktails are seriously refreshing. The Whiskey Sour is a classic cocktail made with rye whiskey. The Bourbon Sour is a favorite in the South for quiet afternoon sipping on the porch. A delicious splash of almond flavor makes the Amaretto Sour distinct and the berry essence of sloe gin gives the Sloe Gin Fizz a sweet, lighter edge.

## Whiskey Sour

1 1/2 oz rye whiskey
1 1/2 oz lemon juice
1/2 oz simple syrup
1/2 egg white
4 dashes of bitters
1 orange boat

1 Fill a rocks glass with ice cubes.

2 Add the whiskey, lemon juice, simple syrup, egg white and bitters to a shaker.

*Note: To make simple syrup, see page 42.*

3 Shake the mixture vigorously for 5 to 10 seconds.

4 Pour the drink into the glass and garnish with an orange boat.

*Note: To make an orange boat, see page 37.*

## Bourbon Sour

1 1/2 oz bourbon
1 1/2 oz lemon juice
1/2 oz simple syrup
1/2 egg white
4 dashes of bitters
1 orange boat

1 Fill a rocks glass with ice cubes.

2 Add the bourbon, lemon juice, simple syrup, egg white and bitters to a shaker.

*Note: To make simple syrup, see page 42.*

3 Shake the mixture vigorously for 5 to 10 seconds.

4 Pour the drink into the glass and garnish with an orange boat.

*Note: To make an orange boat, see page 37.*

**TIP** *What can I use if I run out of fresh lemons?*

If you find yourself without enough fresh lemons to make the lemon juice called for in these Sours, you can substitute 2 oz of lemonade for the lemon juice and simple syrup called for in the original recipes.

**TIP** *How do I make a Ramos Gin Fizz?*

The Ramos Gin Fizz is an effervescent, sour cocktail. It is prepared in the same way and with the same ingredients as the Sloe Gin Fizz, except that the sloe gin is replaced with 1 1/2 oz of gin and the drink is garnished with a lemon wedge.

## Amaretto Sour

- 1 1/2 oz amaretto
- 1 1/2 oz lemon juice
- 1/2 oz simple syrup
- 1/2 egg white
- 4 dashes of bitters
- 1 orange boat

1 Fill a rocks glass with ice cubes.

2 Add the amaretto, lemon juice, simple syrup, egg white and bitters to a shaker.

*Note: To make simple syrup, see page 42.*

3 Shake the mixture vigorously for 5 to 10 seconds.

4 Pour the drink into the glass and garnish with an orange boat.

*Note: To make an orange boat, see page 37.*

## Sloe Gin Fizz

- 1 1/2 oz sloe gin
- 1 1/2 oz lemon juice
- 1/2 oz simple syrup
- 1/2 egg white
- 4 dashes of bitters
- 1 oz club soda
- 1 orange boat

1 Fill a rocks glass with ice cubes.

2 Add the sloe gin, lemon juice, simple syrup, egg white and bitters to a shaker.

*Note: To make simple syrup, see page 42.*

3 Shake the mixture vigorously for 5 to 10 seconds.

4 Pour the drink into the glass and add the club soda.

5 Garnish with an orange boat and stir the drink.

*Note: To make an orange boat, see page 37.*

# CHAMPAGNE Cocktails

Champagne is the ideal celebratory drink and certainly needs no improvement. There are those, however, who figure that there's always room for experimentation and have created cocktails that take advantage of champagne's distinct flavor and tiny bubbles. So the next time you are in the mood for merry-making and have a hankering for something different, try the Classic Champagne Cocktail, sophisticated French 75, seductive Kir Royale or the always-popular Mimosa. You will be pleasantly surprised by champagne's versatility.

## Classic Champagne Cocktail

1/2 oz brandy
1/2 oz simple syrup
2 dashes bitters
4 oz champagne

1. Fill a shaker halfway with ice cubes.
2. Add the brandy, simple syrup and bitters to the shaker.

   *Note: To make simple syrup, see page 42.*
3. Shake the mixture vigorously for 5 to 10 seconds.
4. Strain the contents of the shaker into a chilled champagne flute.
5. Add the champagne to the flute and stir the drink.

## French 75

1 oz gin
1/4 lemon
1/2 oz simple syrup
4 oz champagne

1. Fill a shaker halfway with ice cubes.
2. Add the gin, juice from the lemon and simple syrup to the shaker.

   *Note: To make simple syrup, see page 42.*
3. Shake the mixture vigorously for 5 to 10 seconds.
4. Strain the contents of the shaker into a chilled champagne flute.
5. Add the champagne to the flute and stir the drink.

**TIP** *What is a Kir?*

The Kir cocktail is the bubble-free cousin of the Kir Royale. The Kir uses dry white wine instead of champagne, so while it may not have the same texture, it will have a similar berry-accented flavor. To make a Kir, substitute 5 oz of dry white wine for the 4 oz of champagne called for in the Kir Royale recipe and serve the drink in a wine glass.

**TIP** *Can I use sparkling white wine instead of champagne?*

Essentially, champagne and sparkling white wine are the same drink. Champagne is simply the name for sparkling white wine made in the Champagne region of France. While there are always variations in quality and flavor from one wine to another, feel free to use less-expensive sparkling white wine when mixing your champagne cocktails.

## Kir Royale

1 oz Chambord
4 oz champagne
1 blackberry

1 Pour the Chambord into a chilled champagne flute.

2 Add the champagne to the flute.

3 Garnish the drink with a blackberry and stir the drink.

## Mimosa

1/2 oz Cointreau
1 1/2 oz orange juice
3 oz champagne
1 orange spiral

1 Pour the Cointreau and orange juice into a chilled champagne flute.

2 Add the champagne to the flute.

3 Garnish the drink with an orange spiral and stir the drink.

# APÉRITIFS

Apéritifs are liquid appetizers. Taken before meals, apéritifs are light, crisp-tasting cocktails intended to stimulate the appetite. Sweet and dry vermouth and Campari are widely used as ingredients in apéritif cocktails and the drinks shown below feature vermouth and Campari prominently. Try mixing a few of these delicious, appetite-inducing cocktails for the guests at your next dinner party. You just may avoid leftovers altogether.

## Americano

- 1 oz Campari
- 1 oz sweet vermouth
- 2 oz club soda
- 1 orange spiral

1. Fill a rocks glass with ice cubes.
2. Add the Campari, sweet vermouth and club soda to the glass.
3. Garnish with an orange spiral and stir the drink.

## Bronx

- 1 oz gin
- 1/2 oz sweet vermouth
- 1/2 oz dry vermouth
- 3 oz orange juice
- 1 maraschino cherry

1. Fill a shaker halfway with ice cubes.
2. Add the gin, sweet vermouth, dry vermouth and orange juice to the shaker.
3. Shake the mixture vigorously for 5 to 10 seconds.
4. Strain the contents of the shaker into a chilled cocktail glass.
5. Garnish with a maraschino cherry.

TIP *What is Campari?*

Campari is a famous Italian apéritif. Brilliant red in color, Campari was created in 1860 and has become an important part of many classic cocktails. It is a refreshingly bitter infusion of herbs and fruits that makes for dramatic-looking drinks.

TIP *Should I serve food with my apéritif cocktails?*

Apéritif cocktails can be served all by themselves or with small, bite-sized appetizers. Popular food choices for pairing with apéritif cocktails include pickles, olives, nuts, small biscuits, crackers and cheeses. Serve whatever you like as long as the flavors are complimentary.

## Campari Royal

1 oz Campari
1 oz Grand Marnier
3 oz orange juice
1 orange wheel

1. Fill a highball glass with ice cubes.
2. Add the Campari, Grand Marnier and orange juice to the glass.
3. Garnish with an orange wheel and stir the drink.

## Milanese

1 oz Campari
1/2 oz Galliano
1/2 oz amaretto
1/2 lemon
1 orange spiral

1. Fill a rocks glass with ice cubes.
2. Add the Campari, Galliano, amaretto and juice from the lemon to a shaker.
3. Shake the mixture vigorously for 5 to 10 seconds.
4. Pour the drink into the glass.
5. Garnish with an orange spiral.

# DIGESTIFS

Originally developed as after-dinner drinks to aid in digestion, digestifs tend to be strongly flavored cocktails with a bitter edge. These digestifs are no different. The Moscow Mule lives up to its name with a strong ginger kick. The Sazerac is fueled by bourbon with a hint of licorice-flavored Pernod. The Pink Gin and Tonic is a refreshingly bitter cocktail. And while it takes a bit of time to create, the Old Fashioned is a classic cocktail that is well worth the effort.

## Moscow Mule

2 oz vodka
1 oz lime juice
1/2 oz simple syrup
3 dashes bitters
3 oz ginger beer
1 lime wedge

1 Fill a highball glass with ice cubes.

2 Add the vodka, lime juice, simple syrup and bitters to a shaker.

*Note: To make simple syrup, see page 42.*

3 Shake the mixture vigorously for 5 to 10 seconds.

4 Pour the drink into the glass and add the ginger beer.

*Note: For information on ginger beer, see the top of page 115.*

5 Garnish with a lime wedge and stir the drink.

## Sazerac

1/2 oz Pernod
2 oz bourbon
1/2 oz simple syrup
2 dashes bitters
1 lemon twist

1 Rinse a chilled cocktail glass with Pernod.

*Note: For information on rinsing a glass, see the top of page 115.*

2 Fill a shaker halfway with ice cubes.

3 Add the bourbon, simple syrup and bitters to the shaker.

*Note: To make simple syrup, see page 42.*

4 Shake the mixture vigorously for 5 to 10 seconds.

5 Strain the drink into the glass and garnish with a lemon twist.

**TIP** *What is ginger beer?*

Ginger beer is a carbonated beverage that generally contains no alcohol and is flavored with ginger, lemon and sugar. Closely related to ginger ale, ginger beer is generally less sweet and has a more assertive, almost fiery ginger flavor. If you find the flavor of ginger beer too spicy, ginger ale is an acceptable substitute.

**TIP** *How do I rinse a glass?*

To rinse a glass with liquor, pour a 1/2 oz of the spirit into the glass. Swirl the spirit around the inside of the glass so that the entire surface of the glass' bowl has been coated. Then discard the rest of the spirit and fill the glass with the cocktail. The cocktail will be flavored with just a hint of the rinse.

## Pink Gin and Tonic

1 1/2 oz gin
2 dashes bitters
2 oz tonic water
1 lime wedge

1 Fill a rocks glass with ice cubes.

2 Add the gin, bitters and tonic water to the glass.

3 Garnish with a lime wedge and stir the drink.

## Old Fashioned

1 orange slice
2 maraschino cherries, stems removed
2 oz bourbon
1/2 oz simple syrup
3 dashes bitters
1 orange twist
1 maraschino cherry

1 Add the orange slice and 2 maraschino cherries to a rocks glass.

2 Muddle the ingredients in the glass.

*Note: For information on muddling, see page 44.*

3 Add 1 oz of bourbon and 2 ice cubes to the glass and stir.

4 Add the simple syrup, bitters and 2 more ice cubes to the glass and stir.

*Note: To make simple syrup, see page 42.*

5 Add another 1 oz of bourbon and fill the glass three-quarters full with ice cubes.

6 Garnish with an orange twist and cherry and stir the drink.

# MUDDLED Cocktails

Muddled cocktails are fun. In case you're new to the concept, muddling refers to crushing ingredients such as herbs and fruit to release their flavors into the cocktail. Mixing a muddled cocktail is almost therapeutic. Squashing fresh fruit delivers the same youthful satisfaction as gleefully splashing around in a puddle. The Mojito and Caipirinha are fine examples of the muddled cocktail which you will want to offer at your next get together. After all, who doesn't want to use the line, "Can I muddle you a cocktail?"

## Mojito

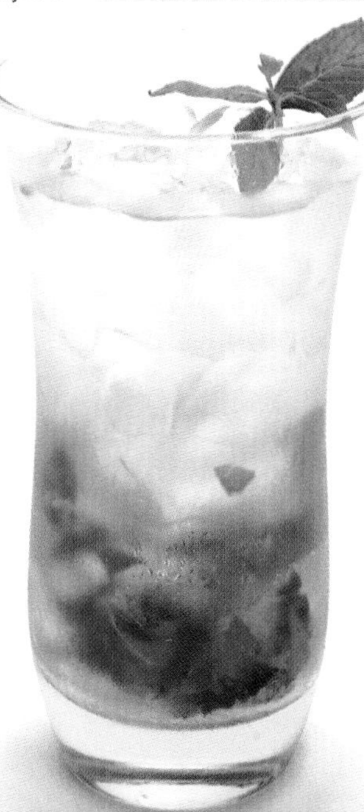

- 12 to 15 mint leaves
- 1/2 lime
- 3/4 oz simple syrup
- 2 oz light rum
- club soda
- 1 sprig of mint

1 Add the mint leaves, the juice of half of a lime and simple syrup to a highball glass.

*Note: To make simple syrup, see page 42.*

2 Muddle the ingredients in the glass.

*Note: For information on muddling, see page 44.*

3 Fill the glass halfway with ice cubes, add the rum and stir the mixture vigorously.

4 Fill the rest of the glass with ice cubes, top the drink with club soda, garnish with a sprig of mint and stir the drink.

## Melon Mojito

- 3 or 4 1-inch melon chunks
- 12 to 15 mint leaves
- 1/2 lime
- 3/4 oz simple syrup
- 2 oz light rum
- club soda
- 1 sprig of mint

1 Add the melon chunks, mint leaves, the juice of half of a lime and simple syrup to a highball glass.

*Note: To make simple syrup, see page 42.*

2 Muddle the ingredients in the glass.

*Note: For information on muddling, see page 44.*

3 Fill the glass halfway with ice cubes, add the rum and stir the mixture vigorously.

4 Fill the rest of the glass with ice cubes, top the drink with club soda, garnish with a sprig of mint and stir the drink.

**TIP** *What other variations of the Mojito and Caipirinha can I make?*

Creating fruity variations of the Mojito and Caipirinha with your favorite fruits is easy. You can muddle in just about any soft, juicy fruit. Consider muddling 12 cranberries, 9 raspberries or 3 to 4 strawberries along with the rest of the ingredients in the recipes listed below the next time you mix up a Mojito or Caipirinha.

**TIP** *What spirit can I use if I can't find cachaca?*

Cachaca is a unique liquor made from sugar cane juice and has a flavor similar to that of light rum. Unless you live in Brazil, where it is the national spirit, cachaca can be difficult to find. If you can't find cachaca, you can easily substitute rum for cachaca in a recipe.

## Caipirinha

4 lime wedges
3/4 oz simple syrup
2 oz cachaca

1. Add 3 lime wedges and simple syrup to a rocks glass.

   *Note: To make simple syrup, see page 42.*

2. Muddle the ingredients in the glass.

   *Note: For information on how to muddle, see page 44.*

3. Fill the glass halfway with crushed ice, add the cachaca and stir the mixture vigorously.

4. Fill the rest of the glass with crushed ice and garnish with the remaining lime wedge.

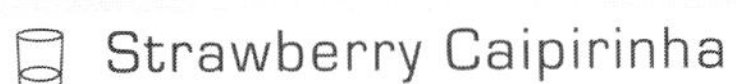

## Strawberry Caipirinha

3 to 4 strawberries
4 lime wedges
3/4 oz simple syrup
2 oz cachaca

1. Add the strawberries, 3 lime wedges and simple syrup to a rocks glass.

   *Note: To make simple syrup, see page 42.*

2. Muddle the ingredients in the glass.

   *Note: For information on how to muddle, see page 44.*

3. Fill the glass halfway with crushed ice, add the cachaca and stir the mixture vigorously.

4. Fill the rest of the glass with crushed ice and garnish with the remaining lime wedge.

# TOMATO-BASED Cocktails

Savory tomato-based cocktails make a refreshing alternative to the typical range of sweet cocktails. Hearty and satisfying, the Bloody Mary and Bloody Caesar are delicious choices as an appetizer. The beefy flavors of the Bloody Bull are sure to please steak lovers. And for an intriguing south-of-the-border twist, the Bloody Maria uses tequila for its base spirit instead of vodka.

## Bloody Mary

salt
1 1/2 oz vodka
2 shakes Worcestershire sauce
2 shakes Tabasco sauce
3 1/2 oz tomato juice
pepper
1 lemon wheel

1 Coat the rim of a highball glass with salt and fill with ice cubes.

*Note: To coat the rim of a glass,* *see page 40.*

2 Add the vodka, Worcestershire sauce and Tabasco sauce to the glass.

3 Add the tomato juice to the glass.

4 Add 2 shakes of salt and pepper to the glass.

5 Garnish with a lemon wheel and stir the drink.

## Bloody Caesar

celery salt
1 1/2 oz vodka
2 shakes Worcestershire sauce
2 shakes Tabasco sauce
3 1/2 oz clam-tomato juice
salt
pepper
1 celery stalk
1 lime wheel

1 Coat the rim of a highball glass with celery salt and fill with ice cubes.

*Note: To coat the rim of a glass,* *see page 40.*

2 Add the vodka, Worcestershire sauce and Tabasco sauce to the glass.

3 Add the clam-tomato juice to the glass.

4 Add 2 shakes of salt and pepper to the glass.

5 Garnish with a celery stalk and lime wheel and stir the drink.

TIP *How can I make my tomato-based cocktails a little more spicy?*

Those who like the heat can add more kick to their tomato-based cocktails by mixing in more spice. To give your cocktails more heat, increase the amount of Worcestershire sauce, hot sauce and pepper in the original recipes to 3 or 4 shakes each.

TIP *What is a Smokin' Hot Bloody Mary?*

The Smokin' Hot Bloody Mary is a fiery, tomato cocktail that is not for amateurs. Instead of the vodka and Tabasco sauce in the Bloody Mary recipe, use Absolut Peppar vodka and Tabasco's Habanero sauce and add 1 teaspoon of horseradish. The Smokin' Hot Bloody Mary delivers an interesting texture and five-alarm flavor. Garnish with a jalapeno pepper if you dare.

## Bloody Bull

- salt
- 1 1/2 oz vodka
- 2 oz beef bouillon
- 2 shakes Worcestershire sauce
- 2 shakes Tabasco sauce
- 2 oz tomato juice
- pepper
- 1 lime wheel

1 Coat the rim of a highball glass with salt and fill with ice cubes.

*Note: To coat the rim of a glass, see page 40.*

2 Add the vodka, beef bouillon, Worcestershire sauce and Tabasco sauce to the glass.

3 Add the tomato juice to the glass.

4 Add 2 shakes of salt and pepper to the glass.

5 Garnish with a lime wheel and stir the drink.

## Bloody Maria

- salt
- 1 1/2 oz tequila
- 2 shakes Worcestershire sauce
- 2 shakes Tabasco sauce
- 3 1/2 oz tomato juice
- pepper
- 1 lime wheel

1 Coat the rim of a highball glass with salt and fill with ice cubes.

*Note: To coat the rim of a glass, see page 40.*

2 Add the tequila, Worcestershire sauce and Tabasco sauce to the glass.

3 Add the tomato juice to the glass.

4 Add 2 shakes of salt and pepper to the glass.

5 Garnish with a lime wheel and stir the drink.

# Tastes of Rye Whiskey

While rye whiskey has quite a strong and distinct flavor, it is still great for mixing in a wide variety of cocktails. For example, both the berry-infused Blue Bomber and citrus-flavored Ruby Red Rye illustrate how rye whiskey is compatible with fruit flavors. The Rye and Dry is perfect for those who like their drinks with very little sweetness. Rye whiskey may seem like an unusual ingredient for a blended drink, but the rich Classic Hummer is sure to change that perception.

## Blue Bomber

- 12 blueberries
- 3 maraschino cherries, stems removed
- 1 1/2 oz rye whiskey
- 1/2 oz cherry brandy
- 1 oz club soda
- 1 maraschino cherry

1. Add the blueberries and 3 maraschino cherries to a rocks glass.
2. Muddle the ingredients in the glass.

   *Note: For information on how to muddle, see page 44.*
3. Fill the glass with crushed ice.
4. Add the rye whiskey, cherry brandy and club soda to the glass.
5. Garnish with a maraschino cherry and stir the drink.

## Ruby Red Rye

- 1 1/2 oz rye whiskey
- 2 1/2 oz red grapefruit juice
- 1 oz tonic water
- 1 orange wheel

1. Fill a highball glass with ice cubes.
2. Add the rye whiskey, grapefruit juice and tonic water to the glass.
3. Garnish with an orange wheel and stir the drink.

**TIP** *What is blended whiskey?*

In the United States, blended whiskey is made from a blend of one or more types of whiskey and neutral grain spirits. Blended whiskey must contain at least 20% straight whiskey. Due to the fact that blended whiskey is mixed with other ingredients, blended whiskey is less expensive than other types of whiskey.

**TIP** *What is rye whiskey?*

Rye whiskey, as the name implies, is a distilled spirit from at least 51% rye grain. It is aged in new charred oak barrels for at least two years. Rye whiskey has a distinctive spicy, sweet oaked flavor and mixes well in cocktails. Popular brands of rye whiskey include Jim Beam Rye, Wild Turkey Rye and Old Overholt.

## Rye and Dry

1 1/2 oz rye whiskey
2 1/2 oz ginger ale
1 lemon wedge

1 Fill a rocks glass with ice cubes.

2 Add the rye whiskey and ginger ale to the glass.

3 Garnish the drink with a lemon wedge and stir the drink.

## Classic Hummer

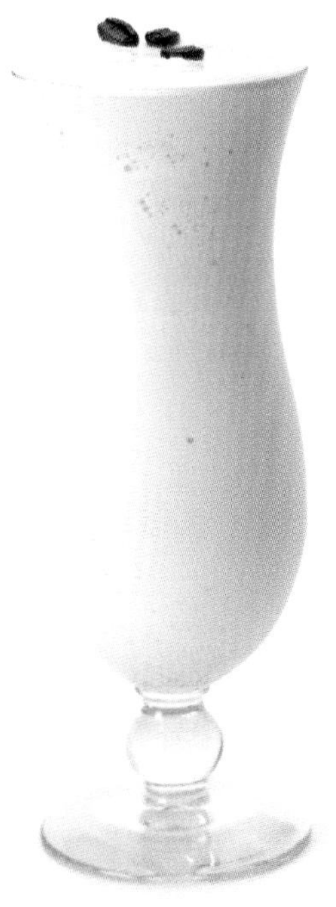

1 oz rye whiskey
1 oz Kahlua
1 oz half & half cream
2 scoops vanilla ice cream
1 cup ice, crushed
3 coffee beans

1 Place the rye whiskey, Kahlua, cream, ice cream and crushed ice in a blender.

2 Blend all of the ingredients until the mixture is smooth.

3 Pour the mixture into a chilled hurricane glass and garnish with coffee beans.

# Tastes of Irish Whiskey

Irish whiskey is a uniquely mellow and somewhat sweet spirit, with much of its flavor derived from aging in barrels that have previously held sherry, rum or bourbon. It may be this familiarity with other spirits that makes Irish whiskey well-suited to mixed drinks. These cocktails highlight the versatility of whiskey from the Emerald Isle. The Dublin Peach and Rugburn cocktails show how nicely Irish whiskey can pair with sweet fruits, while the Dr. J and That's a Corker feature bright citrus flavors.

## Dublin Peach

- 1 oz Irish whiskey
- 1/2 oz vanilla vodka
- 1/2 oz amaretto
- 1 oz peach puree
- 1/2 oz lemon juice
- 1/2 oz simple syrup
- 1 peach slice

1 Fill a rocks glass with ice cubes.

2 Add the Irish whiskey, vanilla vodka, amaretto, peach puree, lemon juice and simple syrup to a shaker.

*Note: To make fruit puree, see page 43. To make simple syrup, see page 42.*

3 Shake the mixture vigorously for 5 to 10 seconds.

4 Pour the contents of the shaker into the glass and garnish with a peach slice.

## Rugburn

- 6 raspberries
- 1 1/2 oz Irish whiskey
- 1/2 oz Chambord
- 1/2 oz lemon juice
- 1/2 oz simple syrup
- 2 oz red cranberry juice
- 3 raspberries

1 Add 6 raspberries to a highball glass.

2 Muddle the raspberries in the glass.

*Note: For information on how to muddle, see page 44.*

3 Fill the glass with crushed ice.

4 Add the Irish whiskey, Chambord, lemon juice, simple syrup and cranberry juice to the glass.

*Note: To make simple syrup, see page 42.*

5 Garnish with 3 raspberries and stir the drink.

**TIP** *Can I make these cocktails using another type of whiskey?*

One of the joys of bartending lies in the freedom to tweak recipes to your personal tastes. Feel free to substitute scotch, bourbon or rye whiskey for the Irish whiskey in these drinks. The end result may be quite different because each type of whiskey has its own distinct character, but that's the whole idea of experimentation. Be creative!

**TIP** *What is the purpose of muddling the lemon pieces into the That's a Corker cocktail?*

Muddling lemon pieces into the cocktail releases essential citrus oils from the peel of the fruit. These oils are potent and give the drink a fresher and more pronounced citrus flavor than you would get from using lemon juice alone. The muddled lemon pieces also become a garnish, lending visual interest to the drink.

## Dr. J

1 1/2 oz Irish whiskey
1/2 oz vanilla vodka
1/2 lime
3 oz ginger ale
1 lime wedge

1 Fill a highball glass with ice cubes.

2 Add the Irish whiskey, vanilla vodka and the juice from 1/2 a lime to a shaker.

3 Shake the mixture vigorously for 5 to 10 seconds.

4 Pour the contents of the shaker into the glass.

5 Add the ginger ale to the glass, garnish with a lime wedge and stir the drink.

## That's a Corker

1/2 lemon, diced
1 1/2 oz Irish whiskey
1/2 oz Galliano
1/4 lemon
1/2 oz simple syrup

1 Add 1/2 a diced lemon to a rocks glass.

2 Muddle the lemon pieces in the glass.

*Note: For information on how to muddle, see page 44.*

3 Fill the glass three-quarters full with crushed ice.

4 Add the Irish whiskey, Galliano, juice from the 1/4 lemon and simple syrup to the glass.

*Note: To make simple syrup, see page 42.*

5 Stir the drink.

# Sun & Sand Cocktails

The next time the Caribbean is calling but your wallet tells you to stay home, you can take a budget-friendly vacation with one of these drinks. If there is one flavor that brings to mind the sun and sand, it is rum. These cocktails all take rum and blend it with luscious fruit flavors like pineapple, lime, banana, pomegranate and raspberry. Sipping on one of these delicious drinks is the next best thing to a plane ticket south.

## Rum Runner

1/2 oz light rum
1/2 oz Chambord
1/2 oz banana liqueur
3 oz pineapple juice
1 oz lime juice
1/2 oz grenadine
1 pineapple flag

1. Fill a hurricane glass with ice cubes.
2. Add the light rum, Chambord, banana liqueur, pineapple juice, lime juice and grenadine to a shaker.
3. Shake the mixture vigorously for 5 to 10 seconds.
4. Pour the drink into the glass and garnish with a pineapple flag.

*Note: To make a pineapple flag,* *see page 36.*

## Planter's Punch

1 1/2 oz light rum
4 oz pineapple juice
1/2 oz grenadine
1 maraschino cherry

1. Fill a highball glass with ice cubes.
2. Add the light rum, pineapple juice and grenadine to a shaker.
3. Shake the mixture vigorously for 5 to 10 seconds.
4. Pour the drink into the glass and garnish with a maraschino cherry.

TIP *Where does the Mai Tai get its name?*

There is a lot of folklore surrounding the creation of the Mai Tai. Legendary bartenders "Don the Beachcomber" and "Trader Vic Bergeron" both claim to have created the drink. According to Trader Vic, he created the drink in 1944 for two friends from Tahiti. Upon taking her first sip, one of his friends exclaimed, "Mai Tai! Roa Ae!" The phrase roughly translates from Tahitian to mean, "This is out of this world! The best!"

TIP *Can I use different types of rum in these cocktails?*

You can use just about any type of rum that you like in these cocktails. Light rum is the standard choice, but for more depth of flavor, you can use both gold and dark rums. Spiced and fruit-flavored rums would also make interesting choices. Beware of using overproof rum, however, as its high alcohol content may prove a little overpowering. For information on different types of rum, see page 52.

## Mai Tai

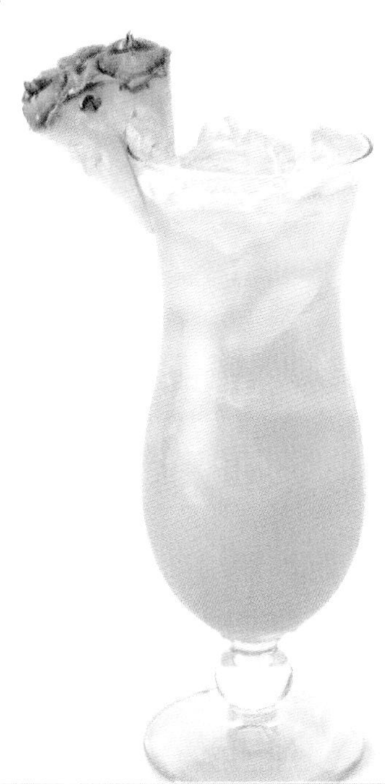

1/2 oz light rum
1/2 oz Grand Marnier
1/2 oz amaretto
3 oz pineapple juice
1 oz lime juice
1 pineapple wedge

1 Fill a hurricane glass with ice cubes.

2 Add the light rum, Grand Marnier, amaretto, pineapple juice and lime juice to a shaker.

3 Shake the mixture vigorously for 5 to 10 seconds.

4 Pour the drink into the glass and garnish with a pineapple wedge.

## Blue Lagoon

1 oz light rum
1/2 oz blue curacao
2 oz pineapple juice
2 oz lime juice
1 orange boat

1 Fill a highball glass with ice cubes.

2 Add the light rum, blue curacao, pineapple juice and lime juice to a shaker.

3 Shake the mixture vigorously for 5 to 10 seconds.

4 Pour the drink into the glass and garnish with an orange boat.

*Note: To make an orange boat, see page 37.*

# Drinks to Beat the Heat

Some drinks are elegant and suave, well suited to black tie affairs. Other cocktails are rich and sweet, pairing well with desserts. On a sweltering summer day, however, you just need a drink that is cold, wet and delicious. Next time the mercury is about to pop out of the top of the thermometer, try one of these drinks to beat the heat. The Bartender's Root Beer, Cuba Libre and Texas Tea are all popular choices, but if you only try one, it has to be the Lynchburg Lemonade.

## Bartender's Root Beer

1 oz Kahlua
1/2 oz Galliano
3 oz cola
1 oz club soda

1 Fill a highball glass with ice cubes.

2 Add the Kahlua, Galliano, cola and club soda to the glass and stir the drink.

## Cuba Libre

1 1/2 oz rum
3 1/2 oz cola
1 lime wedge

1 Fill a rocks glass with ice cubes.

2 Add the rum and cola to the glass.

3 Squeeze the juice from a lime wedge into the drink.

4 Place the lime wedge into the drink and stir the drink.

TIP *Is Jack Daniel's a bourbon?*

While it shares many of the same properties of Kentucky's favorite spirit, Jack Daniel's Tennessee Whiskey is not a bourbon whiskey. Jack Daniels is made from corn, rye and barley and aged in oak barrels like bourbon, but unlike bourbon, Jack Daniel's is filtered through sugar maple charcoal in a process that is designed to mellow the whiskey's flavors.

TIP *Can I substitue Jack Daniel's in the Lynchburg Lemonade?*

Even though Lynchburg Lemonade is named after the hometown of Jack Daniel's Tennessee Whiskey, feel free to substitute 1 oz of bourbon for the Jack Daniel's—the taste is very similar. You can also experiment with using rye whiskey, Irish whiskey or Scotch.

## Texas Tea

- 1/2 oz tequila
- 1/2 oz rum
- 1/2 oz triple sec
- 1/2 lemon
- 1/2 oz simple syrup
- 2 oz cola
- 1 lemon wedge

1. Fill a highball glass with ice cubes.
2. Add the tequila, rum, triple sec, juice from 1/2 a lemon and simple syrup to a shaker.

   *Note: To make simple syrup, see page 42.*
3. Shake the mixture vigorously for 5 to 10 seconds.
4. Pour the mixture into the glass.
5. Add the cola to the glass, garnish with a lemon wedge and stir the drink.

## Lynchburg Lemonade

- 1 oz Jack Daniel's
- 1/2 oz triple sec
- 1/4 lemon
- 1/2 oz simple syrup
- 2 1/2 oz lemon-lime soda
- 1 lemon wedge

1. Fill a highball glass with ice cubes.
2. Add the Jack Daniel's, triple sec, juice from a 1/4 lemon and simple syrup to a shaker.

   *Note: To make simple syrup, see page 42.*
3. Shake the mixture vigorously for 5 to 10 seconds.
4. Pour the mixture into the glass.
5. Add the lemon-lime soda to the glass, garnish with a lemon wedge and stir the drink.

# DANGEROUS Cocktails

Admittedly, these cocktails are not really all that dangerous, but they do have dangerous-sounding names. Killer Kool-aid is a mysterious-looking and delicious cocktail that is very easy to drink. The Hurricane is a furious mix of rum, Galliano and fruit juices. No one in his right mind would run from the Zombie with its delectable fruit flavors and the only sting the Scorpion holds is its bracing splash of lime juice.

## Killer Kool-aid

1/2 oz vodka
1/2 oz Midori melon liqueur
1/2 oz amaretto
4 oz red cranberry juice
1 lime wheel

1 Fill a highball glass with ice cubes.

2 Add the vodka, Midori, amaretto and cranberry juice to the glass.

3 Garnish the drink with a lime wheel and stir the drink.

## Hurricane

1/2 oz light rum
1/2 oz dark rum
1/2 oz Galliano
2 oz orange juice
1 oz pineapple juice
1 oz lime juice
1 lime wheel

1 Fill a hurricane glass with ice cubes.

2 Add the light rum, dark rum, Galliano, orange juice, pineapple juice and lime juice to a shaker.

3 Shake the mixture vigorously for 5 to 10 seconds.

4 Pour the drink into the glass and garnish with a lime wheel.

**TIP** *What is Galliano?*

Galliano is a brilliant yellow, sweet Italian liqueur. Infused with more than 40 herbs, spices and flowers, Galliano has a very distinct vanilla-licorice flavor.

**TIP** *Are there any variations I can make of Killer Kool-aid?*

If you want to change the Killer Kool-aid recipe, you can make a peach-flavored variation called the Big Fella. All you have to do is substitute a 1/2 oz of Southern Comfort for the 1/2 oz of Midori melon liqueur called for in the original recipe.

## Zombie

1/2 oz light rum
1/2 oz dark rum
1/2 oz Grand Marnier
2 oz orange juice
2 oz pineapple juice
1/2 oz grenadine
1 pineapple flag

1. Fill a highball glass with ice cubes.
2. Add the light rum, dark rum, Grand Marnier, orange juice, pineapple juice and grenadine to a shaker.
3. Shake the mixture vigorously for 5 to 10 seconds.
4. Pour the drink into the glass and garnish with a pineapple flag.

*Note: To make a pineapple flag, see page 36.*

## Scorpion

1/2 oz light rum
1/2 oz cognac
1/2 oz amaretto
3 oz orange juice
1 oz lime juice
1 orange flag

1. Fill a highball glass with ice cubes.
2. Add the light rum, cognac, amaretto, orange juice and lime juice to a shaker.
3. Shake the mixture vigorously for 5 to 10 seconds.
4. Pour the drink into the glass and garnish with an orange flag.

*Note: To make an orange flag, see page 36.*

# GLOBAL SUNSHINE Cocktails

All around the world, great sunshine-inspired cocktails abound. Like the country after which it is named, the classic Singapore Sling is both tropical and sophisticated. The Bahama Mama blends two different rums with zingy orange and pineapple flavors for a sweet and refreshing cocktail. The Alabama Slammer is more than just a fun-to-pronounce name, it's a deliciously sweet OJ-based cocktail. The Blue Hawaiian looks stunning, tastes great and will have you doing Elvis impersonations in no time.

## Singapore Sling

1 1/2 oz gin
2 oz orange juice
1 oz lime juice
1/2 oz grenadine
1 oz club soda
1 orange flag

1 Fill a highball glass with ice cubes.

2 Add the gin, orange juice, lime juice and grenadine to the glass.

3 Add the club soda to the mixture.

4 Garnish the drink with an orange flag and stir the drink.

*Note: To make an orange flag, see page 36.*

## Bahama Mama

1 oz light rum
1/2 oz Malibu rum
2 oz orange juice
2 oz pineapple juice
1 pineapple flag

1 Fill a highball glass with ice cubes.

2 Add the light rum, Malibu rum, orange juice and pineapple juice to a shaker.

3 Shake the mixture vigorously for 5 to 10 seconds.

4 Pour the drink into the glass and garnish with a pineapple flag.

*Note: To make a pineapple flag, see page 36.*

**TIP** *What does the Singapore Sling have to do with Singapore?*

The Singapore Sling was created by a Chinese born bartender named Ngiam Tong Boon while he was working at the Long Bar at the world famous Raffles Hotel in Singapore. Since its creation just prior to the First World War, the Singapore Sling has become one of the world's most recognizable cocktails.

**TIP** *Why do Southern Comfort and amaretto pair so well?*

Used in the Alabama Slammer cocktail and Sicilian Kiss shooter (p.175), Southern Comfort and amaretto are a delicious pairing. The reason for this may be that Southern Comfort is a peach-flavored bourbon liqueur and amaretto is a liqueur derived from the pits of apricots, which taste very similar to peaches. It's a match made in the orchard.

## Alabama Slammer

- 1/2 oz vodka
- 1/2 oz Southern Comfort
- 1/2 oz amaretto
- 4 oz orange juice
- 1/2 oz grenadine
- 1 maraschino cherry

1. Fill a highball glass with ice cubes.
2. Add the vodka, Southern Comfort, amaretto, orange juice and grenadine to a shaker.
3. Shake the mixture vigorously for 5 to 10 seconds.
4. Pour the drink into the glass and garnish with a maraschino cherry.

## Blue Hawaiian

- 1 oz Malibu rum
- 1/2 oz blue curacao
- 3 oz pineapple juice
- 1 oz lime juice
- 1 orange flag

1. Fill a highball glass with ice cubes.
2. Add the Malibu rum, blue curacao, pineapple juice and lime juice to a shaker.
3. Shake the mixture vigorously for 5 to 10 seconds.
4. Pour the drink into the glass and garnish with an orange flag.

*Note: To make an orange flag, see page 36.*

# Tastes of Rum

The seemingly endless variety of different rums is a testament to rum's immense popularity. At any liquor store, you will find light rums and dark rums of various ages, gold rums, spiced rums and flavored rums. The cocktails below are just a small sampling of the liquor's range. From the deliciously sharp flavors of the Reggae Rum Punch to the refreshing taste of the Reef Juice, you can dress up rum just about any way you like.

## Reggae Rum Punch

1 1/2 oz dark rum
1/2 oz Chambord
2 oz orange juice
2 oz pineapple juice
1/2 lime
1 pineapple flag

1 Fill a highball glass with ice cubes.

2 Add the dark rum, Chambord, orange juice, pineapple juice and juice from the 1/2 lime to a shaker.

3 Shake the mixture vigorously for 5 to 10 seconds.

4 Pour the contents of the shaker into the glass and garnish with a pineapple flag.

*Note: To make a pineapple flag, see page 36.*

## Bacardi Cocktail

2 oz Bacardi light rum
1 oz lime juice
1 oz water
1/2 oz grenadine
1 maraschino cherry

1 Fill a shaker halfway with ice cubes.

2 Add the Bacardi rum, lime juice, water and grenadine to the shaker.

3 Shake the mixture vigorously for 5 to 10 seconds.

4 Strain the contents of the shaker into a chilled cocktail glass and garnish with a maraschino cherry.

TIP *Should I buy aged rum?*

Rums that have been aged have more mellow and complex flavors than rums that have not been aged. If you will be mixing your rum mostly in cocktails, save your money and don't buy rum that is aged. The subtle flavors of an aged rum are overpowered and lost in mixed drinks.

TIP *Can I use another rum besides Bacardi in the Bacardi Cocktail?*

If you do not have a bottle of Bacardi rum on hand, you can certainly use another brand of rum to make the Bacardi Cocktail. Depending on where you live, however, you may be breaking the law. Believe it or not, a quirky 1936 ruling of the Supreme Court of New York declared that a Bacardi Cocktail must contain Bacardi rum.

## Pain Killer

- 1 1/2 oz dark rum
- 1/2 oz Malibu coconut rum
- 2 oz orange juice
- 2 oz pineapple juice
- 1 pineapple wedge

1. Fill a highball glass with ice cubes.
2. Add the dark rum, Malibu coconut rum, orange juice and pineapple juice to a shaker.
3. Shake the mixture vigorously for 5 to 10 seconds.
4. Pour the contents of the shaker into the glass and garnish with a pineapple wedge.

*Note: To make a pineapple wedge, see page 34.*

## Reef Juice

- 1 1/2 oz dark rum
- 1/2 oz banana liqueur
- 3 oz pineapple juice
- 1/2 lime
- 1/2 oz grenadine
- 1 pineapple flag

1. Fill a highball glass with ice cubes.
2. Add the dark rum, banana liqueur, pineapple juice, juice from the 1/2 lime and grenadine to a shaker.
3. Shake the mixture vigorously for 5 to 10 seconds.
4. Pour the contents of the shaker into the glass and garnish with a pineapple flag.

*Note: To make a pineapple flag, see page 36.*

# Tastes of Tequila

One of Mexico's favorite exports, tequila is the best-known spirit from south of the border. While it is often taken as a shot, tequila also makes great cocktails. The Tequila Sunrise is a must-try—tasting and looking great. If you've never made his acquaintance, Freddy Fudpucker is worth getting to know. The Mayan brings together Mexico's famous spirit with its popular liqueur, Kahlua. The Mexican Mule deliciously combines the Caribbean taste of ginger beer with Mexican flavors of tequila and lime.

## Tequila Sunrise

1/2 oz grenadine
1 1/2 oz tequila
4 oz orange juice

1. Add the grenadine to a highball glass.
2. Fill the glass with ice cubes.
3. Add the tequila to the glass.
4. Add the orange juice to the glass and stir the drink.

## Freddy Fudpucker

1 oz tequila
1/2 oz Galliano
4 oz orange juice
1 maraschino cherry

1. Fill a highball glass with ice cubes.
2. Add the tequila, Galliano and orange juice to the glass.
3. Garnish the drink with a maraschino cherry and stir the drink.

**TIP** *Do bottles of tequila really contain a worm?*

Many people are under the impression that some brands of tequila contain a worm at the bottom of the bottle. This is not true. The misconception dates back to the 1940s when a producer of mezcal, a Mexican liquor related to tequila, started placing a small caterpillar in each of its bottles as a publicity stunt. By Mexican law, bottles of tequila cannot contain either a worm or a caterpillar.

**TIP** *What type of tequila should I buy?*

There are several types of tequila, including silver, gold, rested and aged. Silver and gold tequila have been aged less than 60 days. Rested tequila has been aged between 60 days and one year. Aged, or añejo, tequila has been aged for more than a year. For cocktails and shots, avoid the harsher silver tequila and go for the more mellow gold tequila. You can save the rested and aged varieties for special occasions.

## Mayan

1 1/2 oz tequila
1/2 oz Kahlua
2 oz pineapple juice
3 espresso beans

1. Fill a rocks glass with ice cubes.
2. Add the tequila, Kahlua and pineapple juice to a shaker.
3. Shake the mixture vigorously for 5 to 10 seconds.
4. Pour the drink into the glass and garnish with 3 espresso beans.

## Mexican Mule

2 oz tequila
1/2 lime
1/2 oz simple syrup
3 oz ginger beer
1 lime wedge

1. Fill a highball glass with ice cubes.
2. Add the tequila, juice from the 1/2 lime and simple syrup to a shaker.

   *Note: To make simple syrup, see page 42.*
3. Shake the mixture vigorously for 5 to 10 seconds.
4. Pour the drink into the glass and add the ginger beer.
5. Garnish with a lime wedge and stir the drink.

# Tastes of Bourbon

Bourbon is America's liquor. In 1964, the U.S. Congress passed an act that declared bourbon to be "America's Native Spirit." Produced in Kentucky, this unique form of whiskey has a distinctly complex and sweet character which lends cocktails a subtle lingering sweetness. From the classic Ward 8 to the berry-flavored Bourbon Smash, these cocktails are sure to please a crowd and will be a welcome part of your next bash—whether you are celebrating the Fourth of July or not.

## Ward 8

- 2 oz bourbon
- 1 oz orange juice
- 1/2 lemon
- 1/2 oz grenadine
- 1 maraschino cherry

1. Fill a shaker halfway with ice cubes.
2. Add the bourbon, orange juice, juice from the lemon and grenadine to a shaker.
3. Shake the mixture vigorously for 5 to 10 seconds.
4. Strain the contents of the shaker into a chilled cocktail glass and garnish with a maraschino cherry.

## Kentucky Colonel

- 1 oz bourbon
- 1/2 oz Southern Comfort
- 1/2 oz triple sec
- 2 oz orange juice
- 1/2 lemon
- 1/2 oz simple syrup
- 1 maraschino cherry

1. Fill a highball glass with ice cubes.
2. Add the bourbon, Southern Comfort, triple sec, orange juice, juice from the lemon and simple syrup to a shaker.

   *Note: To make simple syrup, see page 42.*
3. Shake the mixture vigorously for 5 to 10 seconds.
4. Pour the contents of the shaker into the glass and garnish with a maraschino cherry.

**TIP** *What is bourbon?*

Bourbon is a form of whiskey which takes its name from Kentucky's Bourbon County where it originated. The production of bourbon is strictly defined by U.S. law. Bourbon must be made from at least 51% but no more than 79% corn and aged in oak barrels for at least 2 years.

**TIP** *What is the difference between single barrel and small batch bourbons?*

As bourbons age, each barrel takes on a character of its own. Bottles of single barrel bourbon are bottled directly from only one barrel that has usually been selected for its high quality. This means that one bottle of single barrel bourbon may differ from another bottle that was taken from a different barrel. Small batch bourbons are blends from a limited selection of different barrels, creating bourbon with a more uniform character from one bottle to the next.

## Bourbon Smash

- 12 raspberries
- 6 mint leaves
- 2 oz bourbon
- 2 oz red cranberry juice
- 1/2 lime
- 1/2 oz simple syrup
- 1 sprig of mint

1 Place the raspberries and mint leaves in a highball glass. Muddle the ingredients in the glass.

*Note: For information on how to muddle, see page 44.*

2 Fill the glass with crushed ice.

3 Add the bourbon, cranberry juice, juice from the lime and simple syrup to the glass.

*Note: To make simple syrup, see page 42.*

4 Garnish with a sprig of mint and stir the drink.

## Mississippi Punch

- 1 1/2 oz bourbon
- 1/2 oz brandy
- 3 oz water
- 1/4 lemon
- 1/2 oz simple syrup
- 1 orange slice

1 Fill a highball glass with ice cubes.

2 Add the bourbon, brandy, water, juice from the lemon and simple syrup to a shaker.

*Note: To make simple syrup, see page 42.*

3 Shake the mixture vigorously for 5 to 10 seconds.

4 Pour the contents of the shaker into the glass.

5 Garnish with an orange slice.

# Frozen Daiquiris

There are two reasons that blenders have found their way into most households: for pureeing soups and blending daiquiris. In case you've never had the pleasure, frozen daiquiris are a popular sweet and sour drink combining rum and lime juice. Variations abound and are simply made by adding complimentary fruit flavors. Strawberries, bananas and pineapples are all natural choices. If your blender has been limited to blending squash for soups, shift gears and mix up a daiquiri for a change.

## Frozen Lime Daiquiri

1 1/2 oz light rum
3 oz lime juice
1/2 oz lime cordial
1/2 oz simple syrup
1 cup ice, crushed
1 lime wheel

1. Place the rum, lime juice, lime cordial, simple syrup and ice in a blender.

   *Note: To make simple syrup, see page 42.*

2. Blend the mixture until it is smooth.
3. Pour the drink into a hurricane glass and garnish with a lime wheel.

## Frozen Strawberry Daiquiri

superfine sugar
1 1/2 oz light rum
4 strawberries
1 oz lime juice
1/2 oz lime cordial
1/2 oz simple syrup
1 cup ice, crushed
1 lime wheel

1. Coat the rim of a hurricane glass with superfine sugar.

   *Note: To coat the rim of a glass, see page 40.*

2. Place the rum, strawberries, lime juice, lime cordial, simple syrup and ice in a blender.

   *Note: To make simple syrup, see page 42.*

3. Blend the mixture until it is smooth.
4. Pour the drink into a hurricane glass and garnish with a lime wheel.

**TIP** *Is there a faster way to mix frozen daiquiris for a lot of people?*

Lime juice, lime cordial and simple syrup definitely make the best-tasting frozen daiquiris, but when you are mixing for a crowd, you may want to save time. For an adequate substitute, use a quantity of limeade equal to the total amount of lime juice, lime cordial and simple syrup in the recipe. For example, you would use 2 oz of limeade to replace the 1 oz lime juice, 1/2 oz lime cordial and 1/2 oz simple syrup called for in a recipe.

**TIP** *What other types of daiquiris can I make?*

Take a trip to your local grocery store and see what types of fruit juices are available. Don't be afraid to experiment! You can create any type of fruit daiquiri you like by adjusting the Frozen Strawberry Daiquiri recipe. Just add 2 oz of any type of juice instead of the 4 strawberries called for in the recipe.

## Frozen Banana Daiquiri

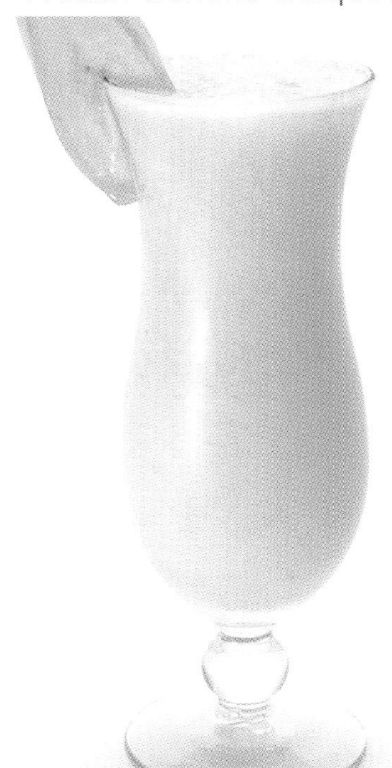

- 1 1/2 oz light rum
- 1/2 ripe banana
- 1 oz lime juice
- 1/2 oz lime cordial
- 1/2 oz simple syrup
- 1 cup ice, crushed
- 1 banana slice

1. Place the rum, banana, lime juice, lime cordial, simple syrup and ice in a blender.

   *Note: To make simple syrup, see page 42.*

2. Blend the mixture until it is smooth.
3. Pour the drink into a hurricane glass and garnish with a banana slice.

## Frozen Pineapple Daiquiri

- 1 1/2 oz light rum
- 1 pineapple ring
- 1 oz lime juice
- 1/2 oz lime cordial
- 1/2 oz simple syrup
- 1 cup ice, crushed
- 1 pineapple wedge

1. Place the rum, pineapple ring, lime juice, lime cordial, simple syrup and ice in a blender.

   *Note: To make simple syrup, see page 42.*

2. Blend the mixture until it is smooth.
3. Pour the drink into a hurricane glass and garnish with a pineapple wedge.

# DAIQUIRIS ON THE ROCKS

Many people do not recognize a daiquiri unless it is a slushy drink poured from a blender. The original versions of these delicious rum-lime drinks, however, were shaken together and served over ice or "on the rocks." These four old-style daiquiris make for a pleasant change of pace and are handy if you don't have a blender. Each of these variations features a fruit liqueur in place of fresh fruit, delivering a daiquiri that is delicious and easy to make.

## Raspberry Daiquiri

- superfine sugar
- 1 oz light rum
- 1/2 oz Chambord
- 2 oz lime juice
- 1 oz lime cordial
- 1/2 oz simple syrup
- 3 raspberries

1 Coat the rim of a margarita glass with superfine sugar and fill with crushed ice.

*Note: To coat the rim of a glass, see page 40.*

2 Place the rum, Chambord, lime juice, lime cordial and simple syrup in a shaker.

*Note: To make simple syrup, see page 42.*

3 Shake the mixture vigorously for 5 to 10 seconds.

4 Pour the drink into the glass and garnish with three raspberries.

## Melon Daiquiri

- 1 oz light rum
- 1/2 oz Midori melon liqueur
- 2 oz lime juice
- 1 oz lime cordial
- 1/2 oz simple syrup
- 1 melon slice

1 Fill a margarita glass with crushed ice.

2 Place the rum, melon liqueur, lime juice, lime cordial and simple syrup in a shaker.

*Note: To make simple syrup, see page 42.*

3 Shake the mixture vigorously for 5 to 10 seconds.

4 Pour the drink into the glass and garnish with a melon slice.

TIP *Can I serve daiquiris without the ice?*

It is quite acceptable to serve daiquiris without ice. Just put your ingredients together in a shaker that has been half-filled with ice cubes. Shake the mixture for several seconds to bring down the temperature and strain the drink into a chilled cocktail glass. A daiquiri that is served without ice is referred to as a "natural daiquiri" or a "daiquiri straight up."

TIP *What is lime cordial?*

Lime cordial is a sweetened, non-alcoholic, lime-flavored syrup. It is added to cocktails to boost the lime flavor and give the drink a noticeable sweetness. Lime cordial should not be used as a substitute for lime juice, which is less concentrated and is not sweet.

## Peach Daiquiri

- 1 oz light rum
- 1/2 oz peach schnapps
- 2 oz lime juice
- 1 oz lime cordial
- 1/2 oz simple syrup
- 1 peach slice

1. Fill a margarita glass with crushed ice.
2. Place the rum, peach schnapps, lime juice, lime cordial and simple syrup in a shaker.

   *Note: To make simple syrup,* *see page 42.*
3. Shake the mixture vigorously for 5 to 10 seconds.
4. Pour the drink into the glass and garnish with a peach slice.

## Pear Daiquiri

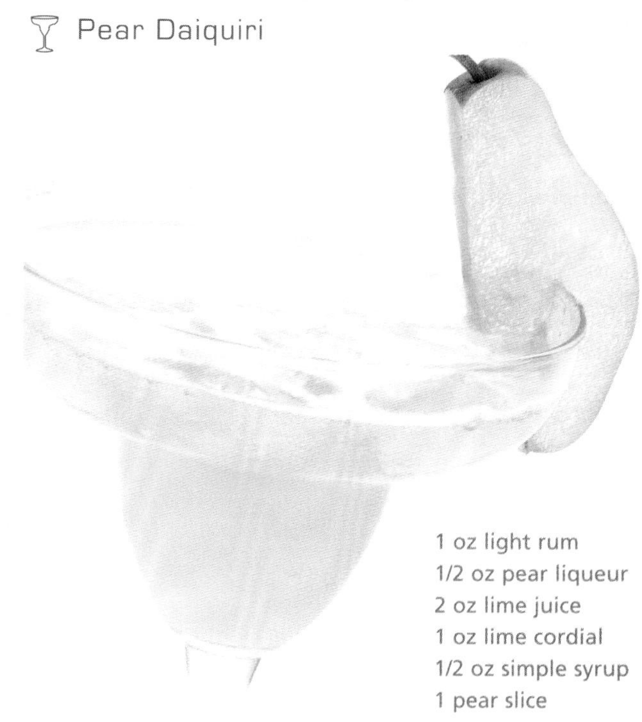

- 1 oz light rum
- 1/2 oz pear liqueur
- 2 oz lime juice
- 1 oz lime cordial
- 1/2 oz simple syrup
- 1 pear slice

1. Fill a margarita glass with crushed ice.
2. Place the rum, pear liqueur, lime juice, lime cordial and simple syrup in a shaker.

   *Note: To make simple syrup,* *see page 42.*
3. Shake the mixture vigorously for 5 to 10 seconds.
4. Pour the drink into the glass and garnish with a pear slice.

# FROZEN Coladas

The Pina Colada is the flavor of the tropics—one taste of that distinctive coconut-pineapple blend and most of us start humming Bob Marley's greatest hits. Mixing up a Pina Colada will have you feeling the bright sun and warm ocean breezes, even if you live in Wisconsin. If you want to add more fruit flavor, simply add strawberries, peaches or bananas to the blend to create a few different but equally delicious frozen coladas.

## Pina Colada

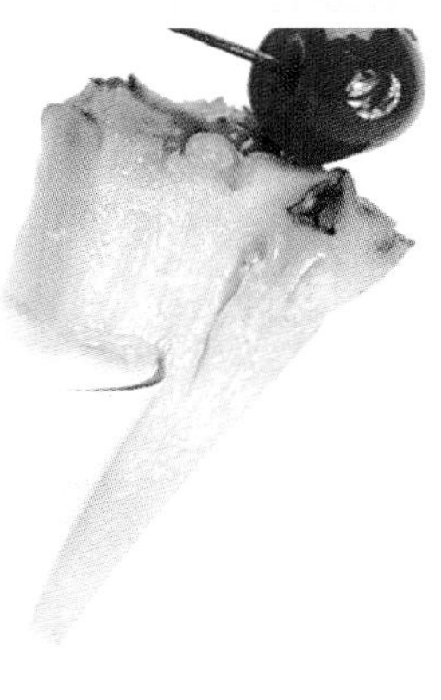

- 1 1/2 oz light rum
- 2 oz pineapple juice
- 1 oz half & half cream
- 1 oz coconut cream
- 1 cup ice, crushed
- 1 pineapple flag

1 Place the light rum, pineapple juice, half & half cream, coconut cream and ice into a blender.

2 Blend the mixture until it is smooth.

3 Pour the drink into a hurricane glass and garnish with a pineapple flag.

*Note: To create a pineapple flag, see page 36.*

## Strawberry Colada

- 1 1/2 oz light rum
- 2 oz pineapple juice
- 4 strawberries
- 1 oz half & half cream
- 1 oz coconut cream
- 1 cup ice, crushed
- 1 strawberry

1 Place the light rum, pineapple juice, 4 strawberries, half & half cream, coconut cream and ice into a blender.

2 Blend the mixture until it is smooth.

3 Pour the drink into a hurricane glass and garnish with a strawberry.

**TIP** *How do I make a Mocha Colada?*

A Mocha Colada is a Pina Colada with an extra caffeinated dimension. Using the Pina Colada recipe, reduce the amount of light rum down to 1 oz and add a 1/2 oz of Kahlua. Garnish this extra creamy cocktail with a maraschino cherry.

**TIP** *What is a Chi Chi?*

To whip up a Chi Chi, simply substitute 1 1/2 oz of vodka for the light rum called for in the Pina Colada recipe. Garnish the drink with a pineapple flag.

## Banana Colada

- 1 1/2 oz light rum
- 2 oz pineapple juice
- 1/2 ripe banana
- 1 oz half & half cream
- 1 oz coconut cream
- 1 cup ice, crushed
- 1 banana slice

1 Place the light rum, pineapple juice, 1/2 banana, half & half cream, coconut cream and ice into a blender.

2 Blend the mixture until it is smooth.

3 Pour the drink into a hurricane glass and garnish with a banana slice.

## Peach Colada

- 1 1/2 oz light rum
- 2 oz pineapple juice
- 1/4 ripe peach
- 1 oz half & half cream
- 1 oz coconut cream
- 1 cup ice, crushed
- 1 peach slice

1 Place the light rum, pineapple juice, 1/4 peach, half & half cream, coconut cream and ice into a blender.

2 Blend the mixture until it is smooth.

3 Pour the drink into a hurricane glass and garnish with a peach slice.

# MARGARITAS

The margarita is a popular tequila-based cocktail that many people know as an icy party drink served from a blender. The original technique for preparing a margarita actually calls for the ingredients to be combined in a shaker, shaken thoroughly and then served in a glass with ice. With only three main flavors—tequila, triple sec and lime—margaritas are perfect for making fruity variations. Strawberries, raspberries and even peaches deliver deliciously complimentary flavors.

## Lime Margarita on the Rocks

salt
1 oz tequila
1/2 oz triple sec
2 oz lime juice
1 oz lime cordial
1/2 oz simple syrup
1 lime wedge

1 Coat the rim of a margarita glass with salt and fill with crushed ice.

*Note: To coat the rim of a glass, see page 40.*

2 Add the tequila, triple sec, lime juice, lime cordial and simple syrup to a shaker.

*Note: To make simple syrup, see page 42.*

3 Shake the mixture vigorously for 5 to 10 seconds.

4 Pour the drink into the glass and garnish with a lime wedge.

## Strawberry Margarita on the Rocks

superfine sugar
4 strawberries
1 oz tequila
1/2 oz triple sec
2 oz lime juice
1 oz lime cordial
1/2 oz simple syrup
1 lime wedge

1 Coat the rim of a margarita glass with sugar and fill with crushed ice.

*Note: To coat the rim of a glass, see page 40.*

2 Muddle the strawberries in the bottom of a shaker.

*Note: For information on muddling, see page 44.*

3 Add the tequila, triple sec, lime juice, lime cordial and simple syrup to the shaker.

*Note: To make simple syrup, see page 42.*

4 Shake the mixture vigorously for 5 to 10 seconds.

5 Pour the drink into the glass and garnish with a lime wedge.

TIP *What is an Italian Margarita?*

An Italian Margarita is a simple variation of the classic Lime Margarita. To mix an Italian Margarita, substitute a 1/2 oz of amaretto for the triple sec called for in the Lime Margarita on the Rocks recipe. The rich, nutty taste helps to balance the sharp tequila-lime flavor.

TIP *Can I make a frozen Lime and Strawberry Margarita?*

Absolutely! To transform a margarita on the rocks into a frozen margarita, simply add one cup of ice to the ingredients and place in a blender. You can also turn a frozen margarita into a margarita on the rocks by removing the cup of ice from the ingredients and following the instructions for how to make a margarita on the rocks.

## Frozen Raspberry Margarita

superfine sugar
12 raspberries
1 oz tequila
1/2 oz triple sec
2 oz lime juice
1 oz lime cordial
1/2 oz simple syrup
1 cup ice, crushed
3 raspberries

1 Coat the rim of a margarita glass with sugar.

*Note: To coat the rim of a glass, see page 40.*

2 Place the raspberries, tequila, triple sec, lime juice, lime cordial, simple syrup and ice into a blender.

*Note: To make simple syrup, see page 42.*

3 Blend the mixture until it is smooth.

4 Pour the drink into the glass and garnish with 3 raspberries.

## Frozen Peach Margarita

1/4 peach
1 oz tequila
1/2 oz triple sec
2 oz lime juice
1 oz lime cordial
1/2 oz simple syrup
1 cup ice, crushed
1 peach slice

1 Place the peach, tequila, triple sec, lime juice, lime cordial, simple syrup and ice into a blender.

*Note: To make simple syrup, see page 42.*

2 Blend the mixture until it is smooth.

3 Pour the drink into a margarita glass and garnish with a peach slice.

# CREAMY Cocktails

These cocktails are not for those who are sensitive to lactose. But if you have a sweet tooth, these creamy cocktails are just what the doctor ordered. The Crème Brûlé offers the luscious flavors of the famous French dessert. The Jamaican Bobsled is a smooth, sweet ride fueled by rum. Turning to the blender, you may want to try the summery Strawberry Shortcake with its vanilla and almond undertones. Or for another sweet and delicious frozen treat, try the Kid in a Candy Store.

## Crème Brûlé

- 1 oz vanilla vodka
- 1/2 oz butterscotch schnapps
- 2 oz half & half cream
- 1/2 oz simple syrup
- 1/2 egg white
- cinnamon

1. Fill a rocks glass with ice cubes.
2. Add the vodka, butterscotch schnapps, cream, simple syrup and egg white to a shaker.

*Note: To make simple syrup,* *see page 42.*

3. Shake the mixture vigorously for 5 to 10 seconds.
4. Pour the drink into the glass and sprinkle with cinnamon.

## Jamaican Bobsled

- 1 oz spiced rum
- 1/2 oz Tia Maria
- 2 oz half & half cream
- 1 maraschino cherry

1. Fill a rocks glass with ice cubes.
2. Add the spiced rum, Tia Maria and cream to a shaker.
3. Shake the mixture vigorously for 5 to 10 seconds.
4. Pour the drink into the glass and garnish with a maraschino cherry.

**TIP** *How can I cut the calorie count of these cocktails?*

Half & half cream and ice cream are definitely not low fat ingredients. Feel free to switch out the half & half cream for whole or even 2% milk. For the ice cream, you can substitute frozen yogurt. For those who are lactose intolerant, soy milk and ice cream alternatives are acceptable substitutes.

**TIP** *What is egg white powder?*

Egg white powder is nothing more than pasteurized egg white that has been dehydrated. Due to the fact that it has been pasteurized, egg white powder is a good alternative for those who do not want to mix raw egg whites into their cocktails. One teaspoon of egg white powder is the equivalent of 1/2 an egg white.

## Strawberry Shortcake

- 1 oz vanilla vodka
- 1 oz amaretto
- 4 strawberries
- 2 scoops vanilla ice cream
- 1 cup ice, crushed
- 1 strawberry

1. Place the vodka, amaretto, 4 strawberries, ice cream and ice into a blender.
2. Blend until the mixture is smooth.
3. Pour the mixture into a hurricane glass and garnish with a strawberry.

## Kid in a Candy Store

- 1 oz Chambord
- 1/2 oz amaretto
- 1/2 oz Baileys
- 4 Oreo cookies
- 6 maraschino cherries, stems removed
- 2 scoops vanilla ice cream
- 1 cup ice, crushed
- 1 maraschino cherry

1. Place the Chambord, amaretto, Baileys, 3 Oreo cookies, 6 maraschino cherries, ice cream and ice into a blender.
2. Blend until the mixture is smooth.
3. Pour the mixture into a hurricane glass and garnish with a maraschino cherry and the remaining Oreo cookie.

# KAHLUA Cocktails

In case you have never been formally introduced, Kahlua is a very popular Mexican coffee liqueur. Cocktails made with this liqueur are perfect after dinner drinks due to their rich and intensely sweet flavors. With names like Brown Cow and Mudslide, however, it should be fairly obvious that Kahlua cocktails are not really intended to be served with quail and caviar. These cocktails are party drinks. Think about serving them with dessert after your next Tex-Mex dinner party.

## Brown Cow

- 1 1/2 oz Kahlua
- 2 1/2 oz half & half cream
- 1 maraschino cherry

1. Fill a rocks glass with ice cubes.
2. Add the Kahlua and cream to the glass.
3. Garnish with a maraschino cherry and stir the drink.

## Mudslide

- 1 1/2 oz vodka
- 1/2 oz Kahlua
- 1/2 oz Baileys
- 2 oz half & half cream
- 1 maraschino cherry

1. Fill a rocks glass with ice cubes.
2. Add the vodka, Kahlua, Baileys and cream to the glass.
3. Garnish with a maraschino cherry and stir the drink.

**TIP** *What is a Friar Tuck?*

A Friar Tuck is a luscious cocktail that uses the hazelnut coffee flavor combination of Frangelico and Kahlua. To make a Friar Tuck, pour 1 1/2 oz of Frangelico, 1 oz of Kahlua and 2 oz of half & half cream into an ice-filled rocks glass and garnish with a maraschino cherry.

**TIP** *Can I use milk instead of half & half cream?*

You can substitute milk for half & half cream in these cocktails to lessen the calorie load, but the results will not be the same. Half & half cream is used to add a creamy texture and rich flavor to these cocktails. While your waistline may thank you, your tastebuds may not.

## Toasted Almond

1 1/2 oz amaretto
1 oz Kahlua
2 oz half & half cream
1 maraschino cherry

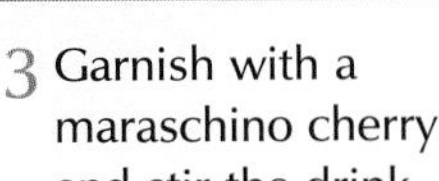

1 Fill a rocks glass with ice cubes.

2 Add the amaretto, Kahlua and cream to the glass.

3 Garnish with a maraschino cherry and stir the drink.

## Butterscotch Mocha Bliss

1 1/2 oz Kahlua
1 oz butterscotch schnapps
2 oz half & half cream
1 maraschino cherry

1 Fill a rocks glass with ice cubes.

2 Add the Kahlua, butterscotch schnapps and cream to the glass.

3 Garnish with a maraschino cherry and stir the drink.

# FROZEN Drinks I

If you were the type of kid who could hear the ice-cream truck a mile away, you are going to love these drinks. The Chocolate Strawberry Blizzard mixes chocolate and strawberry flavors with the coffee tones of Kahlua. Death by Chocolate is a dream come true for chocolate lovers. The Banana Sandwich takes the tropical flavors of rum and banana and combines them with Oreo cookies, while the Banana Boat is a frosty blizzard of banana.

## Chocolate Strawberry Blizzard

- 1 1/2 oz Kahlua
- 2 oz half & half cream
- 1 oz chocolate syrup
- 2 scoops vanilla ice cream
- 1 cup ice, crushed
- 2 strawberries, stems removed
- 1 chocolate-dipped strawberry

1. Place the Kahlua, cream, chocolate syrup, vanilla ice cream, crushed ice and 2 strawberries in a blender.
2. Blend all of the ingredients until the mixture is smooth.
3. Pour the mixture into a hurricane glass and garnish with a chocolate-dipped strawberry.

## Death by Chocolate

- 1 oz dark crème de cacao
- 1/2 oz Baileys
- 2 oz half & half cream
- 2 scoops chocolate ice cream
- 1 cup ice, crushed
- 1 maraschino cherry

1. Place the crème de cacao, Baileys, cream, chocolate ice cream and crushed ice in a blender.
2. Blend all of the ingredients until the mixture is smooth.
3. Pour the mixture into a hurricane glass and garnish with a maraschino cherry.

**TIP** *What is banana liqueur?*

Banana liqueur is a yellow liqueur that, as you might have guessed, tastes like ripe bananas. Sometimes called crème de banane, banana liqueur also contains hints of vanilla and almond. It is the perfect way to boost the tropical flavor in your drinks. Popular brands of banana liqueur include De Kuyper Crème de Banane, Marie Brizard Crème de Banane and Bols Crème de Bananes.

**TIP** *Can I use different types of ice cream in these drinks?*

Don't be afraid to experiment! You can always add your favorite ice cream flavor to these frozen treats to create a custom blend. For example, if you want even more of a strawberry taste in your Chocolate Strawberry Blizzard, just add 2 scoops of strawberry ice cream instead of vanilla.

## Banana Sandwich

- 1 oz light rum
- 1/2 oz banana liqueur
- 2 oz half & half cream
- 2 scoops vanilla ice cream
- 1 cup ice, crushed
- 4 Oreo cookies
- 1/2 banana

1. Place the light rum, banana liqueur, cream, vanilla ice cream, crushed ice, 3 Oreo cookies and 1/2 banana in a blender.
2. Blend all of the ingredients until the mixture is smooth.
3. Pour the mixture into a hurricane glass and garnish with the remaining Oreo cookie.

## Banana Boat

- 1 oz light rum
- 1/2 oz banana liqueur
- 1/2 oz white crème de cacao
- 2 oz half & half cream
- 2 scoops vanilla ice cream
- 1 cup ice, crushed
- 1/2 banana
- 1 banana slice

1. Place the light rum, banana liqueur, crème de cacao, cream, vanilla ice cream, crushed ice and 1/2 banana in a blender.
2. Blend all of the ingredients until the mixture is smooth.
3. Pour the mixture into a hurricane glass and garnish with a banana slice.

# FROZEN Drinks II

Baileys is an extremely versatile liqueur—it excels in both hot beverages and icy blended drinks. These four frozen drinks put Baileys in the spotlight. Named after the famed circus operators, Barnum and Bailey, the Barnumint Bailey is a delicious blend of Irish cream and mint. The FBI is like a frozen cup of creamy coffee enhanced with Baileys, Kahlua and vodka. For stunning-looking drinks, you will be hard-pressed to beat the tasty and eye-catching Frozen Mudslide or Honey Bunny.

## Barnumint Bailey

- 3/4 oz Baileys
- 3/4 oz green crème de menthe
- 2 oz half & half cream
- 2 scoops vanilla ice cream
- 4 Oreo cookies
- 1 cup ice, crushed

1 Place the Baileys, crème de menthe, cream, vanilla ice cream, 3 Oreo cookies and crushed ice in a blender.

2 Blend all of the ingredients until the mixture is smooth.

3 Pour the mixture into a hurricane glass and garnish with the remaining Oreo cookie.

## FBI

- 1/2 oz Baileys
- 1/2 oz Kahlua
- 1/2 oz vodka
- 2 oz half & half cream
- 2 scoops vanilla ice cream
- 1 cup ice, crushed
- 1 maraschino cherry

1 Place the Baileys, Kahlua, vodka, cream, vanilla ice cream and crushed ice in a blender.

2 Blend all of the ingredients until the mixture is smooth.

3 Pour the mixture into a hurricane glass and garnish with a maraschino cherry.

**TIP** *What is Baileys?*

Made in Ireland with dairy cream, cocoa and Irish whiskey, Baileys started the trend toward creamy liqueurs. Today, Baileys is one of the world's most popular liqueurs. While it contains a high percentage of cream, Baileys does not need refrigeration because the whiskey acts as a preservative.

**TIP** *Can I use chocolate instead of honey in the Honey Bunny?*

If you would prefer to pair chocolate with the tasty mixture of Baileys, Frangelico and vanilla vodka, feel free to add chocolate syrup to the inside of the glass rather than honey.

## Frozen Mudslide

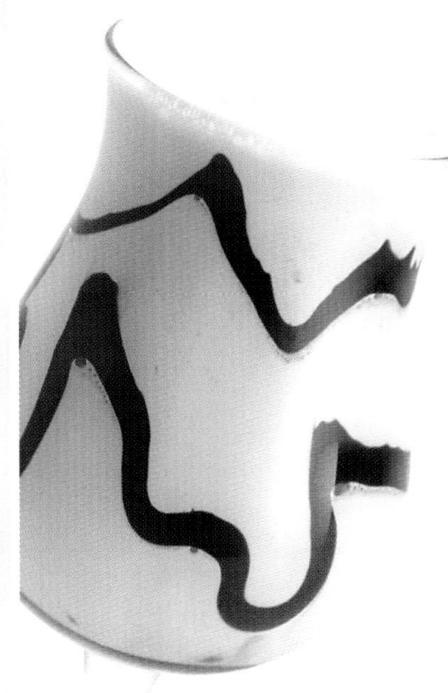

- 1/2 oz Baileys
- 1/2 oz Kahlua
- 1/2 oz vodka
- 2 oz half & half cream
- 2 scoops vanilla ice cream
- 1 cup ice, crushed
- 1 oz chocolate syrup

1 Place the Baileys, Kahlua, vodka, cream, vanilla ice cream and crushed ice in a blender.

2 Blend all of the ingredients until the mixture is smooth.

3 Drizzle 1 oz of chocolate syrup around the inside of the hurricane glass.

4 Immediately pour the mixture from the blender into the glass to freeze the drizzled chocolate syrup on the sides of the glass.

## Honey Bunny

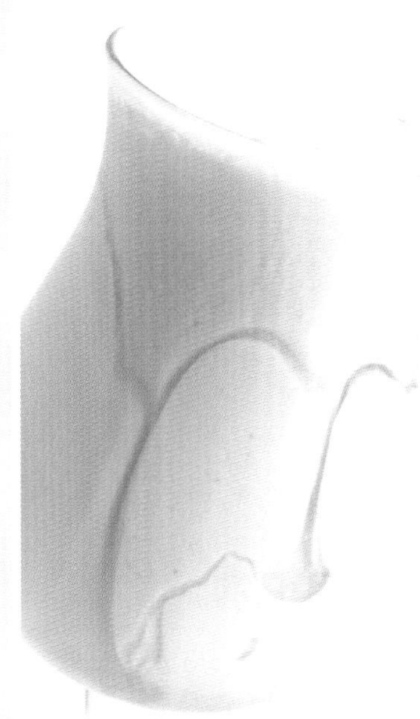

- 1/2 oz Baileys
- 1/2 oz Frangelico
- 1/2 oz vanilla vodka
- 2 oz half & half cream
- 2 scoops vanilla ice cream
- 1 cup ice, crushed
- 1 oz liquid honey

1 Place the Baileys, Frangelico, vanilla vodka, cream, vanilla ice cream and crushed ice in a blender.

2 Blend all of the ingredients until the mixture is smooth.

3 Drizzle 1 oz of liquid honey around the inside of the hurricane glass.

4 Immediately pour the mixture from the blender into the glass to freeze the drizzled liquid honey on the sides of the glass.

# FROZEN Drinks III

Frozen drinks aren't just cool and delicious, they are easy to make. There's no shaking or straining—just throw everything in the blender, hit the switch and then pour the drink into the awaiting glass. If your tastes favor chocolate, whip up the scrumptious Cocobanana, Brazilian Monk or Dreamsicle frozen drinks. For those who aren't crazy about chocolate, you can make the Smile When You're Blue—it's loaded with blueberries, stunning to look at and guaranteed to bring a smile to your face.

## Cocobanana

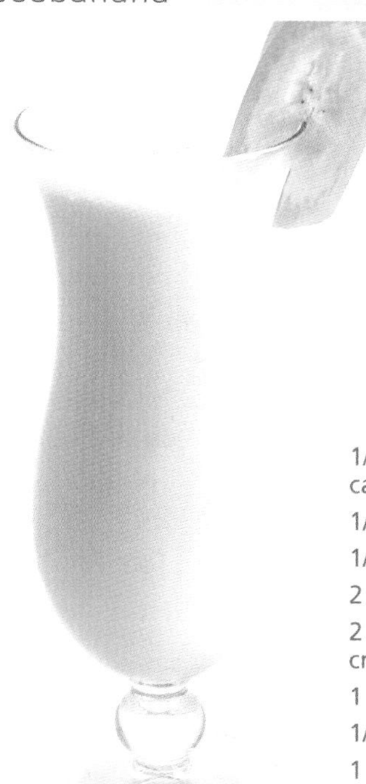

- 1/2 oz dark crème de cacao
- 1/2 oz banana liqueur
- 1/2 oz amaretto
- 2 oz half & half cream
- 2 scoops vanilla ice cream
- 1 cup ice, crushed
- 1/2 banana
- 1 banana slice

1. Place the dark crème de cacao, banana liqueur, amaretto, cream, vanilla ice cream, crushed ice and 1/2 banana in a blender.
2. Blend all of the ingredients until the mixture is smooth.
3. Pour the mixture into a hurricane glass and garnish with a banana slice.

## Brazilian Monk

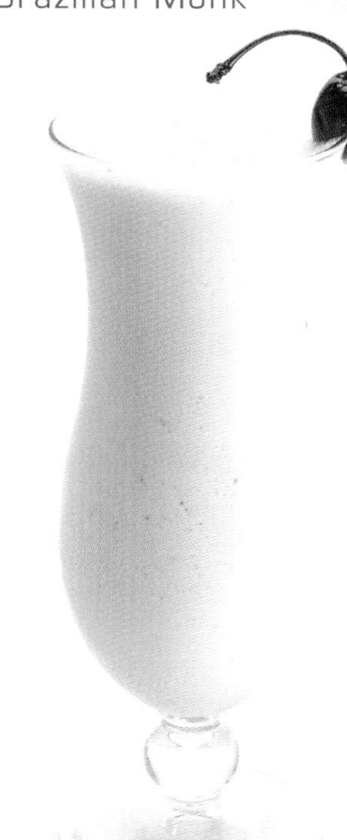

- 1/2 oz dark crème de cacao
- 1/2 oz Frangelico
- 1/2 oz Kahlua
- 2 oz half & half cream
- 2 scoops vanilla ice cream
- 1 cup ice, crushed
- 1 maraschino cherry

1. Place the dark crème de cacao, Frangelico, Kahlua, cream, vanilla ice cream and crushed ice in a blender.
2. Blend all of the ingredients until the mixture is smooth.
3. Pour the mixture into a hurricane glass and garnish with a maraschino cherry.

**TIP** *Can I make less fattening versions of these drinks?*

If you are counting calories but are tempted to try one of these delicious frozen drinks, there are a few ways that you can make them a little more waistline-friendly. Try using whole milk instead of the half & half cream. You could also substitute frozen yogurt for the ice cream. Finally, you could use a little less ice cream, replacing it with a little more crushed ice.

**TIP** *Can I use a different type of berry in the Smile When You're Blue frozen drink?*

Don't be afraid to experiment when you are making frozen drinks! For example, there are several delicious variations you can make on The Smile When You're Blue drink by simply swapping out the blueberries for an equal amount of another berry. Try using raspberries, blackberries or strawberries.

## Dreamsicle

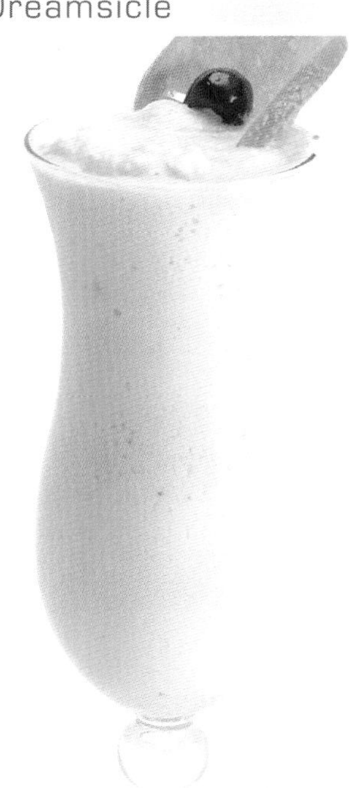

- 1 oz white crème de cacao
- 1 oz triple sec
- 1 oz half & half cream
- 1 scoop vanilla ice cream
- 1 scoop orange sherbet
- 1 cup ice, crushed
- 1 orange boat

1. Place the white crème de cacao, triple sec, cream, vanilla ice cream, orange sherbet and crushed ice in a blender.
2. Blend all of the ingredients until the mixture is smooth.
3. Pour the mixture into a hurricane glass and garnish with an orange boat.

*Note: To make an orange boat, see page 37.*

## Smile When You're Blue

- 1 oz light rum
- 1 oz blue curacao
- 2 oz half & half cream
- 2 scoops vanilla ice cream
- 1 cup ice, crushed
- 12 blueberries
- 1 orange boat

1. Place the light rum, blue curacao, cream, vanilla ice cream, crushed ice and blueberries in a blender.
2. Blend all of the ingredients until the mixture is smooth.
3. Pour the mixture into a hurricane glass and garnish with an orange boat.

*Note: To make an orange boat, see page 37.*

# Tour of North America Shooters

Who knew you could drink a flag? Borrowing the colors from the flags of the United States, Mexico and Canada, the three flag-inspired shooters below allow you to salute the three North American neighbors, one delicious gulp at a time. Raising a flag has never been so enjoyable. And to get you around the continent in style, the '57 T-Bird with Florida Plates shooter offers a zippy grapefruit-fueled ride.

## American Flag

1/3 oz blue curacao

1/3 oz cherry brandy

1/3 oz peppermint schnapps

1 Pour the blue curacao into a shot glass.

2 Layer the cherry brandy over the back of a barspoon onto the surface of the blue curacao.

3 Layer the peppermint schnapps over the back of a barspoon onto the surface of the cherry brandy.

*Note: For information on how to layer drinks, see page 45.*

## Mexican Flag

1/3 oz cherry brandy

1/3 oz white crème de cacao

1/3 oz green crème de menthe

1 Pour the cherry brandy into a shot glass.

2 Layer the crème de cacao over the back of a barspoon onto the surface of the cherry brandy.

3 Layer the crème de menthe over the back of a barspoon onto the surface of the crème de cacao.

*Note: For information on how to layer drinks, see page 45.*

**TIP** *What other types of '57 T-Birds can I mix?*

To change a '57 T-Bird with Florida Plates, just remove the grapefruit juice and replace it with another fruit juice. To make a '57 T-Bird with Hawaiian Plates, use 1/4 oz of pineapple juice. To make a '57 T-Bird with California Plates, use 1/4 oz of orange juice. To make a '57 T-Bird with a Cape Cod Bumper Sticker, use 1/4 oz of red cranberry juice.

**TIP** *Can I travel North America in a Harley Davidson?*

Sure. A Harley Davidson is easy to assemble—in shooter form, at least. Simply shake together 1/2 oz each of Jack Daniels and Kahlua with ice. Strain the drink into a shot glass and you are ready to roll.

## Canadian Flag

1/3 oz grenadine

1/3 oz peppermint schnapps

1/3 oz cherry brandy

1 Pour the grenadine into a shot glass.

2 Layer the peppermint schnapps over the back of a barspoon onto the surface of the grenadine.

3 Layer the cherry brandy over the back of a barspoon onto the surface of the peppermint schnapps.

*Note: For information on how to layer drinks, see page 45.*

## '57 T-Bird with Florida Plates

1/4 oz Grand Marnier

1/4 oz amaretto

1/4 oz vodka

1/4 oz white grapefruit juice

1 Fill a shaker halfway with ice cubes.

2 Add all of the ingredients to the shaker.

3 Shake the mixture 3 to 4 times.

4 Strain the drink into a shot glass.

# FRUITY Shooters I

Lemons, limes, oranges, melons and bananas—sounds like a trip to the local fruit stand. Instead, it is the exciting list of flavors in these shooters that burst with fruit tastes. The refreshing taste of melon liqueur is paired beautifully with OJ in the Melon Ball. The Lemon Drop is a full-contact hit of lemon sure to set your taste buds buzzing. Banana takes center stage in the Banana Popsicle and the Monkey's Lunch.

## Melon Ball

- 1/3 oz vodka
- 1/3 oz Midori melon liqueur
- 1/3 oz orange juice

1. Fill a shaker halfway with ice cubes.
2. Add all of the ingredients to the shaker.
3. Shake the mixture 3 to 4 times.
4. Strain the drink into a shot glass.

## Lemon Drop

- superfine sugar
- 1/3 oz vodka
- 1/3 oz triple sec
- 1/3 oz lemon juice
- 1 lemon wedge

1. Coat the lemon wedge and the rim of a shot glass with superfine sugar and set aside.

   *Note: To coat the rim of a glass, see page 40.*

2. Fill a shaker halfway with ice cubes.
3. Add the vodka, triple sec and lemon juice to the shaker.
4. Shake the mixture 3 to 4 times and then strain into a shot glass.
5. The person drinks the shot and then sucks on the sugar coated lemon in quick succession.

TIP *How can I make a Watermelon shooter?*

A Watermelon shooter is just a variation of the Melon Ball shooter. To make a Watermelon shooter, just replace the orange juice in the Melon Ball with 1/3 oz of red cranberry juice.

TIP *What is a Kamikaze?*

A Kamikaze is the lime version of the Lemon Drop shooter. To make a Kamikaze, use 1/3 oz of fresh lime juice instead of the fresh lemon juice called for in the Lemon Drop.

## Banana Popsicle

1/3 oz banana liqueur
1/3 oz blue curacao
1/3 oz fresh lime juice

1. Fill a shaker halfway with ice cubes.
2. Add all of the ingredients to the shaker.
3. Shake the mixture 3 to 4 times.
4. Strain the drink into a shot glass.

## Monkey's Lunch

1/3 oz Kahlua
1/3 oz banana liqueur
1/3 oz Baileys

1. Pour the Kahlua into a shot glass.
2. Layer the banana liqueur over the back of a barspoon onto the surface of the Kahlua.

   *Note: For information on how to layer drinks, see page 45.*

3. Layer the Baileys over the back of a barspoon onto the surface of the banana liqueur.

# FRUITY
## Shooters II

Mixing great fruit based shooters is all about pairing just the right fruit flavors with one another. These four classic fruit shooters are outstanding examples of what happens when you get those flavor combinations right. Featuring flavor mixes like raspberry-lime and melon-cranberry, these drinks sing with simple straightforward fruit taste. It is almost a shame to down them in just one gulp.

### Purple Haze

1/3 oz vodka
1/3 oz Chambord
1/3 oz lime juice

1. Fill a shaker halfway with ice cubes.
2. Add all of the ingredients to the shaker.
3. Shake the mixture 3 to 4 times.
4. Strain the drink into a shot glass.

### Woo Woo

1/3 oz vodka
1/3 oz peach schnapps
1/3 oz red cranberry juice

1. Fill a shaker halfway with ice cubes.
2. Add all of the ingredients to the shaker.
3. Shake the mixture 3 to 4 times.
4. Strain the drink into a shot glass.

**TIP** *How can I make my shooters stand out?*

For an extra visual effect, take your cue from full sized cocktails and coat the rim of your shot glasses with superfine sugar. Not only will this make your shooters look great, the sugar will add an extra dash of sweetness to the drink. To coat the rim of a glass, see page 40.

**TIP** *What is a Razzy Melon on the Beach?*

A Razzy Melon on the Beach is a delicious twist on the Sex on the Beach shooter. Just swap out the 1/2 oz of peach schnapps for 1/4 oz of Chambord and 1/4 oz of Midori melon liqueur. This shooter provides a delicious balance of raspberry and melon flavors that will surely tempt your taste buds.

## Broken Down Golf Cart

- 1/4 oz vodka
- 1/4 oz Midori melon liqueur
- 1/4 oz amaretto
- 1/4 oz red cranberry juice

1 Fill a shaker halfway with ice cubes.

2 Add all of the ingredients to the shaker.

3 Shake the mixture 3 to 4 times.

4 Strain the drink into a shot glass.

## Sex on the Beach

- 1/2 oz peach schnapps
- 1/4 oz pineapple juice
- 1/4 oz red cranberry juice

1 Fill a shaker halfway with ice cubes.

2 Add all of the ingredients to the shaker.

3 Shake the mixture 3 to 4 times.

4 Strain the drink into a shot glass.

# SWEET TREAT Shooters

If you have a weakness for all things sweet, beware of the recipes below. These seriously sweet shooters will kick your fondness for sweetness into overdrive. Each one of these luscious shooters is more dessert than drink. They offer irresistible flavors like cinnamon, chocolate, orange and butterscotch. Partake and enjoy if you dare, but don't say you weren't warned.

## Apple Pie à la Mode

1/2 oz Goldschlager
1/4 oz apple juice
1/4 oz half & half cream
cinnamon

1 Fill a shaker halfway with ice cubes.

2 Add the Goldschlager, apple juice and cream to the shaker.

3 Shake the mixture 3 to 4 times.

4 Strain the drink into a shot glass and sprinkle with cinnamon.

## Creamy Orange Sherbet

1/4 oz white crème de cacao
1/4 oz amaretto
1/4 oz orange juice
1/4 oz half & half cream

1 Fill a shaker halfway with ice cubes.

2 Add the crème de cacao, amaretto, orange juice and cream to the shaker.

3 Shake the mixture 3 to 4 times.

4 Strain the drink into a shot glass.

**TIP** *How can I make an After Eight shooter?*

The After Eight shooter is a variation of the Butterscotch Mocha shooter. To make an After Eight, use 1/3 oz of peppermint schnapps instead of the butterscotch schnapps. Go ahead and drink it before 8:00, we won't tell.

**TIP** *What is a Black Forest shooter?*

A Black Forest shooter is another delicious variation on the Butterscotch Mocha shooter. Just substitute the butterscotch schnapps with 1/3 oz of cherry brandy to recreate the flavor of the decadent cake.

## Chocolate-Orange Espresso

1/3 oz white crème de cacao

1/3 oz Kahlua

1/3 oz orange juice

1. Fill a shaker halfway with ice cubes.
2. Add the crème de cacao, Kahlua and orange juice to the shaker.
3. Shake the mixture 3 to 4 times.
4. Strain the drink into a shot glass.

## Butterscotch Mocha

1/3 oz Kahlua

1/3 oz butterscotch schnapps

1/3 oz Baileys

1. Pour the Kahlua into a shot glass.
2. Layer the butterscotch schnapps over the back of a barspoon onto the surface of the Kahlua.
3. Layer the Baileys over the back of a barspoon onto the surface of the butterscotch schnapps.

*Note: For information on how to layer drinks,* *see page 45.*

# TOUGH GUY Shooters

You sleep on a bed of rusty nails, eat crushed glass for breakfast and walk on red-hot coals as a pastime. You think you're a tough guy, huh? Then you'll have to try these shooters on for size. In truth, these drinks are not terribly harsh, but they do have tough-sounding names. So even if the only things you ever crunch are numbers, throwing back a shooter like the Raging Bull is bound to leave you feeling a little more macho.

## Raging Bull

1/3 oz Kahlua
1/3 oz sambuca
1/3 oz tequila

1 Pour the Kahlua into a shot glass.

2 Layer the sambuca over the back of a barspoon onto the surface of the Kahlua.

3 Layer the tequila over the back of a barspoon onto the surface of the sambuca.

*Note: For information on how to layer drinks, see page 45.*

## Windex Shooter

1/2 oz vodka
1/2 oz blue curacao

1 Fill a shaker halfway with ice cubes.

2 Add all of the ingredients to the shaker.

3 Shake the mixture 3 to 4 times.

4 Strain the drink into a shot glass.

TIP *What is a Prairie Inferno?*

A Prairie Inferno is a variation of the Prairie Fire shooter with a lot more heat. To create a Prairie Inferno, substitute the Tabasco in the Prairie Fire with an ultra hot sauce like Frank's Red Hot or Dave's Insanity Sauce. Unless you are trying to inflict serious harm, 1 or 2 drops should suffice.

TIP *What is a Flatline?*

A flatline is another variation of the Prairie Fire shooter. Pour 1/2 oz of sambuca into a shot glass and then layer 1/2 oz of tequila on top. Then add a drop of Tabasco on top of the tequila. The Tabasco will fall through the tequila and layer on top of the sambuca.

## Three Wise Men

1/3 oz Jack Daniels

1/3 oz Johnnie Walker Red

1/3 oz Jose Cuervo tequila

1. Fill a shaker halfway with ice cubes.
2. Add all of the ingredients to the shaker.
3. Shake the mixture 3 to 4 times.
4. Strain the drink into a shot glass.

## Prairie Fire

1 oz tequila

2 drops Tabasco

1. Pour the tequila into a shot glass.
2. Add 2 drops of Tabasco onto the surface of the tequila.

# Cinnamon & Licorice Shooters

Cinnamon and licorice: two bold flavors that are difficult to ignore. If you love these strong flavors, these shooters will be right up your alley. Infused with either Goldschlager or sambuca, a potent licorice-flavored liqueur, the Black Gold, Fluglebinder, Schnapple Shooter and Jellybean all promise a pleasant slap to the taste buds. In case you are wondering about the Fluglebinder, it's named after the plastic bits on the ends of a shoelace and it is mentioned in a conversation in the movie *Cocktail*.

## Black Gold

1/2 oz Goldschlager
1/2 oz Jägermeister

1. Pour the Goldschlager into a shot glass.
2. Layer the Jägermeister over the back of a barspoon onto the surface of the Goldschlager.

*Note: For information on how to layer drinks, see page 45.*

## Fluglebinder

2/3 oz Chambord
1/3 oz Goldschlager

1. Pour the Chambord into a shot glass.
2. Layer the Goldschlager over the back of a barspoon onto the surface of the Chambord.

*Note: For information on how to layer drinks, see page 45.*

**TIP** *How do I create a Short Shorts shooter?*

The Short Shorts shooter is a variation of the Jellybean shooter. To whip one up, just replace the Chambord in the Jellybean recipe with 1/2 oz of Grand Marnier.

**TIP** *What is a Black Opal?*

A Black Opal is a shooter that combines 1/2 oz of black sambuca with 1/2 oz of Baileys. To make one, simply pour the black sambuca into a shot glass and then slowly pour the Baileys on top.

## Schnapple Schooter

1/2 oz Goldschlager

1/4 oz apple juice

1/4 oz red cranberry juice

1. Fill a shaker halfway with ice cubes.
2. Add all of the ingredients to the shaker.
3. Shake the mixture 3 to 4 times.
4. Strain the drink into a shot glass.

## Jellybean

1/2 oz Chambord

1/2 oz sambuca

1. Fill a shaker halfway with ice cubes.
2. Add all of the ingredients to the shaker.
3. Shake the mixture 3 to 4 times.
4. Strain the drink into a shot glass.

# TRICK OR TREAT Shooters

Halloween: it's not just for kids anymore. Halloween is adored by many adults because it allows them to shed their personality by putting on a costume and becoming someone or something completely different. These shooters, all named after fictional characters, are like a trick-or-treat costume in a shot glass. At your next Halloween bash, or whenever you want to have a bit of fun, throw some of these eccentrically named shooters together for your guests.

## Extraterrestrial

1/3 oz Midori melon liqueur

1/3 oz Baileys

1/3 oz vodka

1 Pour the melon liqueur into a shot glass.

2 Layer the Baileys over the back of a barspoon onto the surface of the melon liqueur.

3 Layer the vodka over the back of a barspoon onto the surface of the Baileys.

*Note: For information on how to layer drinks, see page 45.*

## Bubble Gum Boy

1/3 oz banana liqueur

1/3 oz blue curacao

1/3 oz Baileys

1 Pour the banana liqueur into a shot glass.

2 Layer the blue curacao over the back of a barspoon onto the surface of the banana liqueur.

3 Layer the Baileys over the back of a barspoon onto the surface of the blue curacao.

*Note: For information on how to layer drinks, see page 45.*

TIP *When I mix up more than one shooter at a time, why do I always end up with a little bit extra?*

Don't forget that as you shake your shooters, the ice in the shaker begins to melt. The small amount of water can change the 4 oz of liquor you put in the shaker into 5 1-oz drinks.

TIP *What is the difference between a shot and a shooter?*

A shot refers to a 1 to 2 oz serving of a single spirit like tequila, vodka or whiskey. A shooter is like a mini cocktail, a combination of various spirits, liqueurs and mixers. Shooters do, however, tend to have a higher alcohol content than larger cocktails.

## Alice in Wonderland

1/3 oz Kahlua
1/3 oz tequila
1/3 oz Grand Marnier

1 Fill a shaker halfway with ice cubes.
2 Add all of the ingredients to the shaker.
3 Shake the mixture 3 to 4 times.
4 Strain the drink into a shot glass.

## Big Green Monster

1/2 oz cognac
1/2 oz Hpnotiq liqueur

1 Fill a shaker halfway with ice cubes.
2 Add all of the ingredients to the shaker.
3 Shake the mixture 3 to 4 times.
4 Strain the drink into a shot glass.

# Crème de Cacao Shooters

Just like Stevie Wonder and Paul McCartney told us in the song *Ebony and Ivory*, chocolate and vanilla go together in perfect harmony. Okay, so they weren't exactly singing about chocolate and vanilla, but they could have been. The very popular crème de cacao liqueur is a perfect example of how these two flavors blend together so beautifully. The shooters below combine crème de cacao with other tasty liqueurs for chocolaty treats sure to please even the most discriminating chocolate lover.

## Blue-Eyed Blonde

1/3 oz white crème de cacao

1/3 oz banana liqueur

1/3 oz blue curacao

1 Pour the crème de cacao into a shot glass.

2 Layer the banana liqueur over the back of a barspoon onto the surface of the crème de cacao.

3 Layer the blue curacao over the back of a barspoon onto the surface of the banana liqueur.

*Note: For information on how to layer drinks, see page 45.*

## China White

1/2 oz white crème de cacao

1/2 oz Baileys

1 Pour the crème de cacao into a shot glass.

2 Layer the Baileys over the back of a barspoon onto the surface of the crème de cacao.

*Note: For information on how to layer drinks, see page 45.*

**TIP** *Why do I have to follow the order of ingredients when layering shooters?*

Each spirit and liqueur has a specific density which affects whether it will sink underneath or float on top of the other ingredients in a layered shooter. Very thick, syrupy liqueurs generally sink to the bottom of the glass, creamy liqueurs will sit in the middle of a shooter and clear spirits, such as vodka, float on top of the other ingredients.

**TIP** *What is a Crispy Crunch?*

The Crispy Crunch shooter is a variation of the Chocolate Martini shooter. To create a Crispy Crunch, just substitute 1/2 oz of Frangelico for the vodka in the Chocolate Martini shooter recipe.

## Chocolate Martini Shooter

1/2 oz white crème de cacao

1/2 oz vodka

1 Fill a shaker halfway with ice cubes.

2 Add all of the ingredients to the shaker.

3 Shake the mixture 3 to 4 times.

4 Strain the drink into a shot glass.

## Polar Bear

1/2 oz white crème de cacao

1/2 oz peppermint schnapps

1 Fill a shaker halfway with ice cubes.

2 Add all of the ingredients to the shaker.

3 Shake the mixture 3 to 4 times.

4 Strain the drink into a shot glass.

# IRISH CREAM Shooters

Few liqueurs are as widely adored as Baileys Irish cream. Its sweet flavor is irresistible for many people and these shooters will not disappoint those folks. The B-52 shooter features the famous combination of Baileys with Kahlua and Grand Marnier. The ABC shooter is named for the three main ingredients—Amaretto, Baileys and Cointreau. The Nutty Irishman infuses coffee (Kahlua) with Irish cream (Baileys) and hazelnut (Frangelico) flavors. The Baby Guinness, meanwhile, looks just like a miniature version of the Emerald Isle's other celebrated alcoholic export.

## B-52

1/3 oz Kahlua
1/3 oz Baileys
1/3 oz Grand Marnier

1 Pour the Kahlua into a shot glass.

2 Layer the Baileys over the back of a barspoon onto the surface of the Kahlua.

3 Layer the Grand Marnier over the back of a barspoon onto the surface of the Baileys.

*Note: For information on how to layer drinks, see page 45.*

## ABC

1/3 oz amaretto
1/3 oz Baileys
1/3 oz Cointreau

1 Pour the amaretto into a shot glass.

2 Layer the Baileys over the back of a barspoon onto the surface of the amaretto.

3 Layer the Cointreau over the back of a barspoon onto the surface of the Baileys.

*Note: For information on how to layer drinks, see page 45.*

**TIP** *Do I need a barspoon to layer shooters?*

While a barspoon is a must for any bar, you can actually use a stemmed cherry to layer drinks in a pinch. Hold the cherry by the stem and rest it inside the shot glass. Then slowly pour the liqueur over the cherry—the fall of the liquid will be slowed as it passes over the fruit. As a bonus, you've got a tasty, liqueur-soaked cherry to snack on when you're done.

## Nutty Irishman

1/3 oz Kahlua
1/3 oz Baileys
1/3 oz Frangelico

1. Pour the Kahlua into a shot glass.
2. Layer the Baileys over the back of a barspoon onto the surface of the Kahlua.
3. Layer the Frangelico over the back of a barspoon onto the surface of the Baileys.

*Note: For information on how to layer drinks, see page 45.*

## Baby Guinness

3/4 oz Kahlua
1/4 oz Baileys

1. Pour the Kahlua into a shot glass.
2. Layer the Baileys over the back of a barspoon onto the surface of the Kahlua.

*Note: For information on how to layer drinks, see page 45.*

# Tastes of the South
## Shooters

Few things bring the Southern States to mind like tree-ripened peaches and barrel-aged bourbon. The splash of Southern Comfort liqueur in these shooters gives you a delicious sample of both. If you can't get enough peach flavor, try the Southern Peach shooter. Bourbon fans will be drawn to the Devil's Manhattan Shooter. Amaretto, a liqueur which is partially derived from peach pits, pairs beautifully with the peach flavors in the Sicilian Kiss and Chase Your Tail shooters.

### Southern Peach

1/2 oz Southern Comfort
1/2 oz peach schnapps

1 Fill a shaker halfway with ice cubes.
2 Add the ingredients to the shaker.
3 Shake the mixture 3 to 4 times.
4 Strain the drink into a shot glass.

### Devil's Manhattan Shooter

1/3 oz bourbon
1/3 oz Southern Comfort
1/3 oz cherry brandy

1 Fill a shaker halfway with ice cubes.
2 Add the ingredients to the shaker.
3 Shake the mixture 3 to 4 times.
4 Strain the drink into a shot glass.

TIP *How can I make shooters for a crowd?*

Shooters are social drinks which are great for a crowd, so mixing one at a time may not be efficient. To mix 5 or 6 shooters at once, just multiply the ingredients. For example, if a shooter calls for 1/2 oz each of vodka and sambuca you can make 6 servings by shaking together 3 oz of each.

TIP *Is there a way to control the pour rate if I'm using pouring spouts?*

Pouring spouts have two holes—one from which the liquid pours and another which lets air into the bottle allowing a smooth pour. If you block the air hole with your finger, you can regulate how much air is allowed in and you will have much better control over the rate at which the liquid comes out.

## Sicilian Kiss

1/2 oz Southern Comfort
1/2 oz amaretto

1. Fill a shaker halfway with ice cubes.
2. Add the ingredients to the shaker.
3. Shake the mixture 3 to 4 times.
4. Strain the drink into a shot glass.

## Chase Your Tail

1/3 oz citrus vodka
1/3 oz Southern Comfort
1/3 oz amaretto

1. Fill a shaker halfway with ice cubes.
2. Add the ingredients to the shaker.
3. Shake the mixture 3 to 4 times.
4. Strain the drink into a shot glass.

# FLAMING SHOOTERS, SLAMMERS & POPPERS

Flaming shooters, slammers and poppers are shooters with attitude. Flaming shooters are set ablaze before drinking. A slammer is a shot that requires a lick of salt before and slurp of lemon after consuming. A popper is a shooter containing soda and is banged on the bar so that it fizzes while being gulped. Part drink and part performance, you will need a little more space than normal to make and serve these shooters. Fire insurance isn't a bad idea, either.

## Flaming Sambuca

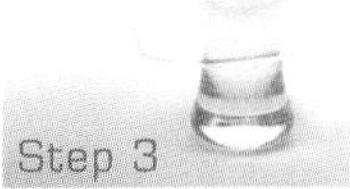

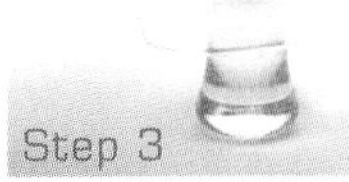

1 oz sambuca

1 Pour the sambuca into a shot glass.

2 Set the surface of the sambuca ablaze with a lighter.

3 The drinker extinguishes the shooter by placing an empty rocks glass over the flames before consuming.

## Hot Apple Pie

1/2 oz Baileys
1/2 oz Goldschlager
1/8 oz, 151-proof rum
cinnamon

1 Pour the Baileys into a shot glass.

2 Layer the Goldschlager over the back of a barspoon onto the surface of the Baileys.

*Note: For information on how to layer drinks, see page 45.*

3 Slowly pour the 151-proof rum on top of the drink.

4 Set the surface of the drink ablaze with a lighter and sprinkle with cinnamon.

5 The drinker extinguishes the shooter by placing an empty rocks glass over the flames before consuming.

TIP *Are there any precautions I should take when making flaming shots?*

You should never play with fire while you're under the influence of alcohol. Instead, have the designated driver or a non-drinking friend prepare these drinks for your crowd. You should also ensure the fire is extinguished before consumption. Last, but not least, do not try to transport, carry or move a drink that is on fire.

TIP *How long should I let the Flaming Sambuca and Hot Apple Pie burn?*

You should extinguish the flames no more than a few seconds after you set the drink ablaze. The longer the drink is on fire, the hotter the shot glass will become. Be careful as you don't want to burn your mouth when drinking the shot!

## Tequila Slammer

Step 2

1 oz tequila
salt
1 lemon wedge

1 Pour the tequila into a shot glass.

2 The drinker licks the skin between his/her thumb and index finger and then sprinkles salt on the area.

3 In quick succession, the drinker licks the salt, drinks the tequila and then sucks on the lemon.

## Tequila Popper

Step 2

3/4 oz tequila
1/4 oz lemon-lime soda

1 Pour the ingredients into a shot glass.

2 The drinker covers the glass with his/her hand or napkin, slams it on the bar and then drinks the shooter while it is still fizzing.

# Classic Coffee Warmers

When people think of coffee warmers, these four classics often come to mind. The Almond Mocha is a delicious warmer reminiscent of chocolate-coated almonds. You can count on the Monte Cristo to deliver delicious coffee liqueur and orange flavors. The B-52 is a famous combo of three popular liqueurs and the Irish Cream Coffee is sure to satisfy whiskey lovers. With these recipes under your belt, you'll be prepared to please any coffee-crazed crowd.

## Almond Mocha

- 1 1/2 oz amaretto
- 1/2 oz chocolate syrup
- 4 oz coffee
- whipped cream
- 1 maraschino cherry

1. Add the amaretto and chocolate syrup to a preheated coffee glass.
2. Slowly add the coffee to the glass.
3. Top the drink with whipped cream, garnish with a maraschino cherry and stir the drink.

## Monte Cristo

- 3/4 oz Grand Marnier
- 3/4 oz Kahlua
- 4 oz coffee
- whipped cream
- 1 maraschino cherry

1. Add the Grand Marnier and Kahlua to a preheated coffee glass.
2. Slowly add the coffee to the glass.
3. Top the drink with whipped cream, garnish with a maraschino cherry and stir the drink.

TIP *What type of whipped cream should I use as a topping?*

For any coffee warmer that is supposed to be topped with whipped cream, you can use aerosol whipped cream or fresh whipped cream that you have prepared. If you plan to top off your coffee warmer with a maraschino cherry, you should use aerosol whipped cream as it has a thicker consistency and will hold the cherry better than fresh whipped cream.

Aerosol Whipped Cream

Fresh Whipped Cream

## B-52 Coffee

superfine sugar
1/2 oz Baileys
1/2 oz Grand Marnier
1/2 oz Kahlua
4 oz coffee
whipped cream
1 maraschino cherry

1. Coat the rim of a preheated coffee glass with superfine sugar.

   *Note: To coat the rim of a glass, see page 40.*

2. Add the Baileys, Grand Marnier and Kahlua to the glass.
3. Slowly add the coffee to the glass.
4. Top the drink with whipped cream, garnish with a maraschino cherry and stir the drink.

## Irish Cream Coffee

3/4 oz Baileys
3/4 oz Irish whiskey
4 oz coffee
whipped cream
1 maraschino cherry

1. Add the Baileys and Irish whiskey to a preheated coffee glass.
2. Slowly add the coffee to the glass.
3. Top the drink with whipped cream, garnish with a maraschino cherry and stir the drink.

# COFFEE
## Warmers I

These tasty warmers let you go café hopping without even leaving the comfort of your own bar. The Café Gates offers the sweet tastes of Grand Marnier and Tia Maria. The Café Oscar is a pleasing almond blend of amaretto and Kahlua. Baileys, Drambuie and Tia Maria mix beautifully in the Café Royal, while the Café Michelle combines Baileys and Kahlua. The most decadent ingredient in these warmers, however, may be the generous dollop of whipped cream.

### Café Gates

3/4 oz Grand Marnier
3/4 oz Tia Maria
4 oz coffee
whipped cream
cocoa powder

1. Add the Grand Marnier and Tia Maria to a preheated coffee glass.
2. Slowly add the coffee to the glass.
3. Top the drink with whipped cream, a sprinkle of cocoa powder and stir the drink.

### Café Oscar

3/4 oz amaretto
3/4 oz Kahlua
4 oz coffee
whipped cream
cocoa powder

1. Add the amaretto and Kahula to a preheated coffee glass.
2. Slowly add the coffee to the glass.
3. Top the drink with whipped cream, a sprinkle of cocoa powder and stir the drink.

**TIP** *Can I use my favorite liqueurs to create a custom coffee warmer?*

Creating a warmer that suits your tastes is easy. You may have noticed that each of these warmers includes 1 1/2 oz of alcohol for every 4 oz of coffee. Keeping this ratio in mind, you can be as creative with new ingredients as you desire.

**TIP** *What is Tia Maria?*

Tia Maria is a Jamaican, rum-based coffee liqueur. This popular liqueur is a deep amber-colored blend of sugar cane, Jamaican coffee, vanilla and caramel. With rich flavors, Tia Maria makes an ideal ingredient for any coffee-based cocktail.

## Café Royal

1/2 oz Baileys
1/2 oz Drambuie
1/2 oz Tia Maria
4 oz coffee
whipped cream
cocoa powder

1. Add the Baileys, Drambuie and Tia Maria to a preheated coffee glass.
2. Slowly add the coffee to the glass.
3. Top the drink with whipped cream, a sprinkle of cocoa powder and stir the drink.

## Café Michelle

3/4 oz Baileys
3/4 oz Kahlua
4 oz coffee
whipped cream
cocoa powder

1. Add the Baileys and Kahlua to a preheated coffee glass.
2. Slowly add the coffee to the glass.
3. Top the drink with whipped cream, a sprinkle of cocoa powder and stir the drink.

# COFFEE
## Warmers II

Bored of your regular cup of java? Then banish the coffee monotony with these four delicious recipes. If you are a fan of chocolate mint pairings, you will adore the Polar Bear Coffee. The Henry XIII Coffee is a sweet coffee warmer that combines brandy with Grand Marnier and Kahlua. You won't be able to help but fall in love with the nutty tones of Murphy's Amore. If you are a fan of chocolate chip cookies, try the Vanilla Chocolate Chip Coffee.

### Polar Bear Coffee

3/4 oz peppermint schnapps
3/4 oz white crème de cacao
4 oz coffee
whipped cream
cocoa powder

1. Add the peppermint schnapps and crème de cacao to a preheated coffee glass.
2. Slowly add the coffee to the glass.
3. Top the drink with whipped cream, a sprinkle of cocoa powder and stir the drink.

### Henry XIII Coffee

1/2 oz brandy
1/2 oz Grand Marnier
1/2 oz Kahlua
4 oz coffee
whipped cream
cocoa powder

1. Add the brandy, Grand Marnier and Kahlua to a preheated coffee glass.
2. Slowly add the coffee to the glass.
3. Top the drink with whipped cream, a sprinkle of cocoa powder and stir the drink.

**TIP** *What is Frangelico?*

Frangelico is a delicious hazelnut liqueur that is made in northern Italy using wild hazelnuts, cocoa and vanilla. Frangelico pairs beautifully with chocolate flavors, such as crème de cacao, and is perfect for adding a rich nuttiness to your cocktails.

**TIP** *How can I make a Raspberry Chocolate Chip Coffee?*

The Raspberry Chocolate Chip Coffee is a fruity variation of the Vanilla Chocolate Chip Coffee. To whip up this raspberry warmer, all you have to do is replace the vanilla vodka in the original recipe with 3/4 oz of raspberry vodka.

## Murphy's Amore

3/4 oz Baileys
3/4 oz Frangelico
4 oz coffee
whipped cream
cocoa powder

1 Add the Baileys and Frangelico to a preheated coffee glass.

2 Slowly add the coffee to the glass.

3 Top the drink with whipped cream, a sprinkle of cocoa powder and stir the drink.

## Vanilla Chocolate Chip Coffee

3/4 oz vanilla vodka
3/4 oz white crème de cacao
4 oz coffee
whipped cream
cocoa powder

1 Add the vanilla vodka and crème de cacao to a preheated coffee glass.

2 Slowly add the coffee to the glass.

3 Top the drink with whipped cream, a sprinkle of cocoa powder and stir the drink.

# INTERNATIONAL COFFEE Warmers

Need a vacation? The tickets to a refreshing international escape lie somewhere between your coffeemaker and your bar. A trip to Spain is only as far as the Spanish Coffee's shots of brandy and Kahlua. To get to Holland, mix a little peppermint schnapps into your Café Dutch. The whiskey-infused Irish Coffee will get you to the Emerald Isle and a quick trip to Jamaica with the Café Reggae requires splashes of rum, Tia Maria and crème de cacao.

## Spanish Coffee

- superfine sugar
- 3/4 oz brandy
- 3/4 oz Kahlua
- 4 oz coffee
- whipped cream
- 1 maraschino cherry

1 Coat the rim of a preheated coffee glass with superfine sugar.

*Note: To coat the rim of a glass, see page 40.*

2 Add the brandy and Kahlua to the glass.

3 Slowly add the coffee to the glass.

4 Top the drink with whipped cream, garnish with a maraschino cherry and stir the drink.

## Café Dutch

- 1 1/2 oz peppermint schnapps
- 1 tsp sugar
- 4 oz coffee
- whipped cream
- 1 maraschino cherry

1 Add the peppermint schnapps and sugar to a preheated coffee glass.

2 Slowly add the coffee to the glass.

3 Top the drink with whipped cream, garnish with a maraschino cherry and stir the drink.

**TIP** *How do I make a Russian Coffee?*

A Russian Coffee is a nutty coffee warmer that includes vodka, of course. To make a Russian Coffee, mix a 1/2 oz each of Kahlua and Frangelico with a 1/2 oz of vodka in a preheated coffee glass. Add 4 oz of hot coffee and top with whipped cream.

**TIP** *What is the recipe for Mexican Coffee?*

To make a Mexican Coffee, simply mix 1 oz of Kahlua with a 1/2 oz of tequila in a preheated coffee glass. Then stir in 4 oz of hot coffee and top with whipped cream.

## Irish Coffee

1 1/2 oz Irish whiskey
1 tsp sugar
4 oz coffee

1 Add the whiskey and sugar to a preheated coffee glass.

2 Slowly add the coffee to the glass and then stir the drink.

## Café Reggae

1/2 oz gold rum
1/2 oz Tia Maria
1/2 oz white crème de cacao
4 oz coffee
whipped cream

1 Add the rum, Tia Maria and crème de cacao to a preheated coffee glass.

2 Slowly add the coffee to the glass.

3 Top the drink with whipped cream and stir the drink.

# CAPPUCCINO Warmers

Unlike many Europeans who cannot get through a day without at least one shot of espresso, inhabitants of the New World seem to prefer the espresso's milder cousin, the cappuccino. This popular beverage is a luscious balance between strong coffee flavor and creamy milk. These warmers add further dimension to the cappuccino with the addition of rich spirits and liqueurs. Sambuca, Kahlua, cognac and crème de cacao all give these beverages distinctly satisfying character.

## Midnight Capp

3/4 oz white crème de cacao
3/4 oz sambuca
2 1/2 oz steamed milk
1 1/2 oz espresso
cocoa powder

1. Add the crème de cacao and sambuca to a preheated coffee glass.
2. Slowly add the steamed milk and then the espresso to the glass.
3. Top the drink with milk foam, a sprinkle of cocoa powder and stir the drink.

*Note: For information on steamed milk and milk foam,* *see the top of page 189.*

## Brown Cow Cappuccino

3/4 oz white crème de cacao
3/4 oz Kahlua
2 1/2 oz steamed milk
1 1/2 oz espresso
cocoa powder

1. Add the crème de cacao and Kahlua to a preheated coffee glass.
2. Slowly add the steamed milk and then the espresso to the glass.
3. Top the drink with milk foam, a sprinkle of cocoa powder and stir the drink.

*Note: For information on steamed milk and milk foam,* *see the top of page 189.*

**TIP** *Are there any shortcuts to making cappuccino warmers?*

Instead of making espresso each time you want to whip up a cappuccino warmer, you can easily make espresso syrup. To make espresso syrup, boil up a 1/2 cup of water and stir in 1 cup of sugar. Once the sugar has dissolved, add 4 oz of espresso. Give it a couple of stirs and then pour the syrup into a sealable container. The syrup will keep in the fridge for a couple of weeks.

**TIP** *Can I use milk in the Dairy-Free Chocolate Cappuccino?*

You can create a variation of the Dairy-Free Chocolate Cappuccino by simply using steamed milk instead of soymilk. Conversely, you can also create dairy-free versions of other warmers by substituting steamed soymilk for the steamed milk called for in the recipes.

## Cognac and Cream Cappuccino

3/4 oz cognac
3/4 oz Baileys
2 1/2 oz steamed milk
1 1/2 oz espresso
cocoa powder

1 Add the cognac and Baileys to a preheated coffee glass.

2 Slowly add the steamed milk and then the espresso to the glass.

3 Top the drink with milk foam, a sprinkle of cocoa powder and stir the drink.

*Note: For information on steamed milk and milk foam,* *see the top of page 189.*

## Dairy-Free Chocolate Cappuccino

1 1/2 oz white crème de cacao
2 1/2 oz steamed soymilk
1 1/2 oz espresso
cocoa powder

1 Add the crème de cacao to a preheated coffee glass.

2 Slowly add the steamed soymilk and then the espresso to the glass.

3 Top the drink with milk foam, a sprinkle of cocoa powder and stir the drink.

*Note: For information on steamed milk and milk foam,* *see the top of page 189.*

# LATTE Warmers

Everybody loves lattes. Steaming hot and oh-so creamy, they are the coffee lovers' answer to hot chocolate—comfort in a cup. These four tempting latte variations prove that it is possible to improve upon a classic beverage. For sheer decadence, you cannot top the Chocolate Butterscotch Latte and Butterscotch Cream Latte. The Café au Contraire combines the mellow tones of gold rum with the sweet, assertive flavor of Cointreau. For sheer off-the-wall fun, try the Nutty Monkey Latte with its banana-hazelnut flavoring.

## Chocolate Butterscotch Latte

3/4 oz dark crème de cacao

3/4 oz butterscotch schnapps

2 1/2 oz steamed milk

1 1/2 oz espresso

cocoa powder

1. Add the crème de cacao and butterscotch schnapps to a preheated coffee glass.
2. Slowly add the steamed milk and then the espresso to the glass.
3. Top the drink with milk foam, a sprinkle of cocoa powder and stir the drink.

*Note: For information on steamed milk and milk foam, see the top of page 189.*

## Butterscotch Cream Latte

3/4 oz butterscotch schnapps

3/4 oz Baileys

2 1/2 oz steamed milk

1 1/2 oz espresso

cinnamon

1. Add the butterscotch schnapps and Baileys to a preheated coffee glass.
2. Slowly add the steamed milk and then the espresso to the glass.
3. Top the drink with milk foam, a sprinkle of cinnamon and stir the drink.

*Note: For information on steamed milk and milk foam, see the top of page 189.*

TIP *What is the difference between steamed milk and milk foam?*

Both steamed milk and milk foam are created when you froth milk. Steamed milk is the hot, liquid milk and milk foam is the airy foam that forms on top of the steamed milk. Separating the steamed milk and milk foam is easy. As you slowly pour the steamed milk out of the container, use a large spoon to hold the milk foam back.

TIP *What type of milk should I use for my lattes?*

Whole milk, also called homogenized milk, is generally the best choice for producing thick, rich foam for lattes. Lower-fat milks such as 2% and skim milk can also be used but they are a little more difficult to froth and produce a thinner foam.

## Café au Contraire

3/4 oz gold rum
3/4 oz Cointreau
2 1/2 oz steamed milk
1 1/2 oz espresso
orange zest

1 Add the rum and Cointreau to a preheated coffee glass.

2 Slowly add the steamed milk and then the espresso to the glass.

3 Top the drink with milk foam, orange zest and stir the drink.

*Note: For information on steamed milk and milk foam, see the top of page 189.*

*Note: To create orange zest, see page 35.*

## Nutty Monkey Latte

3/4 oz banana liqueur
3/4 oz Frangelico
2 1/2 oz steamed milk
1 1/2 oz espresso
cinnamon

1 Add the banana liqueur and Frangelico to a preheated coffee glass.

2 Slowly add the steamed milk and then the espresso to the glass.

3 Top the drink with milk foam, a sprinkle of cinnamon and stir the drink.

*Note: For information on steamed milk and milk foam, see the top of page 189.*

# SPECIAL OCCASION Warmers I

Next Valentine's Day, share a French Kiss with your sweetheart. If you don't have someone special, then mix up Love Potion #9—it's sure to work wonders. These are coffee warmers, of course, and whether you try the butterscotch-flavored French Kiss Latte, the nutty Love Potion #9 or the chocolate-mint Valentine's Day Latte, you are in for a treat. And if things don't work out on Valentine's Day, the Easter Bunny makes a fine companion afterward.

## French Kiss Latte

- 1/2 oz Tia Maria
- 1/2 oz Grand Marnier
- 1/2 oz butterscotch schnapps
- 2 1/2 oz steamed milk
- 1 1/2 oz espresso
- cocoa powder

1 Add the Tia Maria, Grand Marnier and butterscotch schnapps to a preheated coffee glass.

2 Slowly add the steamed milk and then the espresso to the glass.

3 Top the drink with milk foam, a sprinkle of cocoa powder and stir the drink.

*Note: For information on steamed milk and milk foam, see the top of page 189.*

## Love Potion #9

- 3/4 oz amaretto
- 3/4 oz Frangelico
- 2 1/2 oz steamed milk
- 1 1/2 oz espresso
- cinnamon

1 Add the amaretto and Frangelico to a preheated coffee glass.

2 Slowly add the steamed milk and then the espresso to the glass.

3 Top the drink with milk foam, a sprinkle of cinnamon and stir the drink.

*Note: For information on steamed milk and milk foam, see the top of page 189.*

**TIP** *What is advocaat?*

Advocaat is a rich and creamy, yellow liqueur made from egg yolks, sugar, spices and brandy. Its flavor is somewhat similar to that of eggnog, which makes advocaat the perfect ingredient for Christmas-themed warmers.

**TIP** *Are there any secrets to making great espresso?*

The key to making great espresso starts with the espresso bean itself. You should purchase the best quality espresso beans that you can afford. Grinding the beans right before making the espresso will also help to produce great results. The beans should be finely ground, with a sand-like consistency.

## Valentine's Day Latte

1/2 oz white crème de cacao
1/2 oz white crème de menthe
1/2 oz amaretto
2 1/2 oz steamed milk
1 1/2 oz espresso
cinnamon

1 Add the crème de cacao, crème de menthe and amaretto to a preheated coffee glass.

2 Slowly add the steamed milk and then the espresso to the glass.

3 Top the drink with milk foam, a sprinkle of cinnamon and stir the drink.

*Note: For information on steamed milk and milk foam,* *see the top of page 189.*

## Easter Bunny

3/4 oz Baileys
3/4 oz advocaat
2 1/2 oz steamed milk
1 1/2 oz espresso
cinnamon

1 Add the Baileys and advocaat to a preheated coffee glass.

2 Slowly add the steamed milk and then the espresso to the glass.

3 Top the drink with milk foam, a sprinkle of cinnamon and stir the drink.

*Note: For information on steamed milk and milk foam,* *see the top of page 189.*

# SPECIAL OCCASION Warmers II

Raising a glass is often how we celebrate the holidays. Next Fourth of July, you can hoist the Independence-Day Latte which features cherry brandy, Baileys and blue curacao. The flavors of the Orange Nut Latte make it the perfect after-dinner coffee for your next Thanksgiving meal. The Christmas-themed warmers offer yuletide flavors like sambuca, eggnog, cinnamon and peppermint. Sambuca may not be Christmasy, but it sure tastes great with eggnog.

## Independence-Day Latte

1/2 oz cherry brandy
1/2 oz Baileys
1/2 oz blue curacao
2 1/2 oz steamed milk
1 1/2 oz espresso
cinnamon

1 Add the cherry brandy, Baileys and blue curacao to a preheated coffee glass.

2 Slowly add the steamed milk and then add the espresso to the glass.

3 Top the drink with milk foam, a sprinkle of cinnamon and stir the drink.

*Note: For information on steamed milk and milk foam, see the top of page 189.*

## Orange Nut Latte

3/4 oz Grand Marnier
3/4 oz amaretto
2 1/2 oz steamed milk
1 1/2 oz espresso
nutmeg

1 Add the Grand Marnier and amaretto to a preheated coffee glass.

2 Slowly add the steamed milk and then add the espresso to the glass.

3 Top the drink with milk foam and nutmeg and then stir the drink.

*Note: For information on steamed milk and milk foam, see the top of page 189.*

TIP *How do I make steamed milk and eggnog?*

You can make steamed milk and eggnog for your drinks by heating it with the frothing attachment found on most espresso makers. A less expensive alternative is to use a latte whip. Whipping hot milk with a latte whip provides the same type of hot, foamy milk as an espresso maker.

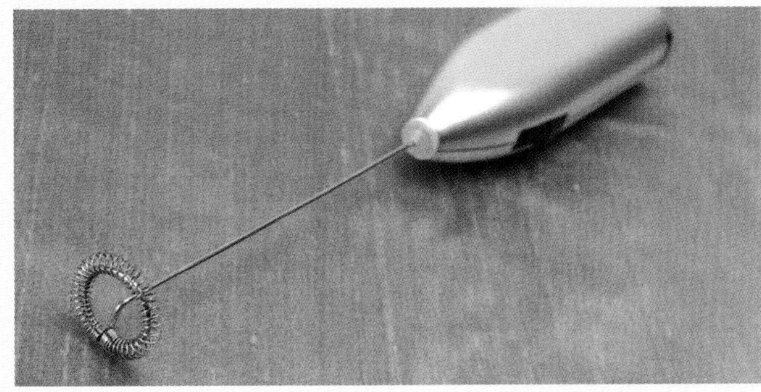

Latte whip

## Christmas Cappuccino

3/4 oz sambuca

3/4 oz advocaat

2 1/2 oz steamed eggnog

1 1/2 oz espresso

cinnamon

1 Add the sambuca and advocaat to a preheated coffee glass.

2 Slowly add the steamed eggnog and then add the espresso to the glass.

3 Top the drink with eggnog foam, a sprinkle of cinnamon and stir the drink.

*Note: For information on steamed milk and milk foam,* *see the top of page 189.*

## Candy Cane Latte

3/4 oz cherry brandy

3/4 oz peppermint schnapps

2 1/2 oz steamed milk

1 1/2 oz espresso

cinnamon

1 Add the cherry brandy and peppermint schnapps to a preheated coffee glass.

2 Slowly add the steamed milk and then add the espresso to the glass.

3 Top the drink with milk foam, a sprinkle of cinnamon and stir the drink.

*Note: For information on steamed milk and milk foam,* *see the top of page 189.*

# HOT CHOCOLATE Warmers

The Mayans had the right idea. More than 2,000 years ago they began using cocoa to create a hot, bitter beverage. This early form of hot chocolate was reserved for nobility. Today, the drink is a sweet-tasting favorite enjoyed by the masses and a great way for kids to warm up after a romp in the snow. But there are more potent versions for grown-ups. Try these delicious variations the next time you need to thaw out.

## Almond Hot Chocolate

1 1/2 oz amaretto
4 1/2 oz hot chocolate
whipped cream
cocoa powder

1 Add the amaretto to a preheated coffee glass.
2 Slowly add the hot chocolate to the glass.
3 Top the drink with whipped cream, a sprinkle of cocoa powder and stir the drink.

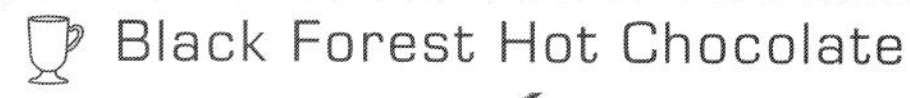

## Black Forest Hot Chocolate

3/4 oz Chambord
3/4 oz white crème de cacao
4 oz hot chocolate
whipped cream
cocoa powder
1 maraschino cherry

1 Add the Chambord and crème de cacao to a preheated coffee glass.
2 Slowly add the hot chocolate to the glass.
3 Top the drink with whipped cream and a sprinkle of cocoa powder. Garnish with a maraschino cherry and stir the drink.

**TIP** *What is a Berry Nutty Hot Chocolate?*

The Berry Nutty Hot Chocolate is a coconut-flavored variation of the Black Forest Hot Chocolate. To make a Berry Nutty Hot Chocolate, simply substitute 3/4 oz of coconut rum for the crème de cacao in the Black Forest Hot Chocolate recipe.

**TIP** *How can I dress up my hot chocolate warmers?*

Marshmallows are an ideal garnish for any type of hot chocolate. Finely grated chocolate or chocolate shavings also look great when sprinkled on top of the whipped cream of a hot chocolate warmer. You can also perch a maraschino cherry on top of it all.

## Brandy Chocolexander

3/4 oz brandy
3/4 oz dark crème de cacao
4 oz hot chocolate
whipped cream
cocoa powder

1 Add the brandy and crème de cacao to a preheated coffee glass.

2 Slowly add the hot chocolate to the glass.

3 Top the drink with whipped cream, a sprinkle of cocoa powder and stir the drink.

## Hot Chocolate Stinger

3/4 oz brandy
3/4 oz white crème de menthe
4 oz hot chocolate
whipped cream
cocoa powder

1 Add the brandy and crème de menthe to a preheated coffee glass.

2 Slowly add the hot chocolate to the glass.

3 Top the drink with whipped cream, a sprinkle of cocoa powder and stir the drink.

# TEAS, CIDERS, & OTHER Warmers

There is nothing like a soothing hot cup of tea on a cold evening. Add a bit of alcohol to that tea and the relaxation factor doubles. The two tea warmers here include a couple of delicious liqueurs—the Almond Tea has amaretto and the Blueberry Tea features Grand Marnier and amaretto and, strangely, no blueberries. With peach schnapps, apple cider becomes the delicious Apple Peach Cobbler. And you cannot ignore the delicious flavors of Hot Buttered Rum.

## Almond Tea

1 1/2 oz amaretto
1 orange pekoe tea bag
boiling water

1. Add the amaretto and orange pekoe tea bag to a preheated coffee glass.
2. Fill the glass with boiling water.
3. Allow the tea to brew to your desired strength and then remove the tea bag. Stir the drink.

## Blueberry Tea

3/4 oz Grand Marnier
3/4 oz amaretto
orange pekoe tea
1 orange wheel

1. Pour the Grand Marnier and amaretto into a preheated brandy snifter.
2. Fill the snifter two-thirds of the way to the top with orange pekoe tea, garnish with an orange wheel and stir the drink.

**TIP** *What is a Warm Cinnamon Roll?*

A Warm Cinnamon Roll is a variation of the Apple Peach Cobbler. To create this cinnamon tasting treat, simply substitute the 1 1/2 oz of peach schnapps with 1 oz of rum and 1/2 an oz of Goldschlager.

**TIP** *What is rum batter?*

Rum batter is a mixture of spices and butter used to flavor hot rum-flavored drinks. To make rum batter, melt 3 tablespoons of butter in a saucepan and then stir in 6 tablespoons of brown sugar, a pinch each of salt, nutmeg and cinnamon. Pour the mixture into a shallow pan and refrigerate to harden. This makes 16 1-tsp servings.

## Apple Peach Cobbler

- 1 1/2 oz peach schnapps
- 4 1/2 oz apple cider, heated

1. Pour the peach schnapps and apple cider into a preheated coffee glass.

   *Note: You can substitute apple juice for the hot apple cider.*

2. Stir the drink.

## Hot Buttered Rum

- 1 1/2 oz gold rum
- 1 tsp rum batter
- 4 oz water, boiling
- 1 cinnamon stick

1. Pour the rum into a preheated coffee glass.
2. Add the rum batter to the glass.

   *Note: For information on rum batter, see the top of page 197.*

3. Add the boiling water to the glass.
4. Garnish with a cinnamon stick and stir the drink.

# CITRUS Mocktails

Oranges, lemons, limes and grapefruit all provide that refreshing zing to these alcohol-free drinks. None is zingier than the Homemade Lemonade. This delicious recipe raises the drink above its status as a mere ingredient for other cocktails and is well worth creating. The Virgin Caipirinha is a citrus-filled, booze-free version of a traditional Brazilian cocktail. The Virgin Seabreeze is refreshing for any occasion—seaside or not. Finally, who can resist the lime-splashed Shirley Temple? It is the first "cocktail" many of us ever tasted.

## Homemade Lemonade

zest of 1 lemon
3 oz simple syrup
8 oz boiling water
8 oz ice-cold water
2 oz lemon juice
2 lemon wheels

- This recipe makes two servings.

1 Add the zest of one lemon, simple syrup and 8 oz of boiling water to a shaker and stir.

*Note: To zest a lemon, see page 35. To make simple syrup, see page 42.*

2 Once the mixture has cooled, stir in 8 oz of ice-cold water and the lemon juice to the shaker.

3 Fill two highball glasses with ice cubes.

4 Pour equal amounts of the lemonade into each glass and garnish each with a lemon wheel.

## Virgin Caipirinha

1/2 lemon, sliced into wedges
1/2 lime, sliced into wedges
1/2 mandarin orange, sliced into wedges
1/2 oz simple syrup
ginger ale
1 sprig of mint

1 Place the lemon, lime, orange, simple syrup and a dash of ginger ale into a highball glass.

*Note: To make simple syrup, see page 42.*

2 Muddle the ingredients in the glass.

*Note: For information on muddling, see page 44.*

3 Fill the glass with crushed ice.

4 Fill the rest of the glass with ginger ale.

5 Garnish the surface of the drink with a sprig of mint and stir the drink.

**TIP** *How can I make Limeade?*

The Homemade Lemonade recipe can be applied to any citrus fruit. To make Limeade, just substitute lime ingredients in place of the lemon. Don't be afraid to experiment with other citrus fruits. Also try white or pink grapefruit, tangerines or even blood oranges. Just keep in mind that sweeter fruits will require less simple syrup.

**TIP** *Why doesn't the Shirley Temple taste like the ones I sipped as a kid?*

We've listed the classic Shirley Temple, a simple ginger ale and grenadine mix with a splash of lime, but the drink has many variations. You can try adding more lime juice or even fresh-squeezed orange juice to adjust the flavor to your liking.

## Virgin Seabreeze

3 oz red cranberry juice

3 oz white grapefruit juice

1/2 oz grenadine

1 lime wheel

1. Fill a highball glass with ice cubes.
2. Add the cranberry juice, grapefruit juice and grenadine to a shaker.
3. Shake the mixture vigorously for 5 to 10 seconds.
4. Pour the contents of the shaker into a highball glass and garnish with a lime wheel.

## Shirley Temple

1/4 lime

6 oz ginger ale

1/2 oz grenadine

1 maraschino cherry

1. Fill a highball glass with ice cubes.
2. Squeeze the lime over the ice cubes.
3. Add the ginger ale and grenadine to the glass.
4. Garnish with a maraschino cherry and stir the drink.

# CRANBERRY-BASED Mocktails

Bright red and refreshingly tart, cranberry juice is one of the most versatile and popular mixers behind the bar—the perfect "sour" component for any sweet-and-sour concoction. When it comes to mixing alcohol-free drinks for your guests, cranberry juice adds a sharp bite that gives your cocktails an interesting depth. These four recipes are great options when you want to give your non-drinking guests cocktail alternatives with crisp complexity.

## Virgin Madras

3 oz red cranberry juice
3 oz orange juice
1 lime wheel

1. Fill a highball glass with ice cubes.
2. Add the juices to the shaker.
3. Shake the mixture vigorously for 5 to 10 seconds.
4. Pour the contents of the shaker into the glass and garnish with a lime wheel.

## Shakers Dream

3 oz lemonade
2 oz red cranberry juice
2 oz pineapple juice
1 lime wheel

1. Fill a highball glass with ice cubes.
2. Add the lemonade, cranberry juice and pineapple juice to the shaker.
3. Shake the mixture vigorously for 5 to 10 seconds.
4. Pour the contents of the shaker into the glass and garnish with a lime wheel.

**TIP** *What other cranberry-based cocktails can I create?*

Cranberry juice is a dry tasting juice and best combined with a sweet mixer. Starting with cranberry juice, you can add just about any sweet fruit juice—such as pineapple, pomegranate, orange, grape, raspberry or passion fruit—and top with club or lemon-lime soda to create a tasty custom-made cocktail.

**TIP** *What is the best way to present a cranberry-based drink?*

Cranberry beverages generally have a striking brilliant red hue. The color of a lemon, lime or orange garnish will provide a perfect contrast to the color of the drink. Also, don't overlook the froth that results from a good shake. Serve your drinks immediately after shaking to ensure maximum texture.

## Cranberry Pucker

- 3 oz lemonade
- 3 oz red cranberry juice
- 1 oz club soda
- 1 lemon wheel

1. Fill a highball glass with ice cubes.
2. Add the lemonade and cranberry juice to the shaker.
3. Shake the mixture vigorously for 5 to 10 seconds.
4. Pour the contents of the shaker into the glass.
5. Add the club soda to the glass, garnish with a lemon wheel and stir the drink.

## Berry Sweetheart

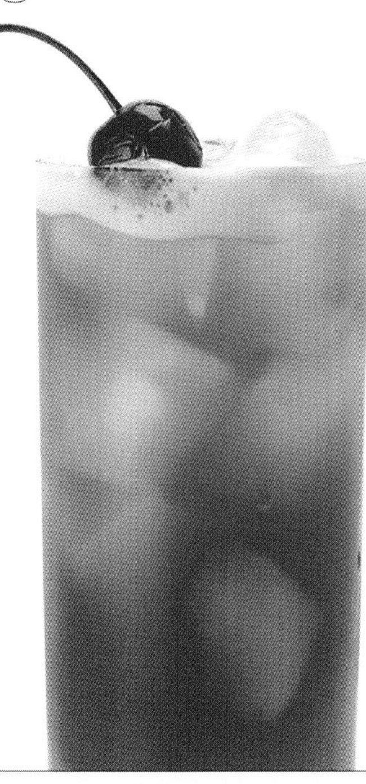

- 3 oz red cranberry juice
- 3 oz apple juice
- 1 oz honey
- 1 maraschino cherry

1. Fill a highball glass with ice cubes.
2. Add the juices and honey to a mixing glass.
3. Stir the ingredients with a barspoon.
4. Pour the contents of the mixing glass into the highball glass and garnish with a maraschino cherry.

# TROPICAL Mocktails

For many people, paradise is sun, sand and a cold, fruity cocktail in hand. With the recipes below, you can at least offer your guests one of those comforts. Inspire thoughts of balmy days on the beach with one of these four non-alcoholic tropical beverages. These beverages also make a great breakfast drink to serve your guests who have stayed the night after an evening of cocktails.

## Virgin Strawberry Sling

2 oz apple juice
2 oz pineapple juice
1 oz strawberry puree
1 oz club soda
1 strawberry

1 Fill a highball glass with ice cubes.

2 Add the apple juice, pineapple juice and strawberry puree to a shaker.

*Note: To make fruit puree, see page 43.*

3 Shake the mixture vigorously for 5 to 10 seconds.

4 Pour the contents of the shaker into the glass.

5 Add the club soda to the glass, garnish with a strawberry and stir the drink.

## Virgin Singapore Sling

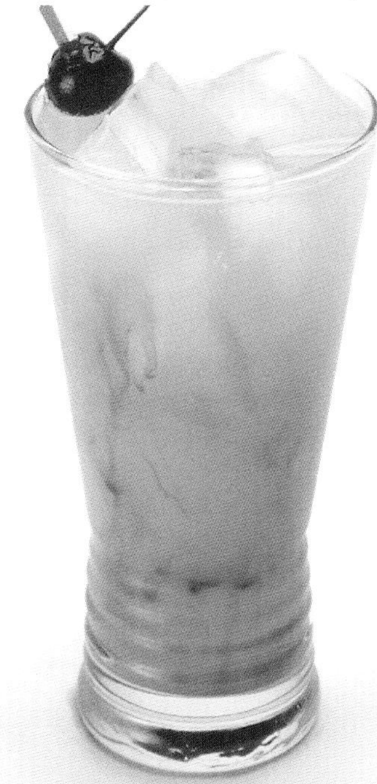

2 oz orange juice
2 oz pineapple juice
1 oz lime juice
club soda
dash of grenadine
1 maraschino cherry

1 Fill a highball glass with ice cubes.

2 Add the orange juice, pineapple juice and lime juice to a shaker.

3 Shake the mixture vigorously for 5 to 10 seconds.

4 Pour the contents of the shaker into the glass.

5 Fill the glass with club soda and add a dash of grenadine to the glass.

6 Garnish with a maraschino cherry and stir the drink.

TIP *What other types of Slings can I make?*

Almost any berry can be used to create a delicious Sling variation. Using the Virgin Strawberry Sling recipe, just swap out the strawberry puree for the puree of another berry such as blueberry, blackberry or raspberry.

TIP *Why is grenadine often used in tropical drinks?*

Grenadine, which is a sweetened syrup made from pomegranates, is used to add a sweet, cherry-like flavor to drinks. Its flavor is ideal for balancing tropical beverages with strong, sour ingredients such as pineapple juice. For a non-tropical twist, you can use grenadine to make homemade cherry cola—just add 1/2 oz of grenadine to a 12 oz cola.

## Tropical Ale

3 oz pineapple juice
3 oz ginger ale
1/2 oz grenadine
1 maraschino cherry

1. Fill a highball glass with ice cubes.
2. Pour the pineapple juice, ginger ale and grenadine into the glass.
3. Garnish with a maraschino cherry and stir the drink.

## Pineapple Passion

2 oz pineapple juice
2 oz orange juice
2 oz lemonade
1/2 oz grenadine
1 maraschino cherry

1. Fill a highball glass with ice cubes.
2. Pour the pineapple juice, orange juice, lemonade and grenadine into a shaker.
3. Shake the mixture vigorously for 5 to 10 seconds.
4. Pour the contents of the shaker into the glass and garnish with a maraschino cherry.

# ELEGANT Mocktails

Elegant but not uptight, these recipes take a few classic cocktails in delicious directions which are both inspiring and nonalcoholic. You will find these concoctions all feature refreshing fruit flavors but are not so sweet that you would label them "fruity drinks." Offer these sophisticated-yet-fun mocktails to your guests who choose not to drink alcohol and there is no way they will feel left out of the festivities.

## Virgin Cosmopolitan

- 4 oz red cranberry juice
- 1/2 oz lime cordial
- 1/2 lime
- 1/4 orange
- 1 orange spiral or orange wheel

1. Fill a shaker halfway with ice cubes.
2. Add the cranberry juice and lime cordial to the shaker.
3. Squeeze the juice from the lime and orange into the shaker.
4. Shake the mixture vigorously for 5 to 10 seconds.
5. Strain the contents of the shaker into a chilled cocktail glass and garnish with an orange spiral or an orange wheel.

## Virgin Lychee-tini

- 2 oz apple juice
- 2 oz red cranberry juice
- 1 oz lychee juice
- 1 oz lime juice
- 1 lychee

1. Fill a shaker halfway with ice cubes.
2. Add the apple, cranberry, lychee and lime juice to the shaker.
3. Shake the mixture vigorously for 5 to 10 seconds.
4. Strain the contents of the shaker into a chilled cocktail glass and garnish with a lychee.

**TIP** *How can I create a Virgin Metropolitan?*

A Metropolitan is just a variation of the ever-popular Cosmopolitan. To create a flavorful Virgin Metropolitan, simply substitute a 1/2 oz of black currant cordial for the lime cordial in the Virgin Cosmopolitan recipe and shake it with the rest of the ingredients. Garnish the Virgin Metropolitan with skewered blackberries or raspberries.

**TIP** *How can I make a Virgin Strawberry Bellini?*

A pleasant variation of the Virgin Bellini is the Virgin Strawberry Bellini. Substitute the peach puree in the Virgin Bellini recipe with 2 oz of strawberry puree. Garnish the cocktail with a strawberry.

## Virgin Bellini

2 oz peach puree

alcohol-free sparkling white wine

1 peach slice

1 Pour the peach puree into a Champagne flute.

*Note: To make fruit puree, see page 43.*

2 Fill the rest of the flute with the alcohol-free sparkling white wine.

3 Garnish with a peach slice and stir the drink.

## Virgin Mojito

1/2 oz lime juice

1/2 oz simple syrup

8 to 10 fresh mint leaves

club soda

1 sprig of mint

1 Place the lime juice, simple syrup and 8 to 10 mint leaves in a rocks glass.

*Note: To make simple syrup, see page 42.*

2 Muddle the ingredients in the glass.

*Note: For information on how to muddle, see page 44.*

3 Fill the glass with crushed ice and then fill the glass with club soda.

4 Garnish with a sprig of mint and stir the drink.

# WINE-BASED Mocktails

If you plan to serve wine-based cocktails to your guests, there is no need for designated drivers and others who choose not to drink to be left out. The wide range of alcohol-free wines available today make it possible to create tasty non-alcoholic wine spritzers, coolers and even Sangria. In fact, if you use premium ingredients, your guests may have a difficult time telling the difference between those drinks that contain alcohol and those that do not.

## Virgin Wine Spritzer

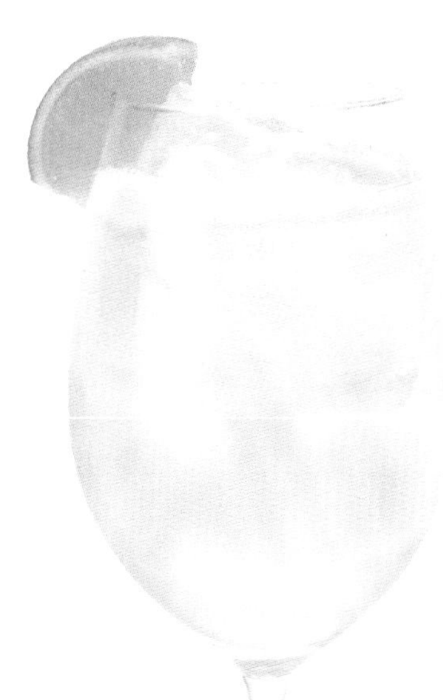

4 oz alcohol-free white wine

2 oz club soda

1 lime wedge

1. Place ice cubes in a wine glass.
2. Pour the alcohol-free wine and club soda over the ice into the wine glass.
3. Garnish with a lime wedge and stir the drink.

## Virgin Wine Cooler

4 oz alcohol-free white wine

2 oz lemon-lime soda

1 lime wedge

1. Place ice cubes in a wine glass.
2. Pour the alcohol-free wine and lemon-lime soda over the ice into the wine glass.
3. Garnish with a lime wedge and stir the drink.

**TIP** *Can I use alcohol-free red wine to make a spritzer or cooler?*

Absolutely. While white varieties are typically used for wine spritzers and coolers, red wines also make delicious cocktails. Just substitute alcohol-free red wine for the white wine called for in the Virgin Wine Spritzer and Virgin Wine Cooler recipes.

**TIP** *What other fruits can I use in Sangria?*

Sangria is endlessly customizable. Feel free to change the fruit ingredients to alter the flavor to your tastes. Experiment with fruits such as papaya, mango, pomegranate, star fruit, lychee, passion fruit or melon.

## Virgin Morning Glory

2 oz orange juice

alcohol-free sparkling white wine

1 orange spiral or orange wheel

1. Pour the orange juice into a Champagne flute.
2. Fill the rest of the glass with the alcohol-free sparkling wine.
3. Garnish with an orange spiral or an orange wheel and stir the drink.

## Virgin Sangria

1 750-ml bottle alcohol-free red wine

4 oz red cranberry juice

4 oz orange juice

2 oz lime juice

1 1/2 oz simple syrup

1 apple, cored and diced

1 pear, cored and diced

1 orange, sliced into wheels

1 lemon, sliced into wheels

1 lime, sliced into wheels

- This recipe makes 10 servings.

1. Place the alcohol-free wine, cranberry juice, orange juice, lime juice and simple syrup into a large pitcher or punch bowl. Stir the mixture.

   *Note: To make simple syrup, see page 42.*

2. Add the diced apple and pear to the wine mixture. Stir the mixture and refrigerate for 4 to 6 hours.
3. Just prior to serving, add the orange, lemon and lime wheels to the mixture.
4. To serve, pour the Sangria into ice-filled highball glasses or wine glasses.

# TOMATO-BASED Mocktails

Not all alcohol-free cocktails and shooters are sweet. These savory, tomato-based drinks are delicious and make a perfect accompaniment to a meal. In fact, the Gazpacho Shooter is a tiny bit of a meal in and of itself—it is a miniature version of the cold soup from which it derives its name. Consider using any one of these recipes as an appetizer for your guests at your next dinner party.

## Virgin Bloody Mary

- salt
- 6 oz tomato juice
- 2 shakes Worcestershire sauce
- 2 shakes Tabasco sauce
- pepper
- 1 lemon wheel

1. Coat the rim of a highball glass with salt and fill with ice cubes.

   *Note: To coat the rim of a glass, see page 40.*

2. Add the tomato juice, Worcestershire sauce and Tabasco sauce to the glass.
3. Add 2 shakes of salt and pepper to the glass.
4. Garnish with a lemon wheel and stir the drink.

## Virgin Bloody Caesar

- celery salt
- 6 oz clam-tomato juice
- 2 shakes Worcestershire sauce
- 2 shakes Tabasco sauce
- salt
- pepper
- 1 celery stalk, leaves attached
- 1 lime wheel

1. Coat the rim of a highball glass with celery salt and fill with ice cubes.

   *Note: To coat the rim of a glass, see page 40.*

2. Add the clam-tomato juice, Worcestershire sauce and Tabasco sauce to the glass.
3. Add 2 shakes of salt and pepper to the glass.
4. Garnish with a celery stalk and a lime wheel and stir the drink.

**TIP** *How can I "turn up the heat" on a Virgin Bloody Mary or Virgin Bloody Caesar?*

If you prefer your drinks with a little more kick, simply add more spice. To give your Virgin Bloody Mary or Virgin Bloody Caesar a moderate or high amount of heat, substitute 3 or 4 enthusiastic shakes each of Worcestershire sauce, Tabasco sauce and pepper for the meek 2 shakes of each called for in the original recipes.

**TIP** *What other variations can I make to the Virgin Bloody Mary and Bloody Caesar recipes?*

To give your Virgin Bloody Marys and Virgin Bloody Caesars a great new flavor and texture, stir in a 1/2 or full teaspoon of horseradish instead of the Worcestershire and Tabasco sauces.

## Virgin Oyster Shooter

- 1 cucumber wheel, finely diced
- 1 fresh oyster, shucked
- 2 oz clam-tomato juice
- 1/2 oz lemon juice
- dash Worcestershire sauce
- dash Tabasco sauce
- dash salt
- dash pepper

1 Place the oyster and cucumber in the bottom of a shot glass.

2 Fill a shaker halfway with ice cubes.

3 Add the clam-tomato juice, lemon juice, Worcestershire sauce, Tabasco sauce, salt and pepper to the shaker.

4 Shake the clam-tomato juice mixture for 5 to 10 seconds and strain into the glass.

## Virgin Gazpacho Shooter

- 4 oz tomato juice
- 1 cucumber wheel, chopped
- 1/8 green pepper, chopped
- 1/4 celery stalk, chopped
- 1/2 tsp lemon juice
- 1/4 tsp horseradish
- dash salt
- dash pepper
- 1 cup ice, crushed
- 8 croutons

- This recipe makes eight large shooters.

1 Place all of the ingredients except for the ice and croutons into a blender.

2 Blend the ingredients until the mixture is smooth.

3 Add the ice to the tomato mixture and then blend again.

4 Pour the mixture into eight large shot glasses and garnish the surface of each drink with one of the croutons.

# FROZEN
## Mocktails I

Most bartenders at tropical resorts will tell you that Pina Coladas and Daiquiris are among the most popular cocktails they serve when temperatures are on the rise. So it only makes sense for you to offer your guests who prefer not to drink alcohol a few tropical cocktails that are alcohol-free. These fruity mocktails are every bit as appealing as the high-octane versions and deliver sweet flavors that refresh in ways a plain old fruit juice cannot.

### Virgin Pina Colada

2 oz pineapple juice
2 oz coconut cream
1 oz half & half cream
1 cup ice, crushed
1 pineapple flag

1. Place the pineapple juice, coconut cream, cream and ice into a blender.
2. Blend all of the ingredients until the mixture is smooth.
3. Pour the mixture into a highball glass and garnish with a pineapple flag.

*Note: To make a pineapple flag, see page 36.*

### Virgin Strawberry Colada

2 oz pineapple juice
1 oz coconut cream
1 oz half & half cream
2 oz strawberry puree
1 cup ice, crushed
1 strawberry

1. Place the pineapple juice, coconut cream, cream, strawberry puree and ice into a blender.

*Note: To make fruit puree, see page 43.*

2. Blend all of the ingredients until the mixture is smooth.
3. Pour the mixture into a highball glass and garnish with a strawberry.

**TIP** *Are there other fruits that I can use in the Colada recipe?*

For a variation of the Virgin Strawberry Colada, try substituting the strawberry puree with 1/2 a mango to create a Virgin Mango Colada. You can also substitute the strawberry puree with 1/2 a banana to create a Virgin Banana Colada. Both of these variations can be garnished with a pineapple flag.

**TIP** *What other kinds of Daiquiris can I make?*

For a variation of the Virgin Strawberry Daiquiri, try substituting the strawberry puree with 1/2 a mango to create a Virgin Mango Daiquiri. You can also substitute the strawberry puree with 1/2 a banana to create a Virgin Banana Daiquiri. Garnish these cocktails with a strawberry.

## Virgin Strawberry Daiquiri

- 3 oz strawberry puree
- 3 oz lime juice
- 1/2 oz simple syrup
- 1 cup ice, crushed
- 1 strawberry

1 Place the strawberry puree, lime juice, simple syrup and ice into a blender.

*Note: To make fruit puree, see page 43. To make simple syrup, see page 42.*

2 Blend all of the ingredients until the mixture is smooth.

3 Pour the mixture into a highball glass and garnish with a strawberry.

## Virgin Miami Vice

- 1 oz pineapple juice
- 1 oz coconut cream
- 1/2 oz half & half cream
- 1 1/2 oz strawberry puree
- 1 1/2 oz lime juice
- 1/4 oz simple syrup
- 1 cup ice, crushed
- 1 strawberry

1 Place the pineapple juice, coconut cream, cream and a half cup of ice into a blender. Blend the mixture until smooth. Pour the mixture into a highball glass.

2 Place the strawberry puree, lime juice, simple syrup and the remaining half cup of ice into a blender. Blend the mixture until smooth.

*Note: To make fruit puree, see page 43. To make simple syrup, see page 42.*

3 Slowly pour the strawberry-lime mixture over the back of a barspoon on top of the pineapple-coconut mixture.

*Note: For information on how to layer drinks, see page 45.*

4 Garnish with a strawberry.

# FROZEN
## Mocktails II

Few things are more refreshing in the heat than frozen berry flavored cocktails. Whether the temperatures outside are high or you just wish they were, these berry-filled recipes are sure to be welcome. Serve these bright beverages to your guests who choose to go alcohol-free and they will not feel the slightest bit of cocktail-envy towards those who are sipping alcohol-infused drinks.

### Big Wave Surfer

- 2 oz orange juice
- 2 oz pineapple juice
- 1 oz strawberry puree
- 1 fresh kiwi fruit, peeled and sliced
- 1 cup ice, crushed
- 1 kiwi fruit wheel

1. Place the orange and pineapple juices, strawberry puree, kiwi fruit and ice into a blender.

   *Note: To make fruit puree, see page 43.*

2. Blend the mixture until it is smooth.
3. Pour the contents of the blender into a highball glass and garnish with a kiwi fruit wheel.

### Banana Berry

- 4 oz red cranberry juice
- 1 scoop orange sherbet
- 1/2 banana, sliced
- 1 cup ice, crushed
- 1/2 lime
- 1 lime wheel

1. Place the cranberry juice, orange sherbet, banana and ice into a blender.
2. Squeeze the juice from the lime into the blender.
3. Blend the mixture until it is smooth.
4. Pour the contents of the blender into a highball glass and garnish with a lime wheel.

TIP *What is a Broken Screwdriver?*

The Broken Screwdriver is an alcohol-free blended drink that you can put together in a hurry. Simply blend 2 oz of orange juice with 2 scoops of orange sherbet. Pour this mixture into a highball glass and garnish with an orange boat. Voila! A refreshing summer cooler that is ready in a flash.

TIP *Do I have to use raw egg whites when called for in a recipe?*

No. If the thought of using raw egg whites in your cocktails makes you a little weary, you can easily substitute egg white powder for the raw egg whites. If a recipe calls for 1 raw egg white, simply substitute 2 teaspoons of egg white powder instead. Another alternative to raw egg whites is pasteurized egg whites, which are available in grocery stores.

## Strawberry Sensation

- 2 oz strawberry puree
- 2 oz pineapple juice
- 2 oz orange juice
- 1 egg white
- 1 tsp honey
- 1 cup ice, crushed
- 1 strawberry

1 Place the strawberry puree, pineapple and orange juices, egg white, honey and ice into a blender.

*Note: To make fruit puree,* *see page 43.*

2 Blend the mixture until it is smooth.

3 Pour the contents of the blender into a highball glass and garnish with a strawberry.

## Strawberry Lassi

- 2 oz plain yogurt
- 4 oz water
- 1 oz honey
- 4 fresh strawberries, halved with stems removed
- 1 cup ice, crushed
- 2 to 3 rose petals or 1 sprig of mint

1 Place the yogurt, water, honey and strawberries into a blender.

2 Blend the mixture until it is smooth.

3 Add the ice to the yogurt mixture.

4 Blend the mixture until it is smooth.

5 Pour the contents of the blender into a highball glass and garnish with rose petals or a sprig of mint.

# FROZEN Mocktails III

While some people turn up their noses at the idea of sweet or fruity beverages, they may shed their inhibitions when they taste these concoctions. These delicious blended mocktails are more dessert than drink and are sure to be crowd pleasers. If you do plan to offer up these tasty beverages, you had better stock up on supplies. These rich, alcohol-free cocktails will leave your guests requesting "just one more."

## Orange Razz Smoothie

- 12 to 15 fresh raspberries
- 2 oz orange juice
- 4 oz plain yogurt
- 1 cup ice, crushed
- 1 sprig of mint

1. Place the raspberries, orange juice and yogurt into a blender.
2. Blend the mixture until it is smooth.
3. Add the ice to the raspberry-orange mixture.
4. Blend the mixture until it is smooth.
5. Pour the mixture into a highball glass and garnish with mint leaves.

## Hawaiian Gold Smoothie

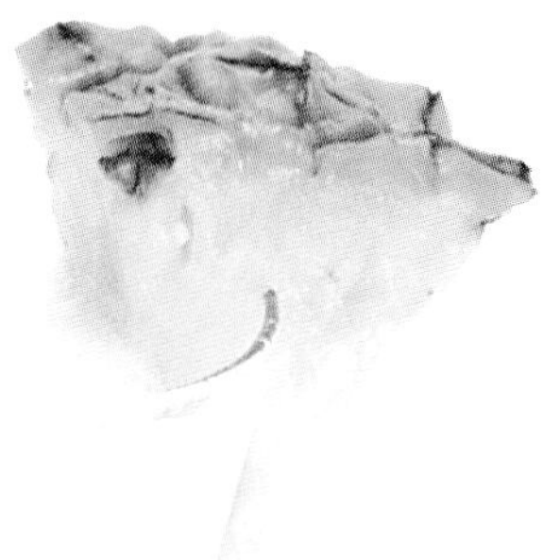

- 3 oz pineapple juice
- 3 oz white grapefruit juice
- 1 1/2 oz coconut cream
- 1 cup ice, crushed
- 1 pineapple wedge

1. Place the pineapple juice, grapefruit juice and coconut cream into a blender.
2. Blend the mixture until it is smooth.
3. Add the ice to the pineapple-grapefruit mixture.
4. Blend the mixture until it is smooth.
5. Pour the mixture into a highball glass and garnish with a pineapple wedge.

TIP *Can I make a smoothie without crushed ice?*

If you don't have access to crushed ice or are tired of smashing up ice cubes, try substituting the crushed ice in your smoothie recipe with vanilla frozen yogurt. It will give your drink a creamy texture and rich taste. If the recipe also calls for regular yogurt, you can substitute it with frozen yogurt as well.

TIP *Any other ideas for blended mocktails that call for ice cream?*

Your cupboards are full of great ingredients for delicious blended frozen drinks. Maple syrup, fruit jams, hazelnut spread, chocolate syrup, instant coffee and even peanut butter all go well with ice cream. Don't be afraid to think creatively and experiment!

## Cookies Gone Bananas

- 2 oz milk
- 2 scoops cookie dough ice cream
- 1 oz chocolate syrup
- 2 dashes cinnamon
- 1/2 banana
- 1 oz espresso (optional)
- 1 cup ice, crushed
- nutmeg
- 1 banana slice

1. Place the milk, ice cream, chocolate syrup, cinnamon, half a banana and espresso into a blender.
2. Blend the mixture until it is smooth.
3. Add the ice to the ice cream mixture.
4. Blend the mixture until it is smooth.
5. Pour the mixture into a highball glass and garnish with nutmeg and a banana slice.

## Ice Cream Sandwich

- 3 oz milk
- 1/2 tsp vanilla extract
- 2 scoops vanilla ice cream
- 4 Oreo cookies
- 1 cup ice, crushed

1. Place the milk, vanilla extract, ice cream, 3 Oreo cookies and ice into a blender.
2. Blend the mixture until it is smooth.
3. Pour the mixture into a highball glass and garnish with the remaining Oreo cookie.

# Wine & Beer

The importance of both wine and beer at any bar cannot be overlooked. This section of the book explores the range of wines from around the world. You will learn about the unique characteristics of red, white and sparkling wines, along with how to serve them. You will also learn about the incredible selection of beer available.

# 12 Wine & Beer Essentials

White Wine

Red Wine

Blush Wine

Champagne & Sparkling Wine

How to Serve Wine

Fortified Wine

Beer

# WHITE Wine

You can tell a lot about a white wine from its label. The name of the grape variety, such as Riesling or Chardonnay, tells you the main type of grape from which the wine is made. The term "body" describes how a wine feels in your mouth, from "light" to "medium" to "full." Acidity describes how tangy a wine tastes, from a soft tasting "low acidity," through crisp "medium acidity," to a sharp tasting "high acidity." The sweetness of a wine is described in terms of "sweet," "semi sweet," "medium dry" or "dry." White wines are best served chilled. The main white wine grape varieties are discussed below.

## Popular Varieties of White Wine

### CHARDONNAY

- Chardonnay is the most popular white wine in the world. White wine drinkers value Chardonnay for its rich taste and buttery smooth texture.
- Chardonnay is traditionally aged in oak barrels and is characterized by a spicy or smoky flavor.
- Due to its popularity, Chardonnay is produced in many wine regions around the world including California, Oregon, Washington State, France, Australia, South Africa and Chile.

### SAUVIGNON BLANC

- Sauvignon Blanc offers white wine drinkers a bright and crisp taste that is characterized by flavors of grass and herbs.
- Sauvignon Blanc is often blended with Sémillon, another variety of white wine grape, to create a more complex tasting wine.
- Many wine regions including France, California and New Zealand produce quality Sauvignon Blanc wine.

**TIP** *Why is white wine clear?*

To produce white wine, the grapes are crushed and the juice, which is pale or light in color, is immediately separated from the skins of the grapes. This prevents the grape skins from passing on any additional color or flavor to the wine, resulting in a light-colored wine.

**TIP** *What is dessert wine?*

A dessert wine is a very sweet wine that is typically served after a meal, often with or in place of dessert. These syrupy wines are generally made from white wine grapes that have been left on the vine past the time when they would usually be harvested. When grapes are left to over ripen, their concentration of sugar rises, which makes for a delicious dessert wine.

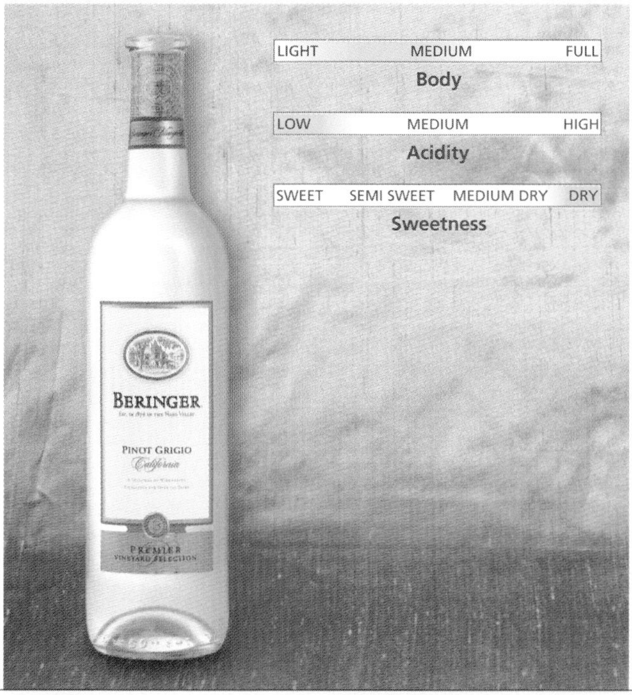
LIGHT MEDIUM FULL
Body
LOW MEDIUM HIGH
Acidity
SWEET SEMI SWEET MEDIUM DRY DRY
Sweetness
BERINGER
PINOT GRIGIO
California
PREMIER
VINEYARD SELECTION

LIGHT MEDIUM FULL
Body
LOW MEDIUM HIGH
Acidity
SWEET SEMI SWEET MEDIUM DRY DRY
Sweetness
WOLF BLASS
Gold Label
RIESLING

### PINOT GRIGIO

- Pinot Grigio is currently enjoying new found popularity among white wine drinkers. Pinot Grigio is also known as Pinot Gris.
- Pinot Grigio has a delicate flavor and aroma and is darker in color than most other white wines.
- Italy produces the most popular Pinot Grigio wines but other wine regions, including France and Oregon, also produce Pinot Grigio wines of distinction.

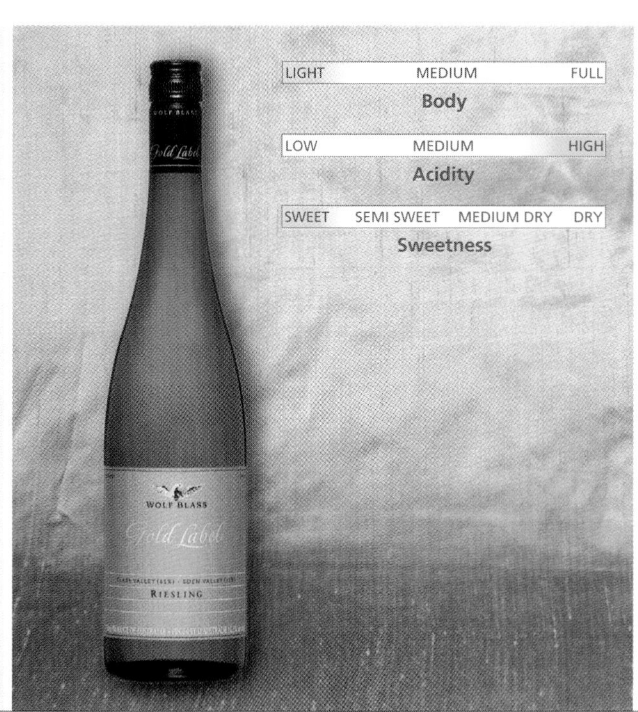

### RIESLING

- Riesling is generally a refreshing tasting wine that is best known for its floral and fruity aromas.
- Riesling wines can often be stored longer than other types of white wine and may improve with age.
- Although Germany is famous for its Riesling wine, France, Australia, the United States and Canada all produce quality Rieslings.

# Red Wine

Red wines are generally more complex tasting than white wines. Much of this complexity comes from tannins, which are compounds that come from the skin and seeds of a grape. Tannins give red wine a dry, bitter flavor. When tannins are used in the right proportions, they create a balanced taste and help improve the wine as it ages. The grape variety on the label, such as Cabernet Sauvignon and Shiraz, tells you the main type of grape used to make the wine. Red wines are best served at room temperature. Some of the most popular red wine varieties are described below.

## Popular Varieties of Red Wine

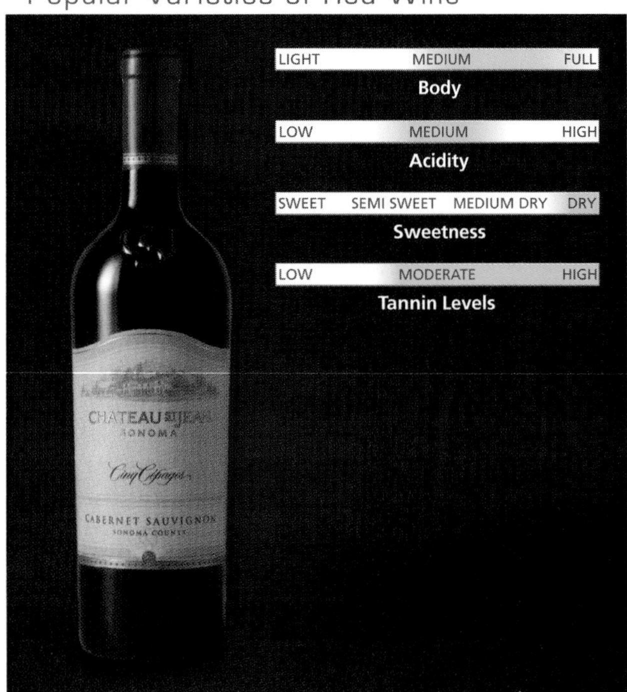


### CABERNET SAUVIGNON

- Cabernet Sauvignon, often referred to as Cabernet or Cab, is generally considered to be the finest red wine in the world. It is prized for its deep color and intense fruit flavor that can be described as dark, rich and complex.

*Note: For information on the body, acidity and sweetness of wine, see the top of page 218.*

- Cabernet Sauvignon wine typically ages very well.
- Cabernet Sauvignon is produced in many wine regions including France, Australia, California, Chile and Italy.

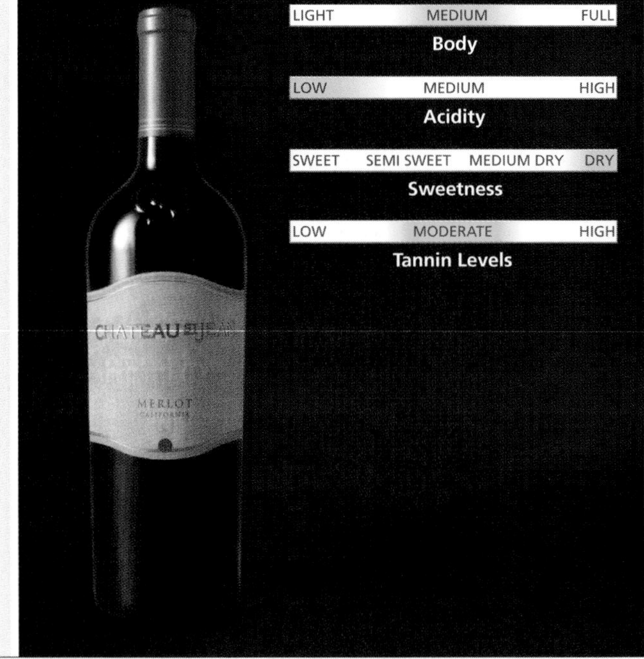


### MERLOT

- Merlot is a popular red wine due to its soft, lush, easy to drink nature. If you are new to red wine, Merlot is a great place to start.
- Merlot is darkly colored and is characterized by flavors of fruit, often plum, and chocolate.
- Merlot is often blended with Cabernet Sauvignon to create a balanced and complex wine.
- Quality Merlots are produced in many wine regions including France, California, Washington State and Chile.

**TIP** *Why is red wine red?*

The color of red wine comes from the skin and seeds of the grapes used to make the wine. After the juice has been extracted from the grapes, the skins and seeds are allowed to sit in the juice during the fermentation process. This passes on color, tannins and flavors to the wine.

**TIP** *How can I tell if a wine is a blend of more than one variety of grape?*

If a wine is a blend that contains significant amounts of two grape varieties, the name of both of the varieties may appear on the label. For example, if the wine is a blend of Cabernet Sauvignon and Merlot, the label would say Cabernet Merlot. The label on the back of the bottle may tell you how much of each variety of grape was used to create the wine.

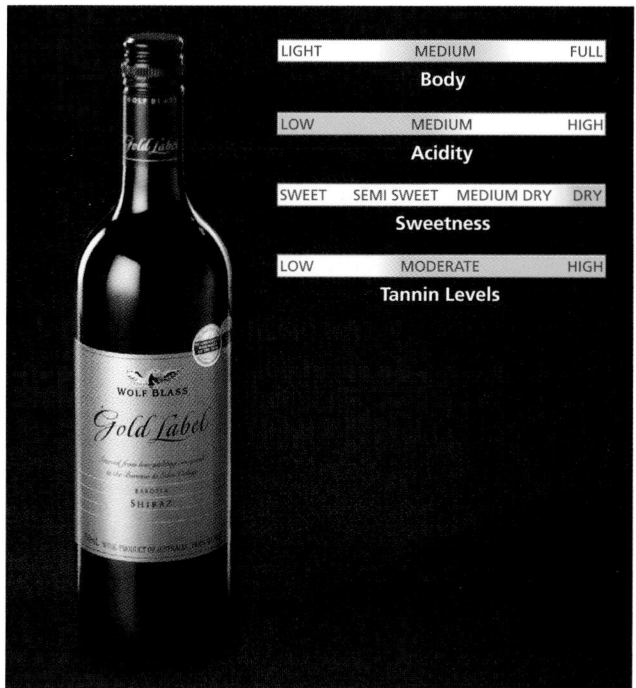

## SHIRAZ

- Shiraz, also known as Syrah, is a deeply colored wine that is appreciated by red wine drinkers for its spicy flavor and aroma.
- Although France and Australia produce some of the best known Shiraz wines, other wine regions, including California and South Africa, also produce Shiraz wines of distinction.

## PINOT NOIR

- Pinot Noir is valued for its fruit flavor, often tasting of berries, and its velvety smooth feel in the mouth.
- Pinot Noir is lighter in color than other red wines.
- The fruit flavor and velvety texture of Pinot Noir are so prized that this grape is rarely blended with other grapes.
- More difficult to grow than other types of grapes, Pinot Noir has succeeded in the wine regions of France, California and Oregon.

# BLUSH Wine

Blush wines, which are also called rosés, are light and fruity wines that have a pinkish hue. Because blush wine is generally sweet and easy-drinking, it is often the first type of wine people try. Like white wine, blush wine should be served chilled. White Zinfandel is the most popular blush wine variety.

## Blush Wine Overview

- Blush wine, also called rosé, is a pink-colored wine made from red wine grapes.
- In the production of blush wine, the grapes are crushed and the skins are separated from the juice after a short period of time. The skins, which are red or purple, impart only a small amount of color to the wine, coloring the wine pink.
- Because blush wine is generally sweet and easy-drinking, it is often the first type of wine people try.

## White Zinfandel

- California's White Zinfandel is the most popular blush wine and is made from Zinfandel grapes.
- White Zinfandel offers a fresh and fruity taste that is characterized by flavors of strawberry and melon. This pink wine is medium sweet to sweet, easy to drink and low in alcohol, making it a good choice for those who are new to drinking wine.

*Note: For information on the sweetness of wine, see the top of page 218.*

- White Zinfandel is best served chilled and enjoyed shortly after it is bottled.

# Champagne & Sparkling Wine

Champagne is the perfect special occasion drink—it's the bottle many reach for when they have something to celebrate. What makes Champagne and sparkling wines so special are the millions of tiny, tongue-tickling bubbles pent up in each bottle. When not being sprayed by victorious athletes, Champagne and sparkling wines are best served chilled in tall, slender champagne flutes which keep the lovely little bubbles from escaping too quickly. To avoid injury the next time you break out the bubbly, check out the instructions for opening a bottle of Champagne or sparkling wine below.

## Champagne & Sparkling Wine Overview

- Only wine produced in the Champagne region of France can be properly labeled "Champagne." All others are sparkling wine. Chardonnay is the grape variety most commonly used to make Champagne and sparkling wine.
- Champagne and sparkling wine labeled brut are dry, doux are sweet and sec fall between dry and sweet.
- Champagne and sparkling wine are white or pink in color, with the pink ones labeled rosé.

## Opening Champagne or Sparkling Wine

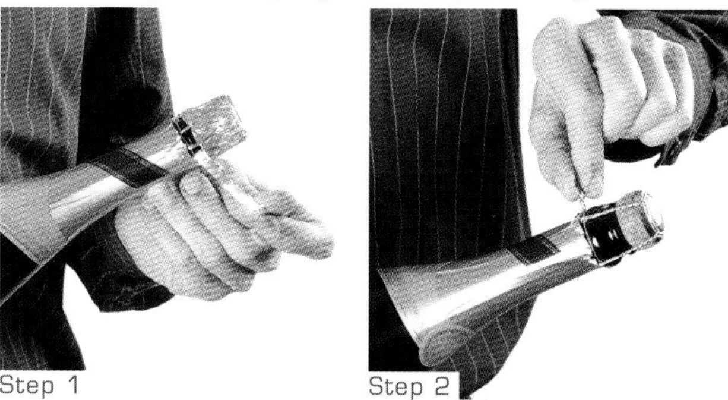

Step 1

Step 2

Steps 3 & 4

1. To open a bottle of Champagne or sparkling wine, remove the foil covering.
2. Remove the wire cage covering the cork.
3. Hold the bottle on a 45 degree angle, with one hand on the cork and the other hand on the body of the bottle.
4. Slowly twist the bottle away from the cork until you feel a gentle pop.

- Champagne and sparkling wine should be served chilled in tall, narrow glasses called champagne flutes. For information on champagne flutes, see page 19.

# How to Serve Wine

Serving and examining wine in the glass can be intimidating for those who are new to the world of wine. Once you understand the basics, however, serving wine is pretty straightforward. These instructions are designed to give you the skills and confidence to properly pour and appreciate wine. With a little practice, you will easily avoid rookie mistakes like allowing bits of cork to fall into your wine and making a loud pop as you remove the cork.

## Opening a Wine Bottle

Step 1

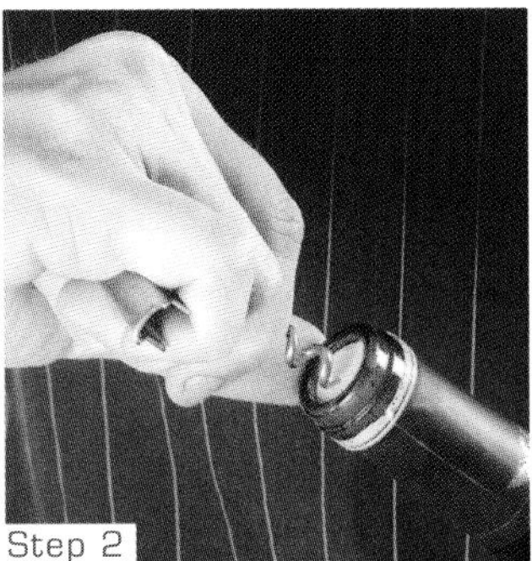

Step 2

Step 3

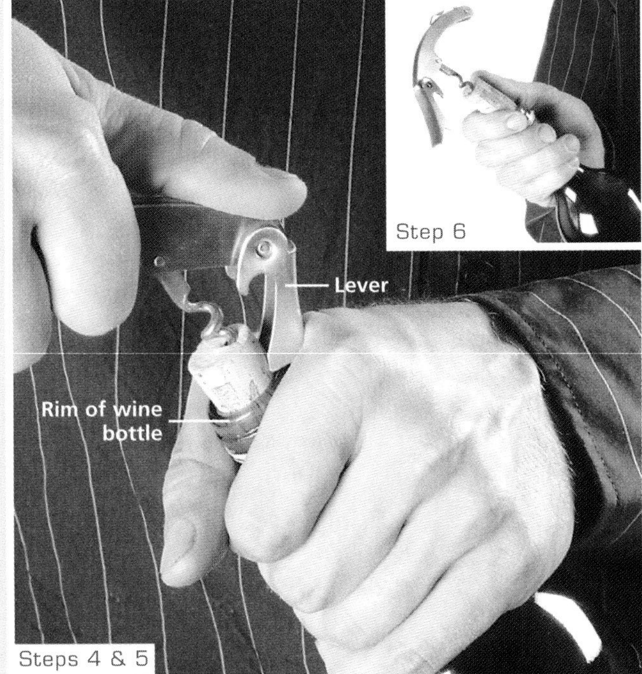


Step 6

Steps 4 & 5

1 Remove the foil covering from the top of the wine bottle.

2 Insert the sharp point of your waiter's corkscrew into the cork just off center.

3 Slowly rotate the corkscrew until 1 1/2 turns of the corkscrew are left visible above the cork. This helps ensure the corkscrew does not penetrate through the bottom of the cork, breaking pieces of the cork into the wine.

4 Place the lever of your corkscrew against the rim of the wine bottle and hold it securely with your hand.

5 With your other hand, pull the corkscrew upwards to begin removing the cork.

6 When the cork is almost out of the bottle, release the corkscrew and finish removing the cork with your hand. This helps prevent a loud popping sound.

**TIP** *Should I smell the cork once it is removed from the bottle?*

There is not much you will be able to tell from smelling the cork, but you should examine it for moisture. A moist cork is an indicator the wine has been stored properly on its side and the bottle's seal has not been compromised. When a bottle of wine is stored upright, the cork may dry out and shrink. This allows air into the bottle and may ruin the wine.

**TIP** *What types of glasses should I use to serve wine?*

In a wine glass, exposure to oxygen tends to impair the flavor of white and blush wines, while it usually improves the flavor of red wine. To keep oxygen from getting at white and blush wines, they are generally served in glasses that feature a small bowl and narrow opening. To permit the maximum amount of oxygen to interact with red wine, it is served in glasses that feature a large bowl and wide opening. For more information on wine glasses, see page 19.

## Pouring Wine

1 When pouring wine, you should hold the wine bottle by the body, not by the neck.

2 Pour the wine into a wine glass until the glass is half full.

3 As you finish pouring the wine, turn the bottle a quarter turn to catch the last drip.

## Examining Wine

1 Hold the wine glass by its stem to prevent the temperature of your hand from affecting the temperature of the wine.

2 Move the wine glass in a circular motion for a few seconds to gently swirl the wine. If the wine moves slowly down the sides of the glass, the wine is said to have *legs*. Legs can indicate a higher quality wine.

3 To smell the wine, place your nose deeply inside the glass and inhale.

4 To taste the wine, take a sip and move the wine over your tongue. Then swallow the wine.

# Fortified Wine

Fortified wine is a type of wine that has an extra dose of alcohol added to it before or during the fermentation process. To add that extra kick, Brandy is often the spirit used to "fortify" wines. Vermouth is a popular fortified wine that is generally used as a cocktail ingredient. Port, Sherry and Madeira are fortified wines that are usually served without mixers in small sherry glasses. The alcohol content of fortified wines typically falls somewhere between that of wine and spirits at 15 to 22% by volume.

## Vermouth

- Vermouth is a fortified and flavored white wine produced mainly in France and Italy. Vermouth is infused with the flavor of various flowers, herbs and spices.
- The two most commonly used types of vermouth are dry white vermouth, known as bianco, and sweet red vermouth, known as rosso.
- Vermouth is most often consumed as an ingredient in cocktails.

## Port

- Port is a sweet fortified wine that is served at room temperature as an after dinner drink. Port comes from Portugal and is the only fortified wine based on red wine. The three most common types of Port are Vintage, Tawny and Ruby.
- Vintage is the highest quality, but requires long aging before it can be consumed.
- Tawny, named for its pale brown color, has a smooth, mellow flavor.
- Ruby is richer in color and stronger in flavor than the other types.

**TIP** *Once opened, how long will fortified wine last?*

Fortified wines were originally created to keep wines from spoiling during long sea voyages. Fortified wines made today continue to remain drinkable longer than ordinary wines. Vermouth, for example, will last up to a year after being opened. Port, Sweet Sherry and Madeira typically stay drinkable for a month after opening. Dry Sherries, however, only keep for a few days after opening and should be refrigerated.

**TIP** *What types of cocktails are made with Vermouth?*

Dry Vermouth is best known as an indispensable ingredient for the Classic Martini. For the recipe, see page 66. Sweet Vermouth is used to make sweeter drinks like the Classic Manhattan and Rob Roy martinis. To learn how to make the Classic Manhattan and Rob Roy martinis, see page 70.

## Sherry

- True Sherry comes from Spain and is made by fortifying dry white wine.
- There are two types of Sherry—Fino and Oloroso.
- Finos are pale in color and are usually dry with a delicate flavor. Finos are typically served chilled as a before dinner drink.
- Olorosos range in color from medium to dark brown and are generally sweet and richly flavored. Olorosos are usually served at room temperature as an after dinner drink.

## Madeira

- Madeira is produced on a small island of the same name off the coast of Portugal. This fortified wine has a subtle smoky flavor and is usually served at room temperature.
- The four types of Madeira are named after the white wine grape used to make each type —Sercial, Verdelho, Bual and Malmsey.
- Sercial and Verdelho are dry and usually served before dinner.
- Bual and Malmsey are sweet and typically served as an after dinner drink.

# BEER

Beer is a simple drink made from just four basic ingredients—water, malted barley, hops and yeast. Barley lends the beverage a sweet taste, while the hops create a bitter flavor. Different beers use blends of these and sometimes other ingredients to create unique beers balanced between sweet and bitter. There are two main types of beer: ale and lager. Ales are more complex, flavorful and darker in color than lagers. Ales also tend to be less carbonated and more full-bodied. There are numerous styles of ale, including Brown Ale, Pale Ale, Wheat Beer and Stout.

## Popular Styles of Ale

### BROWN ALE

- Brown ale originated in Britain and is a sweet, mild-tasting ale with a nutty or caramel flavor.
- This type of ale ranges in color from reddish brown to dark brown and is medium to full-bodied.
- Brown ales brewed in Britain are often lower in alcohol while North American brewers produce drier versions of the ale.
- Newcastle Brown Ale is a popular example of this ale.

### PALE ALE

- Originally brewed in Britain, pale ale is now produced around the world.
- American-style pale ale has a crisp taste with a flavor and aroma dominated by hops. Pale ale brewed in Britain often has a strong malt character and buttery taste.
- Pale ales range in color from gold to copper and are medium-bodied.
- Two well known examples of pale ale are Bass Pale Ale and Sierra Nevada Pale Ale.

**TIP** *What is Fruit Beer?*

Fruit beer, which is also called fruit lambic, is a unique form of beer that originated in Belgium. The brewers add various fruit ingredients to the beer and make use of wild yeasts in the fermentation process. There are several types of fruit beer—kriek includes cherries, pêche uses peaches and framboise is made with raspberries.

**TIP** *How should I store beer?*

Unlike wine, most types of beer do not improve with time in the bottle. Heat and light quickly lower the quality of beer. To keep beer tasting fresh, it should be stored in a refrigerator or a cool, dark room. When beer begins to go "off," it takes on an unpleasant skunky aroma and flavor.

### WHEAT BEER

- An ale of German origin, wheat beer is made from malted wheat as well as malted barley.
- Wheat beer is golden in color and often has a slightly cloudy appearance.
- Wheat beer is popular during the summer due to its high carbonation and crisp, refreshing taste. This type of beer is often served with a lemon wedge.
- You will often see the term *Weisse*, *Weizen* or *Weissbier* on the label of wheat beer. Hoegaarden and Paulaner Hefe-Weizen are popular wheat beers.

### STOUT

- Stout is brewed using roasted barley, which gives this ale its dark color.
- Stout is a rich, full-bodied beer that is known for its complex roasted flavor, slight bitterness and malt sweetness.
- Low in carbonation, stout has a smooth, creamy texture.
- Stout was originally brewed in Ireland and some of the most popular examples of this beer, including Murphy's Irish Stout and Beamish Genuine Irish Stout, all hail from Ireland.

# BEER

While the two main types of beer—ale and lager—are made from the same ingredients, they taste very different from one another. Lagers are brewed for longer periods of time at low temperatures and tend to be lighter in both taste and color as a result. Lagers are also more carbonated and crisp in flavor than ales. Lagers are the most popular form of beer around the world. There are a number of different styles of lagers, including American-Style Lager, Pilsner, Bock and Oktoberfest.

## Popular Styles of Lager

### AMERICAN-STYLE LAGER

- This style of lager was developed in the United States and is usually produced by large brewing companies.
- American-style lagers are pale yellow to light gold in color and tend to be highly carbonated.
- American-style lagers are usually light bodied and are characterized by a crisp, refreshing taste. The flavor and aroma is an even balance between the malt and hops.
- Budweiser and Corona Extra are examples of American-style lager beer.

### PILSNER

- Pilsner is a very popular style of lager and is characterized by its slightly bitter, dry flavor. This type of beer was originally brewed in the city of Plzen in the Czech Republic.
- Pilsners are light yellow to golden in color and clear in appearance.
- Hops generally dominate the taste of this lager and produce a beer that has a floral flavor and aroma.
- Labatt Blue, Beck's, Heineken and Pilsner Urquell are examples of Pilsner beer.

**TIP** *How do I pour beer?*

To pour beer, tilt the glass on a 45-degree angle and pour the beer so that it lands on the side of the glass. As the glass reaches three-quarters full, tilt the glass back upright and stop pouring as the foamy head reaches the top of the glass.

### BOCK

- A beer of German origin, Bock is stronger tasting, higher in alcohol and aged longer than most lagers. Bock is the German word for goat and a goat is often displayed on the label.
- Bocks are dark in color and characterized by a robust malt flavor and full body.
- Doppelbock and Eisbock are stronger versions of Bock lager.
- Michelob Amber Bock and Shiner Bock are two well known examples of this type of beer.

### OKTOBERFEST

- Oktoberfest, also known as Märzen or Märzenbier, is a lager of German origin that was traditionally consumed during the fall festival of the same name.
- Oktoberfest is dark copper in color and has a medium to high alcohol content.
- This lager offers beer drinkers a distinctive toasty flavor and is medium to full-bodied.
- Two popular examples of this beer are Samuel Adams Octoberfest and Paulaner Oktoberfest.

# REFERENCE

It's never a good idea to be caught low on supplies. Gauging how much alcohol is needed for any event is crucial for any bartender. This section of the book will help you figure out how much alcohol you will need on hand to serve your guests. The Glossary provides a handy explanation of common bartending terms.

# 13 Measurements & Reference

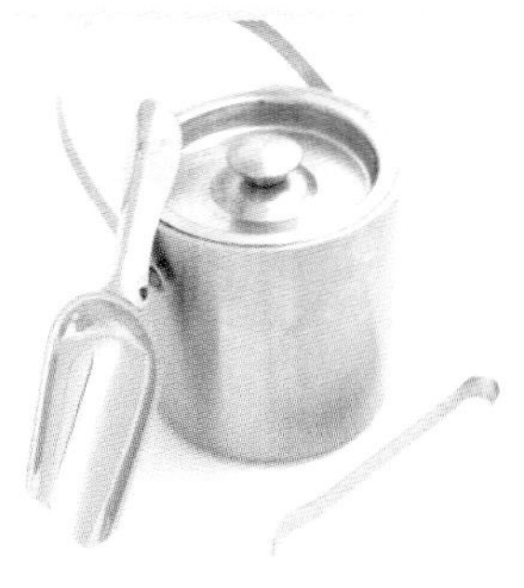

# Bar Measurements

Deciding how far a supply of alcohol will go can be a daunting task for the home bartender. These charts should help you figure out how much alcohol you have, how much you will need and how long it will last you.

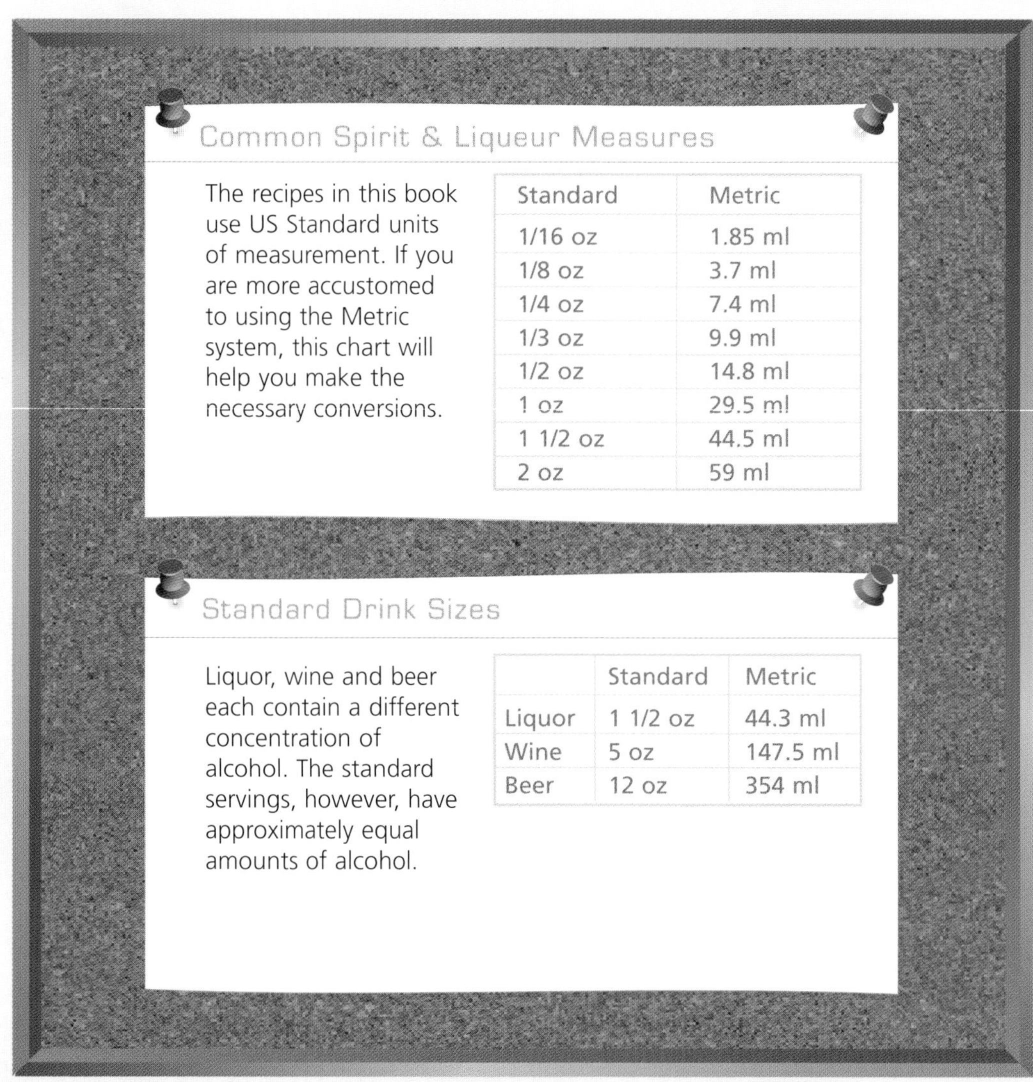

## Common Spirit & Liqueur Measures

The recipes in this book use US Standard units of measurement. If you are more accustomed to using the Metric system, this chart will help you make the necessary conversions.

| Standard | Metric |
|---|---|
| 1/16 oz | 1.85 ml |
| 1/8 oz | 3.7 ml |
| 1/4 oz | 7.4 ml |
| 1/3 oz | 9.9 ml |
| 1/2 oz | 14.8 ml |
| 1 oz | 29.5 ml |
| 1 1/2 oz | 44.5 ml |
| 2 oz | 59 ml |

## Standard Drink Sizes

Liquor, wine and beer each contain a different concentration of alcohol. The standard servings, however, have approximately equal amounts of alcohol.

| | Standard | Metric |
|---|---|---|
| Liquor | 1 1/2 oz | 44.3 ml |
| Wine | 5 oz | 147.5 ml |
| Beer | 12 oz | 354 ml |

## Spirit Bottle Sizes & Servings

It can be difficult to estimate how many drinks a bottle of liquor will give you. This chart will help you determine how many servings you will be able to pour from your bottles of spirits.

| Bottle Size | Ounces | 1-oz Servings | 1 1/2-oz Servings |
|---|---|---|---|
| 375 ml | 12.7 | 12 | 8 |
| 750 ml | 25.4 | 25 | 17 |
| 1 liter | 33.8 | 33 | 22 |
| 1.75 liters | 59.2 | 59 | 39 |
| 3 liters | 101.4 | 101 | 7 |

## Wine Bottle Sizes & Servings

It is not always easy to determine whether you have enough wine to serve your guests. This chart will take the guesswork out of estimating how far the bottles you have will go.

| Bottle Size | Ounces | 5-oz Servings |
|---|---|---|
| 375 ml | 12.7 | 2.5 |
| 750 ml | 25.4 | 5 |
| 1 liter | 33.8 | 6.5 |
| 1.5 liters | 50.9 | 10 |

## Keg Sizes & Servings

For serving beer to a crowd, nothing beats the keg. This chart will help you figure out the size of keg you will need.

| Keg Size | Gallons | 1/2-pint Servings* | 1-pint Servings** | 1 bottle (12 oz) |
|---|---|---|---|---|
| 1 Keg | 15.5 | 248 | 124 | 165 |
| 1/2 Keg | 7.75 | 124 | 62 | 82 |
| 1/4 Keg | 3.88 | 62 | 31 | 41 |

*1/2 pint = 8 oz = 236 ml

**1 pint = 16 oz = 472 ml

# Glossary

A

**Acidity** A term that describes how tangy a wine tastes. Wines range in acidity from soft-tasting "low acidity" through crisp "medium acidity" to a sharp-tasting "high acidity."

**Aging** A process in which wines and spirits are stored for a period of time after the distillation or fermentation process. Aging, which is often the last step in the production of wine and spirits, generally allows for more complex and mellow characteristics to develop.

**Alcohol by Volume (ABV)** A measurement of the percentage of alcohol in an alcoholic beverage.

**Ale** One of two main types of beer. Ales are more complex, flavorful and darker in color than lagers, which is the other main type of beer. Ales also tend to be less carbonated and more full bodied. There are numerous styles of ale, including brown ale, pale ale, wheat beer and stout.

B

**Barspoon** A type of spoon that is long enough to reach the bottom of a large cocktail shaker and is used to stir cocktails that are not shaken. Barspoons can also be used to layer spirits and liqueurs in cocktails.

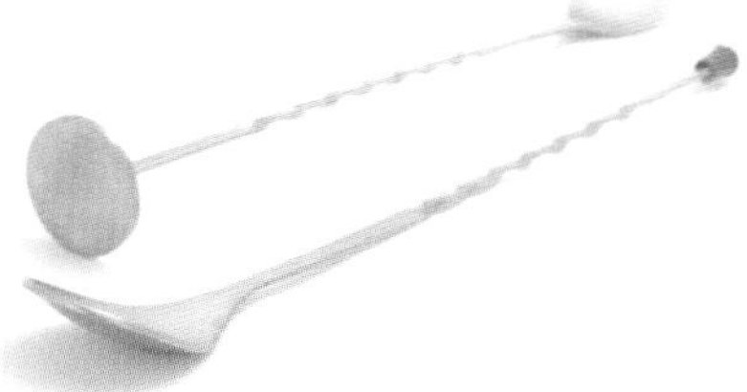

**Blush wine** A wine that is pink in color. The color of a blush wine is derived from grape skins that have been allowed to sit in the grape juice for only a limited time during the wine's production.

**Body** A term that describes how wine feels in your mouth. The body of a wine can range from "light" to "medium" to "full."

**Boston Shaker** A type of cocktail shaker that is composed of two pieces: a tapered stainless steel can and a smaller tapered glass. Boston shakers are preferred by professional bartenders because they are generally bigger and allow more drinks to be mixed at once.

**Brandy** A distilled spirit made from wine or fermented fruit juice. There are a number of different types of brandy, including cognac, armagnac and fruit brandies.

**Brut** A term that describes the sweetness of a champagne or sparkling wine. Brut indicates a wine that is dry and not sweet.

C

**Cabernet Sauvignon** A red wine that is generally considered to be the finest in the world. Sometimes called Cabernet or Cab, this wine is dry, medium-to-full bodied with moderate acidity and moderate-to-high tannin levels. Cabernet Sauvignon wine typically ages very well.

**Champagne** A sparkling white wine produced in the Champagne region of France. Only sparkling wine produced in the Champagne region of France can be properly labeled "Champagne."

**Channel Knife** A hand-held tool featuring a square or rounded head that contains a small blade for cutting long slices of peel from citrus fruits.

**Chardonnay** A white wine with a rich taste and smooth texture. Chardonnay is traditionally aged in oak barrels and is characterized by a spicy or smoky flavor. A good quality Chardonnay is medium-to-full bodied and medium dry with moderate acidity.

**Chilling a Glass** A technique whereby a glass is cooled prior to a drink being poured into the glass.

**Citrus Slice**
A thin, semicircular piece of citrus fruit that is used as a cocktail garnish. A citrus slice is created by cutting a citrus wheel in half.

**Citrus Spiral**
A long piece of citrus peel that is normally 3 to 4 inches long and used as a cocktail garnish. Longer spirals of 6 to 8 inches can also be created for a more dramatic effect.

**Citrus Twist** A 1 to 1 1/2 inch long strip of citrus peel that is used as a cocktail garnish.

**Citrus Wheel** A thin, circular slice of citrus fruit that is used as a cocktail garnish.

**Citrus Zest** Fine threads of citrus fruit peel. Citrus zest contains flavorful oils and is often used as a cocktail garnish. Citrus zest is removed from the peel of a fruit with a citrus zester.

**Citrus Zester** A hand-held tool with five or six small, sharp stainless steel rings used to remove threadlike strips of peel from the rind of a citrus fruit. Combination tools featuring both a channel knife and zester are common.

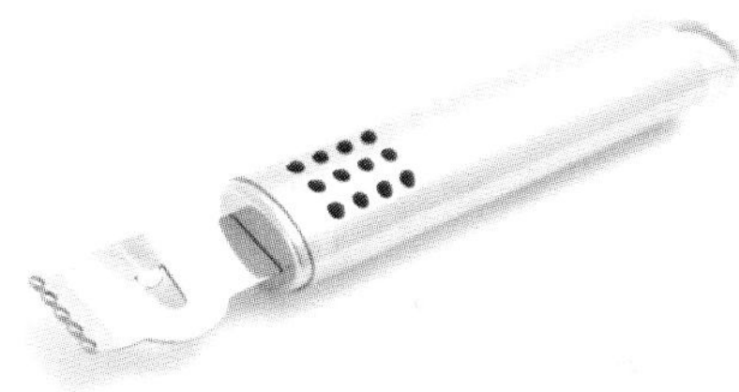

## D

**Density** A term that describes the thickness of a liqueur or spirit. Density is an important factor when layering drinks— thick, denser liquids will sink to the bottom of a glass and less-dense liquids will float on top of ingredients that have a higher density.

**Dessert Wine** A sweet wine that is typically served after a meal, often with or in place of dessert. These syrupy wines are generally made from white wine grapes that have been allowed to over-ripen on the vine, concentrating their sugars and flavors.

# Glossary

**Distillation** A process in which a fermented liquid, which contains small amounts of alcohol, is heated so the alcohol evaporates. The vapor is then condensed into a liquid that contains a much higher amount of alcohol. Gin, vodka, rum, whiskey, tequila and brandy are all made by the process of distillation.

**Doux** A term that describes the sweetness of a champagne or sparkling wine. Doux indicates a wine that is sweet.

**Dry** A term that describes the relative sweetness of a wine. Dry is the absence of sweetness in a wine. Wines range in sweetness from sweet to dry.

## F

**Fermentation** A process in which the sugar in a liquid is converted to alcohol. Fermentation is an initial step in the production of spirits, wines and beers.

**Filtration** A process in which impurities or other substances are removed from wines, beers or spirits. Filtration creates a clearer, smoother-taste.

**Fine Straining** An extra filtration step performed when a drink is poured out of a shaker. You may need to fine strain a cocktail when mixing drinks that contain fruit pulp or small seeds.

**Fortified Wine** A type of wine that has had an extra dose of alcohol added to it before or during the fermentation process. Brandy is the spirit often used to "fortify" wines. Vermouth, Port, Sherry and Madeira are all types of fortified wines.

**Fruit Puree** A thoroughly blended, liquid mixture of fruit that is used to add fresh flavor and texture to cocktails. Purees can be bought at grocery stores or made at home.

## G

**Garnish** A flavorful, decorative item that is added to a drink just before it is served. Garnishes should complement the flavor of a beverage and enhance the drink visually. Popular garnishes include maraschino cherries, citrus spirals and wheels.

**Gin** A clear, distilled spirit that is flavored with juniper berries and other botanical ingredients. When a recipe lists "gin" as an ingredient, it is referring to a specific type of gin called London dry gin.

## H

**Hawthorn Strainer** A slotted, metal disc that has a coil on its underside and is attached to a handle. The Hawthorn strainer fits on top of a Boston shaker's metal can to filter ice and citrus seeds out of a cocktail as it is being poured.

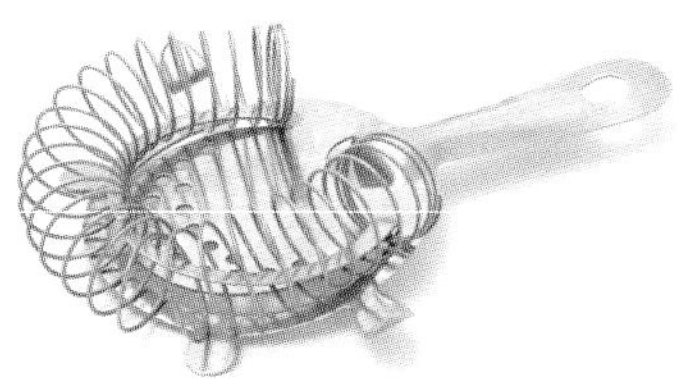

## J

**Jigger** A measuring tool made up of two different-sized cups stacked end-to-end like an hourglass. One cup is normally half the size of the other cup. Some jiggers also feature a handle.

**Julep Strainer** An oversized, metal spoon studded with holes. Julep strainers fit inside a mixing glass to strain ice and citrus seeds out of a stirred cocktail as it is being poured.

## L

**Lager** One of two main types of beer. Lagers tend to be lighter in both taste and color than ales, which is the other type of beer. Lagers are also more carbonated and crisp in flavor. There are a number of different styles of lager, including American-Style Lager, Bock, Oktoberfest and Pilsner.

**Layering**
A bartending technique for pouring drinks that feature liqueurs and liquors which stay separated in distinct layers in a glass. It is possible to achieve this effect because liquids of different densities will stay separate if poured slowly and layered from most-dense to least-dense, bottom to top.

**Legs** A term that describes the character of a wine. If a wine moves slowly down the sides of a glass after being swirled around in the glass, the wine is said to have legs. Legs can indicate a quality wine.

**Liqueur** An alcoholic beverage that is generally made up of a spirit that has been flavored with fruits, herbs, spices and other ingredients. Baileys Irish Cream and Grand Marnier are examples of liqueurs.

## M

**Merlot** A red wine with a lush, easy-to-drink nature. Merlot is darkly colored and characterized by flavors of fruit and chocolate. It is typically a dry, medium-bodied wine with low acidity and moderate levels of tannin.

**Mixing Glass**
A glass that is used for making drinks that need to be stirred rather than shaken.

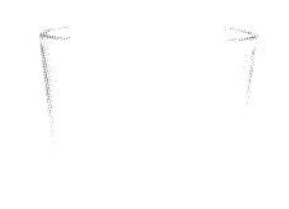

**Mocktail** A cocktail that contains no alcohol. Mocktails are often made with flavors similar to popular alcoholic cocktails and are ideal for designated drivers and others who choose not to drink alcohol.

**Muddler** A wooden bat that is used to crush ingredients such as fruit, herbs and sugar in the bottom of a glass or cocktail shaker. Most muddlers are six or more inches long and flattened on one end.

**Muddling** A bartending technique that involves mashing up cocktail ingredients to release their flavors. Typically, ingredients are placed at the bottom of a sturdy glass and mashed firmly with a muddler, a small wooden bat used for muddling.

# Glossary

N

**Nutmeg Grater**
A tool that is used for grating nutmeg, cinnamon and other spices over drinks.

O

**On the Rocks** A term that describes a spirit or liqueur that is served with ice cubes. For example, serving Scotch whisky with ice is called "Scotch on the Rocks."

P

**Pinot Grigio** A white wine with a delicate flavor and aroma. Pinot Grigio, also called Pinot Gris, is darker in color than most other white wines and is usually light-to-medium bodied and dry with low acidity.

**Pinot Noir** A red wine with fruit flavor and a smooth feel in the mouth. Pinot Noir is lighter in color than other red wines and is dry, light-to-medium bodied with moderate-to-high acidity and low-to-moderate levels of tannin.

**Pourer**
A small spout that is plugged into a bottle to regulate the flow of liquor. Bartenders use pourers to measure out ingredients by the number of seconds they pour.

**Preheat a glass** A technique whereby a glass is heated prior to a hot drink being poured into the glass.

**Proof** A measurement of the amount of alcohol in an alcoholic beverage. Proof is equal to double the percentage of alcohol in the liquid. For example, a spirit that contains 40% alcohol by volume (ABV) is said to be 80 proof.

R

**Riesling** A white wine that is light bodied and sweet with high acidity. Riesling is known for its floral and fruity aromas. Riesling wines can be stored longer than other types of white wine and may improve with age.

**Rimming a Glass** A technique for garnishing a glass by coating the outside of the glass' rim with a powdered or crystallized ingredient such as sugar or salt. The ingredient used to coat the rim of a glass is called a rimmer.

**Rum** A spirit that is distilled from sugar cane. There are several types of rum, including light, dark and gold rums, as well as spiced rum and overproof rum. Much of the world's rum is produced in the Caribbean.

S

**Sauvignon Blanc** A white wine with a bright and crisp taste that is characterized by flavors of grass and herbs. Sauvignon Blanc is typically light-to-medium bodied and dry with high acidity.

**Sec** A term that describes the sweetness of a champagne or sparkling wine. Sec indicates a wine that is neither overly doux (sweet) or brut (dry).

**Shiraz** A red wine with a spicy flavor and aroma. Shiraz, also known as Syrah, is a deeply colored, dry wine that is medium bodied with low-to-moderate acidity and moderate-to-high levels of tannin.

**Shooter** A drink that is comprised of several ingredients and served in a shot glass.

**Shot** A drink that is comprised of a single spirit or liqueur and served in a shot glass.

**Simple Syrup** A mixture of water and sugar that has been heated so the sugar is dissolved and easily mixes into beverages. A common cocktail ingredient used instead of sugar.

**Sparkling Wine** A carbonated wine which is characterized by bubbles which make it appear to sparkle while in the glass. Sparkling wines are usually white wines, the most well-known being champagne.

**Spirit** An alcoholic beverage that has been distilled after it has been fermented. Spirits are also referred to as liquors. Rum and vodka are examples of spirits.

**Standard Shaker**
A type of cocktail shaker that is comprised of three pieces: a can of between 8 and 24 ounces, a lid that contains a strainer and a tight-fitting cap.

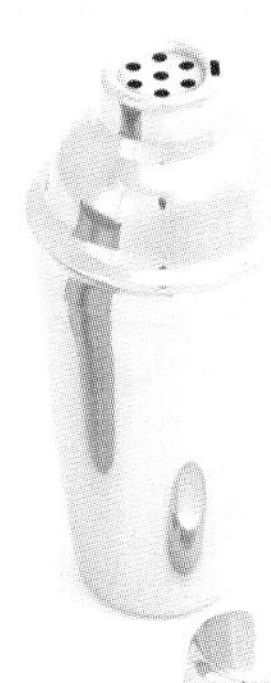

**Straight Up** A term that describes a drink that is mixed in a shaker or mixing glass with ice and then served without ice in a glass. For example, a martini served without ice is a "martini straight up."

**Sweet** A term defining the relative sweetness of a wine. Wines can range in sweetness from sweet to dry.

## T

**Tannins** Bitter compounds that provide red wines with much of their character. Tannins come from grape skins and seeds and give red wine a dry, bitter flavor. When tannins are used in the right proportions, they create a balanced taste and improve the wine as it ages.

**Tea Strainer**
A fine-mesh strainer that is useful for removing small seeds and ice chips from cocktails in a process called fine straining.

**Tequila** A distilled spirit from Mexico that is made from the blue agave plant and is known for its distinct flavor and aroma. Tequila comes in several varieties such as blanco (white), gold, reposado (rested) and añejo (aged).

## V

**Vodka** A colorless and odorless distilled spirit which originated in Eastern Europe.

## W

**Wedge** A thick slice of fruit that is commonly placed on the rim of a glass to garnish a drink. Wedges can be made from pineapples and citrus fruits. Citrus wedges can be squeezed over a drink to add flavor.

**Whiskey** A distilled spirit which is made from various grains, such as barley, rye and wheat, and aged in wooden barrels to mellow and flavor the spirit. Whiskey is made in various forms around the world including Irish whiskey, Scotch whisky, Canadian whisky, rye whiskey, bourbon and Tennessee whiskey. Depending on where the spirit is produced, it may be spelled "whiskey" or "whisky."

**White Zinfandel** A blush wine with a fresh and fruity taste that is characterized by flavors of strawberry and melon. White Zinfandel is a pink wine that is medium-sweet to sweet in flavor and easy to drink. White Zinfandel is best served chilled.

# Index

## C

# Index

## G



## H



## I



## J

# Index

# Index

## V



## W



## X

Did you like this book? MARAN ILLUSTRATED™ offers books on the most popular computer topics, using the same easy-to-use format of this book. We always say that if you like one of our books, you'll love the rest of our books too!

Here's a list of some of our best-selling computer titles:

## Guided Tour Series - 240 pages, Full Color

**MARAN ILLUSTRATED's Guided Tour series features a friendly disk character that walks you through each task step by step. The full-color screen shots are larger than in any of our other series and are accompanied by clear, concise instructions.**

| | ISBN | Price |
|---|---|---|
| MARAN ILLUSTRATED™ Computers Guided Tour | 1-59200-880-1 | $24.99 US/$33.95 CDN |
| MARAN ILLUSTRATED™ Windows XP Guided Tour | 1-59200-886-0 | $24.99 US/$33.95 CDN |

## MARAN ILLUSTRATED™ Series - 320 pages, Full Color

**This series covers 30% more content than our Guided Tour series. Learn new software fast using our step-by-step approach and easy-to-understand text. Learning programs has never been this easy!**

| | ISBN | Price |
|---|---|---|
| MARAN ILLUSTRATED™ Access 2003 | 1-59200-872-0 | $24.99 US/$33.95 CDN |
| MARAN ILLUSTRATED™ Computers | 1-59200-874-7 | $24.99 US/$33.95 CDN |
| MARAN ILLUSTRATED™ Excel 2003 | 1-59200-876-3 | $24.99 US/$33.95 CDN |
| MARAN ILLUSTRATED™ Mac OS® X v.10.4 Tiger™ | 1-59200-878-X | $24.99 US/$33.95 CDN |
| MARAN ILLUSTRATED™ Office 2003 | 1-59200-890-9 | $29.99 US/$39.95 CDN |
| MARAN ILLUSTRATED™ Windows XP | 1-59200-870-4 | $24.99 US/$33.95 CDN |

## 101 Hot Tips Series - 240 pages, Full Color

**Progress beyond the basics with MARAN ILLUSTRATED's 101 Hot Tips series. This series features 101 of the coolest shortcuts, tricks and tips that will help you work faster and easier.**

| | ISBN | Price |
|---|---|---|
| MARAN ILLUSTRATED™ Windows XP 101 Hot Tips | 1-59200-882-8 | $19.99 US/$26.95 CDN |

## maran illustrated PIANO

**MARAN ILLUSTRATED™ Piano** is an information-packed resource for people who want to learn to play the piano, as well as current musicians looking to hone their skills. Combining full-color photographs and easy-to-follow instructions, this guide covers everything from the basics of piano playing to more advanced techniques. Not only does MARAN ILLUSTRATED™ Piano show you how to read music, play scales and chords and improvise while playing with other musicians, it also provides you with helpful information for purchasing and caring for your piano.

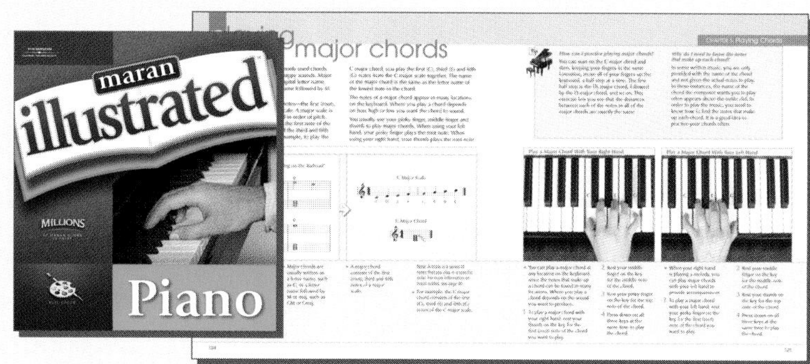


ISBN: 1-59200-864-X

Price: $24.99 US; $33.95 CDN

Page count: 304

## maran illustrated DOG TRAINING

**MARAN ILLUSTRATED™ Dog Training** is an excellent guide for both current dog owners and people considering making a dog part of their family. Using clear, step-by-step instructions accompanied by over 400 full-color photographs, MARAN ILLUSTRATED™ Dog Training is perfect for any visual learner who prefers seeing what to do rather than reading lengthy explanations.

Beginning with insights into popular dog breeds and puppy development, this book emphasizes positive training methods to guide you through socializing, housetraining and teaching your dog many commands. You will also learn how to work with problem behaviors, such as destructive chewing.

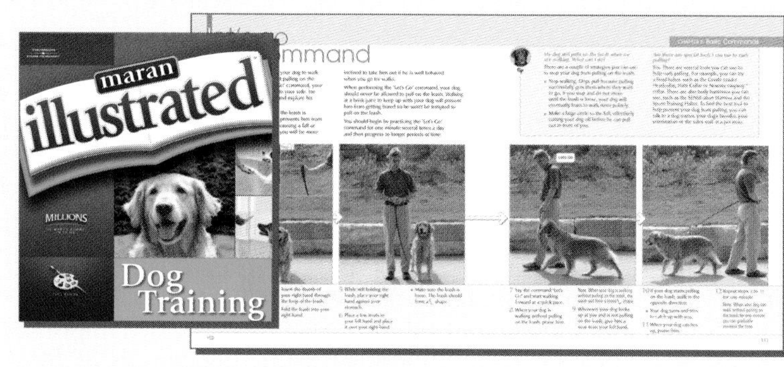


ISBN: 1-59200-858-5

Price: $19.99 US; $26.95 CDN

Page count: 256

## maran illustrated KNITTING & CROCHETING

**MARAN ILLUSTRATED™ Knitting & Crocheting** contains a wealth of information about these two increasingly popular crafts. Whether you are just starting out or you are an experienced knitter or crocheter interested in picking up new tips and techniques, this information-packed resource will take you from the basics, such as how to hold the knitting needles or crochet hook, to more advanced skills, such as how to add decorative touches to your projects. The easy-to-follow information is communicated through clear, step-by-step instructions and accompanied by over 600 full-color photographs—perfect for any visual learner.

ISBN: 1-59200-862-3
Price: $24.99 US; $33.95 CDN
Page count: 304

## maran illustrated YOGA

**MARAN ILLUSTRATED™ Yoga** provides a wealth of simplified, easy-to-follow information about the increasingly popular practice of Yoga. This easy-to-use guide is a must for visual learners who prefer to see and do without having to read lengthy explanations.

Using clear, step-by-step instructions accompanied by over 500 full-color photographs, this book includes all the information you need to get started with yoga or to enhance your technique if you have already made yoga a part of your life. MARAN ILLUSTRATED™ Yoga shows you how to safely and effectively perform a variety of yoga poses at various skill levels, how to breathe more efficiently and much more.

ISBN: 1-59200-868-2
Price: $24.99 US; $33.95 CDN
Page count: 320

# maran illustrated WEIGHT TRAINING

**MARAN ILLUSTRATED™ Weight Training** is an information-packed guide that covers all the basics of weight training, as well as more advanced techniques and exercises.

MARAN ILLUSTRATED™ Weight Training contains more than 500 full-color photographs of exercises for every major muscle group, along with clear, step-by-step instructions for performing the exercises. Useful tips provide additional information and advice to help enhance your weight training experience.

MARAN ILLUSTRATED™ Weight Training provides all the information you need to start weight training or to refresh your technique if you have been weight training for some time.

ISBN: 1-59200-866-6
Price: $24.99 US; $33.95 CDN
Page count: 320